Albert Mansbridge

WILLIAM ROTHENSTEIN, *A. Mansbridge*, DRAWING, 1918

THE UNIVERSITY OF LEEDS ART COLLECTION

# Albert Mansbridge

## The Life and Work of the Founder of the WEA

Bernard Jennings

**UNIVERSITY OF LEEDS**
*with the* WORKERS' EDUCATIONAL ASSOCIATION
**LEEDS STUDIES IN CONTINUING EDUCATION**

*First published in 2002 in the series*
*Leeds Studies in Continuing Education*
*by the School of Education, University of Leeds*
*Leeds LS2 9JT, Great Britain*

*with the Workers' Educational Association*

*Leeds Studies in Continuing Education*

ISSN 0965–0342

*Albert Mansbridge*

ISBN 1 901981 11 8

Design and composition by 'Leeds Studies in Continuing Education'
Printed by Media Services at the University of Leeds

# Contents

# Preface

This book, which appears as the WEA is preparing to celebrate its centenary in 2003, is the last of a series of works by the author dealing with the founder of the Association, which began with the Mansbridge Memorial Lecture, *Albert Mansbridge*, delivered in the University of Leeds in 1973. The late Professor Sidney Raybould of Leeds invited me to undertake research into the life and work of Albert Mansbridge, and he and his successor Professor Norman Jepson gave me every help and encouragement. I have had the privilege of conversations with Mansbridge's son John and niece Mary, and with Dorothy Jones, for many years his personal assistant. Other friends and colleagues of Mansbridge who were generous with their support include F H Bentley, Leonard Clark, Dr Ronald Hope, W H Hosford, Bill Lowth, Ernest Wimble and the officers of the Nationwide (formerly Co-operative Permanent) Building Society.

As the Oxford University was so closely involved in the foundation of the WEA and the tutorial-class movement, the advice and comments of H P Smith and Frank Pickstock were particularly valuable. I have been helped also by colleagues at several other universities, Professor Roger Fieldhouse, Geoffrey Hickson, Dr John Lowe, Professor Harold Wiltshire and Frank Withers. WEA districts and branches have freely opened their records, and I have learned much from colleagues in the Association, including Mel Doyle, Ernest Green, Billy Hughes, Frank Jacques, Reg Jefferies, Robert Lochrie, Elizabeth Monkhouse, Harry Nutt, Fred Padley, Fred Sedgwick and Jack Taylor. On the other side of an ancient ideological divide, I enjoyed a fruitful discussion with Jim Millar, the long-serving general secretary of the National Council of Labour Colleges.

The officers of the National Central Library (now the British Library, Lending Division) were kind enough to deposit the Mansbridge MSS in the care of Professor Raybould at the University of Leeds. The Mills Memorial Library of McMaster University, Hamilton, Ontario, photocopied or transcribed for me the entire Leonard Clark collection, known at McMaster as the Mansbridge MSS. I am most grateful to these libraries, and to the librarians and archivists of the public libraries of Beverley, Birmingham, Manchester, Oxford and Rochdale; the National Library of Scotland, Edinburgh; the National Institute of Adult Continuing Education, Leicester; the Public Record Office; the Royal Library, Windsor Castle; Balliol College, Oxford; Ruskin College, Oxford; and the university libraries of Cambridge, Hull, Leeds and Oxford. Extracts from documents in the Public Record Office appear by kind permission of the Keeper of the Public Records, and material from the Royal Library is used by the gracious permission of Her Majesty the Queen.

I would like to express my thanks to colleagues in Australia: Vernon Crew, Tony Delves, Michael Newman, Richard Pinder, George Shipp and Keith Wake; to Professor J B Condliffe of New Zealand; to Colonel Keith Bryan of the Royal Army Educational Corps; and to my wife Jean for research on WEA records in England and Australia. I owe a double debt to my friend and colleague Professor Stuart Marriott, for his wise editorial guidance, and his enterprise in securing publication of the book.

Finally, I am most grateful to Albert Mansbridge and his associates for having created the movements to promote the dialogue between education and experience, between labour and learning, which have afforded me a fascinating career; to the students in my first WEA classes who cheerfully undertook the task of training their own tutor without my being aware of this at the time; to the members of later classes whose talent and enthusiasm extended the frontiers of collective research in regional and local history; and to the many voluntary workers in the Association whose friendship I have enjoyed.

Bernard Jennings
Institute for Learning
Loten Building,
University of Hull

*February 2002*

# About the Author

Bernard Jennings began his career in adult education in 1950 as a tutor-organiser for the Workers' Educational Association in Yorkshire. In 1961 he became lecturer in history in the Department of Adult Education and Extramural Studies at the University of Leeds, where he was responsible for liaison with the WEA across the extramural region. Eventually he became senior lecturer and head of the Liberal Studies Division. In 1974 he moved to the University of Hull as Professor of Adult Education, and subsequently held a series of senior university positions, including Dean of the Faculty of Social Sciences and Pro-Vice-Chancellor. He became Professor of Regional and Local History in the Department of Adult Education in 1990 and retired three years later.

In 1955, 1958 and 1961 he was elected to represent the borough of Richmond on the former North Riding County Council. From 1981 to 1991 he was National President of the WEA.

Professor Jennings has research interests in two areas. He has written extensively, and edited books produced by WEA classes, in the field of regional and local history, his most recent work being *Yorkshire Monasteries: Cloister, Land and People* (Otley, 1999). On the history, policy and organisation of adult education, he has lectured in twenty countries and had work published in eight.

## Editor's Acknowledgements

The editor is grateful for financial and administrative support given by the University of Leeds and the Workers' Educational Association, which has ensured publication of *Albert Mansbridge*, the concluding title in the present series of 'Leeds Studies in Continuing Education'. Acknowledgement is also due to the Curator of the University Art Collection for permission to reproduce Sir William Rothenstein's crayon portrait of the subject of this book—a portrait which once graced the Leeds University building known thirty years ago as the Albert Mansbridge College.

# 1

## The Young and Enthusiastic Co-operator

Albert Mansbridge was born in Gloucester in January 1876, the youngest of four brothers. The family moved to London in 1880, and settled in Battersea in the following year. Albert's father was a carpenter, who rose to be a general foreman and then a clerk of works. His mother was an active member of the Women's Co-operative Guild from the time of its foundation in 1883. The Mansbridges were Congregationalists, regular chapel-goers who sent their boys to Sunday school. It was entirely in character that Albert made one of his first public appearances reciting poetry to the Band of Hope.[1]

In later life Albert Mansbridge looked back upon his childhood—perhaps through the rosy glow of his own success—and counted himself fortunate to have been brought up as 'a normal child in a decent working-class home'. Battersea was 'a highly favoured locality', with a pleasant park and easy access both to the museums of South Kensington and to the great commons south of the river Thames.

> Childhood has for me no memories of frustration. It was full of inspiration and happiness. It proved to me that the less anyone has, provided he has sufficient plain food, warm clothes and shelter, the greater his chances of happiness. Any little extra or change produces it.[2]

After brief experiences of two schools in Gloucester and London, Mansbridge spent five years as a pupil at board schools in south London. This was the era of 'payment by results' in elementary schools. The curriculum was dominated by reading, writing and arithmetic. Both teaching methods and discipline were rigid and mechanical, partly because classes were so large. At one stage Albert Mansbridge was one of a class of seventy children. As a bright boy, with a good memory and early signs of literary ability, he found school enjoyable, at least in retrospect. 'The teachers, men and women alike, were helpful and kind. They encouraged ambition to excel and were ever ready to stimulate interest.'[3]

Shortly before his tenth birthday, Mansbridge won a scholarship to Sir Walter St John's Middle School, and two years later he passed a second examination which took him to Battersea Grammar School. His teachers wanted him to stay at school until he could enter for a university scholarship, but he was sent to work as an office boy at the age of fourteen. Very few working-class boys, however intelligent, were able to pursue their education beyond that stage. Albert had in fact managed to go further than any of his brothers, who were all talented in different ways. William, the eldest, worked in a candle factory during the day and studied chemistry at night. He became a successful analytical chemist in the oil and fat trade, and was awarded an honorary degree by the University of Liverpool for his contribution to the work of scientific societies in that city. The second son, Allan, left Sir Walter St John's school to go into the civil service and rose to a senior position in Customs and Excise. Henry, two years older than Albert, inherited his father's craft skills, and contrived to combine, very profitably, the careers of woodwork teacher, house builder and cabinet maker.[4]

William Mansbridge tried unsuccessfully to persuade his father that with three out of the four boys at work, it was financially possible to keep Albert at school. Albert seems to have taken the same view, although he never criticized his father directly in any of his autobiographical works. In *The Making of an Educationist* (1929) (writing of himself in the third person) he observed: 'The traditions of his people, moulded by circumstances which never took into account the possibilities or perhaps the necessity for education at school beyond thirteen or fourteen, determined the future to be daily work.'[5]

Harold Begbie included in his book *Living Water* an account of the same experience based upon an interview with Mansbridge in 1917 or 1918.

> Without much trouble to himself he made remarkable progress at school, winning all sorts of scholarships, and inspiring some of his masters with inordinate ambitions for his future. But his father decided that he must take his place in the world; and when he was just over fourteen years of age this vivacious and scholarly boy, who ought to have gone to the University, was bundled into a merchant's office in the City of London to earn a few shillings a week.[6]

Mansbridge did not, however, bemoan his fate. In retrospect he was by no means sure that he had lost on balance by having to leave school at the age of fourteen. He was fond of quoting the academic achievements of men who had been sent to work much younger.

> There is abundant evidence that genius has arisen more often in the cottage than the manor, and has revealed itself apart from the assistance of schools and colleges … The truth is that nothing short of actual catastrophe can damp the fires of the spirit when they have started to flame.[7]

On the credit side were the educative influences and educational opportunities of London. Soon after starting work Mansbridge attended a university extension course given by Professor Vivian Lewes on 'The Chemistry of Air, Fire and Water', and gained a certificate with distinction in the examination. A few years later he heard the lectures of Alfred Milnes, who was 'endowed with powers of clear and constructive exposition of the intricacies of economics in relation to industry'.[8]

When he was nearly sixteen Mansbridge joined the civil service and soon became a boy clerk in the Education Department. He attended evening classes to prepare for the examination for entry to a second-division clerkship, a secure but modest career. His attention was, however, soon diverted from this objective by his other interests, primarily religious. At about the age of fourteen he had left the Congregationalists and joined the Church of England. He offered no explanation for his conversion except that he was attracted by the style of the services which he attended in Gloucester cathedral during holiday visits to the town of his birth. He was confirmed, became a Sunday school teacher, and spoke at mission services and open-air temperance meetings. By the time he was seventeen he had decided to try for holy orders. He applied for teaching posts in the hope of moving on later to Oxford or Cambridge, but was unsuccessful.[9]

In terms of literary parallels, Mansbridge combined the objective of Jude the Obscure with the methods of H. G. Wells's Mr Lewisham. Like the latter he had a 'schema' which provided for systematic daily study. Neither Jude nor Lewisham, however, could match Mansbridge for restlessness. He worked at different times for the civil service examination, London matriculation and the Excise examination as well as taking up the study of Latin and Greek in preparation for holy orders. He founded and edited the *Union*

*Observer*, the journal of the Junior Civil Service Prayer Union, and later became superintendent of a Sunday school and of a Band of Hope. In summer he played cricket, sometimes three or four times a week. In all, he found more satisfaction in active pursuits than in systematic study. 'I turned increasingly to the quicker results of public speaking and preaching, which I obviously enjoyed.'[10]

In October 1894, when he was eighteen, Mansbridge went to Oxford to sit for the Hughes–Neale scholarship, tenable at Oriel College. 'It was', he wrote later, 'a never-to be forgotten experience, those three days, struggling in a college hall with mysterious Latin and Greek.' Mansbridge may have found the papers in Mathematics, History and English rather less daunting, but he never had a serious chance. Not only was his own classical knowledge rather thin, but the scholarship was by no means a poor man's preserve. It was open to anyone who was a member, or whose father was a member, of a Co-operative society which had contributed to the scholarship fund set up to commemorate the work of two Christian Socialist activists in the Co-operative movement, Thomas Hughes and Vansittart Neale.[11]

Mansbridge wrote to his father after the first day of the examination, 'Now I have done as well as I expected, but the men against whom I have to compete are far my superiors in every way. All of them except one teacher are public school men and have read most everything … One fellow is from Owens College, Manchester.' Mansbridge could not have been surprised when the scholarship was awarded to one of the 'superior' men, in fact to the candidate from Owens College.[12]

Mansbridge's 'career as a would-be undergraduate', he wrote over thirty years later, 'commenced and ended in the hall of Oriel College'. He did not, however, consider his visit to Oxford to be entirely without fruit. 'Oxford, incomparable city, lit into undying flame a young man's affection … It was a very beautiful experience, invaluable to me afterwards.' More immediate consolation came in December 1894, when he passed the examination to become a licensed lay reader in the Church of England.[13]

Albert Mansbridge found a substitute for a university in Westminster Abbey where 'he heard with passionate delight the great preachers of the nineties'. One of the greatest of the preachers was Charles Gore, appointed canon of Westminster in December 1894. In the following Lent, Gore delivered in the abbey a course of lectures on 'The Sermon on the Mount', which were later published and became famous. They made a great impact on Mansbridge, and he wrote to Gore, asking him to contribute an article to the *Union Observer*. Gore refused, but invited Mansbridge to his house. Over supper the young man met churchmen and other guests whose conversation enthralled him, and gave him a glimpse of a promised land of wisdom and authority which lay at the end of the road of learning. 'As I listened ... I remember realising for the first time that the newspapers were not to be relied on as records of actual happenings. These men knew, and as they talked of incidents and scenes, not only in the House of Commons, but in many important institutions and places, I gained new views of life and manners.'[14]

Gore virtually adopted Mansbridge, inviting him frequently to his house not only for stimulating conversation with the canon' s guests, but also for lessons in Greek and a good deal of sound advice. Gore tried to persuade Mansbridge to settle down to steady work at his books instead of exhausting himself in a whirl of varied activities. Mansbridge went to see a Cambridge vicar who acted as host to non-collegiate students, but nothing came of it. He became interested in the foreign missions, and made contact with the bishops of British Honduras and New Caledonia. He toyed with the idea of taking a missionary post and seeking ordination abroad, but was warned by a friend that 'there is some restriction on men ordained as you propose to be, returning to England'.[15]

As the year 1895 drew to its close, Mansbridge faced a personal crisis. The prospect of a university place and holy orders was receding. As he had failed to progress in the civil service, he was due to leave his position as a boy clerk in January 1896, when he would be twenty years of age. In November 1895 he took a job, at a poor salary, as a ledger clerk in the office of a city company. Less than a year later he became a clerk in the tea department of the Co-operative Wholesale Society. The move did little to improve Mansbridge's material prospects. 'My work was once again monotonous ... It soon became clear that there was little or no hope of advancement.' He took the job presumably because it gave him a base for active work in the Co-operative movement, through which he hoped to realize some of his ideals.[16]

Mansbridge became involved in Co operative affairs at the time when a 'great debate' about Co-operative education was in progress. Consumer Co-operation was the strongest element in the working-class campaign to build a fairer and more democratic society from the bottom upwards. As working-class radicals gradually abandoned the strategy of demanding political reform through mass rallies and petitions and turned instead to collective self-help, a key instrument became the Co-operative society modelled on the Rochdale Pioneers Co-operative Society (1844). The Pioneers distributed profit as a dividend on purchases, which spread the financial benefits more widely and encouraged more people to play an active role in running their societies. The education of members in the principles and practice of Co-operation, and in related aspects of citizenship, was seen as a necessary feature of the movement. In 1852 the Rochdale Pioneers resolved to allocate 2½ per cent of profits to education, and this became the target urged upon societies by the Co-operative Union. In fact, in the mid 1890s the national average figure was ½ per cent. Furthermore two-fifths of this was spent on libraries and reading rooms, and a comparable sum on social events which came under the umbrella of education committees because they had some propaganda value. Less than £10,000 was used nationally for direct class provision and the support of university extension lectures.[17]

The founder of the university extension movement, James Stuart of Cambridge, had tested the demand for academic adult education through a series of experimental lectures on scientific subjects, one of them hosted by the Rochdale Pioneers. Stuart was greatly influenced by his contact with the intelligent artisans of Rochdale, at whose prompting he added a discussion class to his original scheme of formal lectures. He became convinced that 'the highest class of education, if properly adapted, was capable of being appreciated by, and of real use to, the general mass of the people'. In asking his own university to embark upon a regular series of extension courses, Stuart argued that the liberal education of adults, particularly those with a limited educational background, required teachers of university quality. Only the expert could make his subject both accessible and challenging.[18]

Cambridge began extension work in 1873. Oxford followed suit in 1878, but did little until 1885. Other universities gradually came into the field, but most of the provision was made by Cambridge and Oxford, which ranged throughout England, and in the metropolis by the London Society for the Extension of University Teaching, set up because London was not at that time a teaching university. In 1889/90 Oxford provided courses at over a hundred centres and Cambridge at sixty-seven.[19]

Although the university extension movement had arisen partly out of a sense of guilt in the older universities about the use of their wealth for the benefit of a privileged few, it was launched and maintained without the diversion of more than a tiny part of that wealth. The vice-chancellor of Oxford defended this policy in 1887. 'Our business is not to spread learning but to make learning, and for the funds for spreading it in different towns it is necessary that we should look to others outside.'[20] The cost to Oxford was about £500 a year, and at Cambridge similar expenses were met out of the profits of the Local Examinations system. Apart from these contributions, and limited help from a few Oxford and Cambridge colleges, the financial burden—the lecturer's fee and expenses, the hire of a hall, printing and publicity—fell on the local centre. With an audience of a hundred people, the fee required to cover costs in the absence of a local subsidy was twelve to fifteen shillings for a twelve-lecture course, and seven to eight shillings for one of six lectures.

In response to these financial problems, and in the hope of bringing its programme within the reach of a wider cross-section of the community, Oxford cut its standard course to six fortnightly lectures when it entered the field seriously in 1885. London and Cambridge courses normally lasted for twelve meetings.[21]

In order to attract a large enough lecture audience to cover the costs, and cater at the same time for the serious student, an ingenious pyramid of learning was constructed. A formal lecture lasting for one hour was followed by an optional tutorial class of up to one hour in length, for questions and discussion. Members of the class could, if they wished, submit a weekly or fortnightly essay (according to the pattern of the course) for correction by the lecturer. Those who had written a prescribed number of essays were allowed to sit for an examination. In the years 1893–1902 Cambridge had average attendances of ninety at the lecture and thirty at the class, with an average per course of thirteen weekly papers submitted and eight successful candidates in the examination. Oxford had more people in attendance, but fewer committed students. The latter were helped by the provision of a detailed printed syllabus, which included lecture notes and a reading list, and travelling book boxes.[22]

Additional opportunities for serious study were provided by the summer meetings, which began in Oxford in 1888 and came to be held in alternate

7

years in Oxford and Cambridge. In the period 1896–1914 attendances at Oxford ranged between 866 and 1752, and at Cambridge between 457 and 950, including in both cases visitors from overseas. The meeting was normally divided into two fortnightly periods; students could attend one or both of these. Costs were kept as low as possible, with a tuition fee of twenty-one shillings for the month and lodgings arranged for about twenty-five shillings per week. Financial help for a limited number of students was available in the form of scholarships offered by the University, by extension centres or by the Co-operative movement, usually on the basis of an essay competition.[23]

The leaders of the extension movement were disappointed at the limited working-class response. One of their aims, according to Dr R. D. Roberts (an extension administrator first at Cambridge, later in London), was 'the breaking down of intellectual caste and the universal extension of the intellectual franchise'. A prominent Oxford lecturer, the Revd Hudson Shaw, lamented in 1892, 'The one great blot on the movement was this—it was becoming very largely a middle class movement.' His estimate that workers made up 'only one sixth' of the sixty thousand extension students almost certainly exaggerates the proportion.[24]

The twin obstacles were finance—it was risky for working-class organizations sponsoring extension courses to fix a low fee in the hope of attracting a large audience—and alienation. Workers interested in education for the advancement of their class and the promotion of social and political reform had learned to mistrust middle-class benevolence. This point was well understood by Dr Roberts, who as assistant secretary at Cambridge devoted a great deal of time and energy to the promotion of working-class extension centres, especially in the north-east coalfield. The successful artisan centres, he wrote, 'are all alike found to present the characteristic feature that the management of the lectures is in the hands of an artisan committee'.[25]

The importance of ideology as well as resources is illustrated by the record of extension work in Hebden Bridge, a stronghold of both producer and consumer Co-operation. Extension lectures were financed by the Hebden Bridge Fustian Co-operative Manufacturing Society, often cited as one of the most successful of the 'productives'. The activists of the society looked forward to the creation of a co-operative commonwealth which would displace capitalism without concentrating power in the hands of the state.

They believed that their success would be proportionate to the wisdom and character of their members. For their broad purposes, knowledge was power. Where could they look for the knowledge? Robert Halstead, a fustian weaver who was a keen extension student, argued,

> The great drawback to the working man at the present time is that he is largely at the mercy of political tacticians and extravagant socialists for his knowledge of history. [He was probably thinking of the pamphlets and lectures of bodies such as the Social Democratic Federation and the Socialist League.] ... We need contact with men whose great work is to impart knowledge from sources as uncontaminated as anything that is human can be ... The success of the [labour] movement will finally depend, not so much upon large demonstrations and vigorous harangues, as upon the ability of working men to form large and correct views of the great economic questions ... For the supply of the knowledge ... it would be difficult to turn to any organisation as well qualified as University Extension ...

Knowledge would do more than help them to fulfil their roles as workers and citizens. 'Fortunately for the poor the highest pleasures of life are not inseparably connected with material possessions ... those who are poor in worldly goods need not succumb to the greater curse of poverty of ideas.'[26]

The success of the work in Oldham was due to two factors, the contribution of the Co-operative movement in financing the lectures and providing a congenial environment, and the skill and devotion of Hudson Shaw, one of the greatest of extension lecturers. In eleven out of the twelve years between sessions 1887/88 and 1898/99 he lectured in Oldham on a succession of historical topics. His average audience grew steadily in size—five hundred, seven hundred and in 1895/96, a thousand. Often a class of between one hundred and two hundred remained after the lecture for a question-and-answer session. A much smaller number wrote regular essays, and fewer still entered for the end-of-course examination. The largest number of successful candidates in any year was fifteen. However, Shaw cherished his band of devoted students, and was well rewarded for his efforts. His most successful pupil was Joseph Owen, a young working man who won an essay prize of £10 to take him to the 1894 summer meeting at Oxford. Largely through Shaw's influence an exhibition at Balliol was arranged for Owen. He went up to Oxford in 1895, and a few months after his arrival

9

won the coveted Brackenbury scholarship. He graduated with first-class honours, gained a research scholarship and then a fellowship, and had a distinguished career as an HMI. Oldham and the Co-operative movement were immensely proud of Joseph Owen as 'a splendid example of working-class ability', but the frequency of the references in Co-operative journals to his achievement was a testimony to its rarity.[27]

There were short-lived successes with working-class students at Toynbee Hall in east London, where the warden, Canon Barnett, was an enthusiastic supporter, and in the north-east coalfield. However, the members of the Northumberland Miners Union declined to change the rules of the union so as to allow its funds to be used for educational purposes. It was clear by the mid 1890s that if extension was to attract a substantial working-class clientele, Co-operative societies would have to play a leading role.[28]

At the annual Co-operative Congress in 1896 a special committee, of which Robert Halstead was a member, was appointed to review the movement's educational activities, particularly in the light of the increasing provision by local authorities of technical classes and libraries. The committee recommended to the 1897 congress that all societies should allocate at least 2 ½ per cent of profits to education; that the movement should concentrate on the teaching needed to make good Co-operators, particularly in industrial economics and citizenship; and that a new central education committee should be established, with a full-time paid secretary. The report had a mixed reception, and the full-time post was not instituted.[29]

In the meantime leading Co-operators and university extensionists had been holding a series of conferences with the aim of bringing the two movements closer together. Other Co-operative societies were urged to follow the example of Oldham and Hebden Bridge. Robert Halstead's campaign for the creation of a Co-operative wing to the extension summer meetings achieved a limited success. He was able to organize a Co-operative group admitted on reduced terms with some special lectures and discussions laid on. J. A. R. Marriott, secretary of the Oxford Extension Delegacy, arranged for Hudson Shaw to give 'missionary' lectures about university extension to Co-operative societies. Roberts of Cambridge urged the creation of a central higher education board to draw up schemes of work, and offer diplomas, for non-university adult education. A system of examinations under university extension auspices was instituted for Co-operative Union teachers of such subjects as industrial history and Co-operation. It was realized on all sides, however, that Co-operation was a democratic movement. Power rested with the general meetings of the individual societies, which could be exhorted, but not ordered, to give some priority to education.[30]

In the middle of these discussions and developments, letters and articles written by Albert Mansbridge began to appear in the Co-operative journals. He argued in favour of education to realize the ideals of Co-operation and condemned the obsession with dividend. In essence he repeated what Co-operative radicals had been saying for many years, and were still saying, but in a windier rhetoric than was fashionable even in those days. His self-education through wide reading and listening to sermons had made him addicted to purple passages. For example:

> Men for the cause; men, who, losing themselves, have found themselves; men who are men, who cling to what is noble and right, and pass by in their strength possessions and ease—such is the need of Co-operation ... with faith renewed, with a carelessness of self we will rise to the battle, and in triumph spread our borders ...[31]

On occasion Mansbridge seemed to be barely in control of his own verbosity:

> The abuse of forced-up dividends, the condemnation of the same, possess no healing power. The corrective influence of wise education will do all that is necessary, for upon education noble ideals are reared simultaneously with the power to fulfil them. The educated life is instinct with prevision, is a 'deliberate proceeding controlled by reasonable motives'. Will it be long before the cry of 'Dividend, dividend,' from morn till night is but the opposition screech, rather than, as sometimes now, the verdict of profound and sympathetic humanists?[32]

Insofar as Mansbridge made a distinctive contribution to the debate on Co-operative education, it was in relation to the Hughes–Neale scholarships at Oxford. Some means should be found, he argued, to give the 'poor and ill-trained' a chance at scholarships which tended to go to the 'rich and well-trained'. He described the hopeless task of the one competitor in a recent scholarship examination who had left school at fourteen—himself, although he did not mention this fact in the article concerned:

> societies are callous with regard to these scholarships. The competitor who had been at work since fourteen heard not a word from his own society, which would have been glad to claim a share in his success had he succeeded, although they would have had no more to do with it than the biggest store-hating shopkeeper in the vicinity.

Mansbridge had a dual solution to offer. First, the number of university scholarships should be increased, and they should be better publicized throughout the movement. Secondly, societies should found exhibitions of, say, £10 a year to enable clever boys from Co-operative families to continue at school long enough to prepare for university entrance.[33]

Mansbridge was able to attend the Co-operative Congress at Peterborough in 1898, with a scholarship awarded to him for attaining an 'extremely high standard of excellence' in a Co-operative Union examination in industrial history. During the congress a joint Co-operative–university conference was held, and Mansbridge joined in the discussion. His own account of this is misleading, not to say absurd. 'With the intrepidity of youth I jumped up and urged an alliance between the two great forces there represented.' Not only was he several years late for 'urging an alliance', but he rose after the bishop of Peterborough, Marriott, Roberts, George Jacob Holyoake and eight other delegates, who had spoken at length about both the principles and the practical needs of such an alliance. The only additional point he was able to make was a suggestion that the number of Hughes–Neale scholarships at Oxford should be increased. His enthusiasm made a favourable impression, however, and he was coming to be known as a promising young activist.[34]

There is no evidence that Mansbridge was reflecting on the experience of the Pennine Co-operative heartland, where attempts to form local federations of educational societies to provide a base for university extension prefigured the WEA.[35] He was suffering not only from the brashness of youth, but also from some of the disadvantages of being London based. The working-class movement in the capital lacked the cohesion found in places such as Oldham and Hebden Bridge, partly because people often lived and worked in different areas. London may have been the best place for the birth of a national movement for workers' education. It was not necessarily the ideal location for its conception.

In October 1898 Mansbridge became the teacher of a class in industrial history under the auspices of Battersea Co-operative Society. At the opening meeting he spoke on 'The Co-operative Ideal' with 'eloquence and verve', according to a report in the *Co-operative News*. All of the eight students who entered for the examination at the end of the course were successful. One won a scholarship to the extension summer meeting at Oxford, and three more gained distinctions, out of the six awarded nationally. These achievements earned further praise in the Co-operative press for the 'young and enthusiastic Co-operator'.[36]

It was planned to continue the educational debate at the Oxford extension summer meeting in August 1899. The Oxford Co-operative Society, one of the sponsors of the conference, invited Mansbridge to give a paper on 'The Relation of the Co-operative Movement to the Education of Citizens'. No copy of Mansbridge's paper has been found, but its contents can be pieced together from reports in the Oxford newspapers and the *Co-operative News*.[37] He began with routine attacks on Co-operative societies for allocating less than one per cent of profits to their education committees, and on the latter for using a large part of their limited funds for 'amusement and advertisement'. Referring to current discussions about closer links between the Co-operative Union and university extension, he argued that the Co-operative movement should concentrate its own teaching on book-keeping and the principles of Co-operation, and should train promising employees in these subjects during working hours. The study of citizenship, political economy and industrial history (the other subjects in the educational programme of the Co-operative Union) should be developed in alliance with university extension.

> In any consideration of the possible relationship between University Extension education and Co-operative education, it must ever be borne in mind that the former is more perfect, is better equipped in every way than the latter and must, where a common basis of teaching is agreed upon, be the controlling power.

Mansbridge was no doubt thinking of his own experience when he demanded that a full university education 'must ultimately be placed within the reach of every Co-operator whose capacities demand it. Co-operative societies must build a golden stairway from store to college.' He urged Co-operators to form study groups, open to extension students, which would not only study 'municipal and parliamentary affairs', but would also promote the election of Co-operators to local councils and parliament.

According to the *Co-operative News*, Mansbridge's address was 'of an aggressive nature'. He had failed to realize that he was preaching not merely to the converted, but to the missionaries, including David Smith (chairman of the Co-operative Union Educational Committee), Robert Halstead, Marriott and Hudson Shaw. He seemed to be telling them what they already knew, and to be blaming them for the difficulties against which they had been struggling. In the discussion which followed Mansbridge was criticized by Halstead for not acknowledging the progress which had already been made; by Smith for failing to appreciate that the pace of Co-operative advance was dictated not by the leaders but by 'those members of the quarterly meetings [of societies] who had control of the funds'; and by Marriott, who was reported in the *Co-operative News* as having 'severely condemned the main positions taken up by the writer of the paper'.

A few days later Mansbridge received a postcard from Gore which read, 'Marriott was much displeased at the report in the Co-op. News.' Marriott himself wrote to the journal, saying

> I did not 'severely condemn' the main position of Mr. Mansbridge's paper, and that for two reasons:
> (1) The paper itself was so heavily overlaid with rhetorical ornament that I was unable to understand clearly what its 'main position' was; and (2) because it seemed to me that in spite of its gratuitously aggressive tone, there was much in Mr. Mansbridge's paper well worth serious consideration ...
> I ... should be very sorry if my words were to have any effect in damping an enthusiasm which, if wisely directed and disciplined, will, I trust, bear rich fruit for both the movements represented at the conference, and especially for the cause which they are anxious in common to promote—the higher education of citizens.

Another cryptic postcard from Gore to Mansbridge commented, 'Certainly Marriott spoke his mind. I expect there is a good deal of truth in what he says.'[38]

In his own accounts of the conference compiled at intervals over the next forty years, Mansbridge readily admitted, and laughed at, his own clumsiness, but clung to the belief that he had been a pioneer in the advocacy of an extension–Co-operative partnership. His farewell speech to the WEA Central Council in 1916 included this passage:

> I well remember how, flushed with enthusiasm, I pleaded for an alliance between the University Extension Movement and the Co-operative Movement for the development of the study of history and Citizenship. My impetuosity was very marked and the conclusions I had come to, accompanied as they were by criticisms, gave great and perhaps justifiable occasion for the wrath of men who had been bearing the burden and heat of the day. In any case I was soundly trounced.[39]

In *The Making of an Educationist* (1929) he described how he had 'sought to prove to the conference that the co-operative movement could only achieve its highest educational work in alliance with the universities. He convinced no one, and was indeed so badly battered that he retired forthwith into private life.' Mansbridge's autobiography, *The Trodden Road* (1940) contains a similar account. 'In my enthusiasm for the new unity I made, perhaps, the youthful mistake of not eulogizing sufficiently the work which the Co-operative Movement had already done. A prominent co-operator [David Smith] said that I had aimed at the moon and hit a haystack.'[40]

Mansbridge retired to lick his wounds, and to concentrate for the time being on personal matters. Since the age of nineteen he had been engaged to marry Frances Jane Pringle, a fellow Sunday-school teacher. She shared his ambition 'to do good work … We … often discussed our future. We both felt that somehow we had to try to do something in addition to earning our living.' Mansbridge also received much stimulus and encouragement from talks with his fiancée's father, 'a very perfect gentleman and a ripe scholar', who had been a student at Trinity College, Dublin. If, however, Mr Pringle had asked his prospective son-in-law about his material prospects, he could not have received a very encouraging answer. Mansbridge was still working in the CWS tea department. His employers declared in a testimonial that he was 'an exceptionally able Clerk, being honest, sober and industrious in his work', but he had no hope of promotion and told a friend that he was 'very dissatisfied' with his employment situation.[41]

In the spring of 1899 Mansbridge began to learn shorthand in the hope

15

of improving his job prospects. He wrote to Michael Sadler, whom he had met at the Co-operative Congress in 1898, enquiring about openings in the Special Reports branch of the Education Department, and alternatively asking for help in finding a job in journalism. Sadler could not help with either request, but advised Mansbridge to consult Marriott. In a subsequent letter Sadler thanked Mansbridge for telling him 'of the work which Mr. Marriott has been able to put in your way'. (This was a few weeks before the conference at the 1899 summer meeting.) The work concerned was probably the part-time appointment as a teacher in an evening continuation school for the London School Board which Mansbridge secured at this time. In the following September he presented himself at Sherbrooke Road School, Fulham, as a teacher of economics, industrial history and typewriting. The typewriting class was very successful. Economics failed to recruit the necessary numbers. The industrial history class survived because Mansbridge persuaded some of his typewriting pupils to join it, and because 'an attractive girl student decided to enter it, and the class as a result received an immediate addition of a number of young men'. The latter class went on for several winters, and Mansbridge no doubt gained valuable insights into the nature of student motivation.[42]

Mansbridge's two jobs meant a very long working day during the winter months, but he presumably needed the money to marry and establish a home. In August 1900 he and Frances Pringle were married by Canon Gore. In the following year Mansbridge's search for a better job was at last successful. He was appointed cashier to the Co-operative Permanent Building Society. The latter was small, but was entering upon a period of rapid growth. In Mansbridge's first year with the society receipts increased by forty-two per cent, and he wrote, 'The work called for all my enthusiasm.' In the same year, 1901, the Mansbridges had a son, John.[43]

Albert Mansbridge was still searching for the field of practical idealism which could replace his frustrated vocation for the priesthood. A few months after their marriage, the Mansbridges gathered a few friends together at their home to form a 'Christian Economics Society'. They proposed to examine possible fields for Christian action in social reform, and produce ideas which they hoped might be ventilated through organizations such as the Christian Social Union. Their first subject of study was Gore's *Exposition of the Sermon on the Mount*.[44]

Several churchmen to whom Mansbridge wrote about his new society offered their moral support in general terms, but little progress was made for nearly two years, probably because the work depended too much upon Mansbridge himself, who was still busy with evening-school teaching. The editors of the *Economic Review* promised in May 1901 to consider an article by Mansbridge, but when one was finally submitted late in 1902 it was rejected. The editors explained that they were 'in thorough agreement with your line of argument and fully recognise the importance of the work you are doing' but thought that 'oral addresses to local Co-operative Societies are far more likely to bring about reform than any amount of repetition of the lesson in the E.R.'

Mansbridge accepted the rebuff with good grace and immediately wrote back to the Revd John Carter, one of the editors of the *Economic Review*, offering to write an article on 'The Co-operative Conscience'. Carter agreed to consider it in 1903, but repeated the argument that for Mansbridge's purposes 'the spoken word is much more effective than the printed type'. At about the same time, Mansbridge had a paper on 'The Ethical Basis of Co-operation' printed in pamphlet form. It is not known whether this was the article rejected by the *Economic Review*, or the offprint of a different article in another journal.[45]

Mansbridge spoke from time to time at Co-operative meetings, principally in the London area. In April 1902 he was one of the speakers at a conference of Co-operative employees held at Worcester, where he stayed with his old friend Charles Gore, the newly-appointed bishop of that see.[46] Mansbridge seemed destined for the twin roles of minor Co-operative functionary and minor Co-operative prophet. The latter was, however, both an over-crowded and a rather ineffectual calling. No major Co-operative conference was complete without a progressive bishop or dean to tell the delegates that Co-operation was a movement for moral regeneration and not merely an arrangement to secure honest trading and a dividend, but to most rank-and-file members Co-operation meant the 'divi' and the annual children's treat. For all his immense moral authority in the movement, George Jacob Holyoake's long-fought campaign for a universal '2½ per cent for education' and for profit-sharing in all Co-operative enterprises ('The consumer spends only his money; the worker spends his life') had left most Co-operators unmoved.[47]

17

If Mansbridge felt any sense of frustration at the slow progress of his Christian Economics Society or the limited impact of his Co-operative preaching, it is not revealed in such of his correspondence as has been preserved. At the end of 1902, however, he turned his attention again to the relationship between working-class movements and university extension, and sent an article entitled 'Co-operation, Trade Unionism and University Extension from the Co-operator's standpoint' to the *University Extension Journal*. The article appeared in January 1903, and was well received by both extension and Co-operative activists. Mansbridge was encouraged to develop his ideas more fully in two further articles. Robert Halstead contributed an article in support, and by the summer of 1903 the Association to Promote the Higher Education of Working Men, later re-named the Workers' Educational Association, was born.

# 2

# The Founding of the WEA

The reception given, particularly in university circles, to Albert Mansbridge's articles in the *University Extension Journal* in 1903 was very different from that accorded to his speech at Oxford in August 1899. The main reason was the contrast, in both tone and content, between the speech and the articles. Marriott, Hudson Shaw and other Oxford extension men were, however, more disposed in 1903 to encourage a new initiative in working-class education because of two disappointments which they had recently suffered in this field.

One of the reasons why Mansbridge had been 'so sadly battered' and 'soundly trounced' by both university extensionists and Co-operative leaders in 1899 was that he gave scant credit to his hearers for two modest schemes of partnership which had just been drawn up. The first created a joint examination system. Co-operative Union teachers of economics, industrial history and citizenship who passed an examination set by the Oxford Extension Delegacy could become 'approved' teachers of advanced Co-operative Union classes held under the joint auspices of the Educational Committee of the Co-operative Union and the Delegacy. By session 1902/ 03 eight approved teachers were available to take the joint advanced classes, but there was virtually no response from the Co-operative movement.[1]

The second scheme offered by the Oxford Delegacy to the Co-operatives was for the employment on an experimental basis of Joseph Owen, recently graduated with first class honours, to conduct jointly-arranged tutorial classes. Again there was no response, and Owen's paper given to a joint Co-operative–extension conference at Oxford in August 1901 was very pessimistic in tone: '… he saw very little hope of the spread of such a scheme as University education amongst Co-operative societies … The root of the difficulty was not the expense; it was the feebleness of the demand.'[2]

Another possible ally for university extension had recently appeared on the scene, based conveniently in Oxford, in the form of the Ruskin Hall movement. Ruskin Hall (later College) Oxford was founded in February 1899 by the Americans Walter Vrooman (with financial support from his wife) and Charles Beard. The Oxford hall, the development of which is discussed in Chapter 5, was intended to be the headquarters of a nationwide system of workers' education, involving branch halls, local lecture courses and study by correspondence. The five or six branch halls were short-lived, but many short lecture courses were given, particularly in the north-west of England, where Charles Beard established his base for a time. By 1902 about four thousand students had registered with the correspondence department. Students were encouraged to form local study groups in which they discussed the material for their monthly essays. There were ninety of these by 1902, and they had been grouped together to form the Ruskin Hall Educational League. Eighteen of the thirty-four branches of the league were in Lancashire and Yorkshire, often meeting in Co-operative premises. Working-class extension students in the Co-operative strongholds became involved also with the Ruskin Hall movement. Students who had won essay prizes to the Oxford or Cambridge summer meeting now won Ruskin Hall prizes, in some cases earning a short stay in Oxford. The sense of fellowship was strengthened by regional gatherings of the 'Leaguers'.[3]

Here, therefore, was an ideal organization to provide a popular base and support for working-class university extension. However, the Ruskin leaders, especially Vrooman, rejected any such co-operation. The ivory-tower institution and the bookworm don were often mocked, in articles and cartoons, in *Young Oxford*, the Ruskin magazine which was published monthly from 1899 to 1902. University extension was attacked as totally unsuited to working-class needs. By contrast. 'Ruskin Hall Extension ... gives the great truths of science and history in simple speech and form ... The Co-operative Society ... should no longer waste effort in the vain endeavour to adapt a Medieval System to its Twentieth Century needs.'[4]

Two joint Co-operative–university projects had come to nothing, and the Ruskin Hall leaders had slammed the door on partnership with university extension. The time was therefore ripe for another attempt to solve the problems of bringing the workers and the universities together. The article by Mansbridge published in the *University Extension Journal* in

January 1903—entitled 'Co-operation, Trade Unionism and University Extension from a Co-operator's Standpoint'—was very different in tone and content from his 'gratuitously aggressive' speech of August 1899. He had matured considerably in the interval. He was now twenty-seven, a husband and father, with a responsible job.

Without quenching the fires of his own enthusiasm, he had acquired a degree of self-discipline which not only brought his style under control but enabled him to select the arguments best calculated to sway his readers or hearers. He no longer belaboured the Co-operative and extension movements for their half-heartedness, but took as his theme the social dangers of ignorance in the increasingly active working-class movements.

> Working men today are all afire to act politically. Their Mecca is Parliament, their local temple the Municipality. The plank of their platform is Labour Representation. A state of affairs highly to be desired if it be the result of normal evolution preconditioned by wise education, but at present it bears no such evidence.

It was not enough to have sensible labour leaders, as their good work could be nullified by 'lack of thinking power in the rank and file'. The development of elementary education had opened up 'the beautiful and true' but also exposed people to the 'cheap and changing opinions' of the popular press.

> An Education which merely promotes an unthinking absorption of facts, however numerous, places men more at the mercy of the opinion of the hour, however irresponsible, and renders them more susceptible to flights of mere rhetoric. Democracy is in this parlous condition.

It was in any case a mistake for the workers to concentrate upon immediate issues.

> The appeal of the hour to Trade Unionists and Co-operators is that they make political strokes, promote Bills, register protests and send deputations to responsible Ministers. The true appeal is that they lift themselves up through higher knowledge to higher works and higher pleasures, which, if responded to, will inevitably bring about right and sound action upon Municipal, National and Imperial affairs ...

To break through 'the veneer' of a superficial elementary education and

21

provide the labour movement with the necessary 'wise and forceful educational corrective', the resources of university extension must be used. Extension had hitherto made some modest progress in working with ᴗo-operators, who in general had a broader outlook than trade unionists and so had 'realised in some measure the glory of Education'. It had not 'allied itself with Trade Unionism as such', but the time was ripe for it to do so. 'Trade Unionists and Co-operators are … evincing a tendency to recognise unity of interests, and it will be impossible for friends of Education who look forward into the future to consider the two Movements apart.'

Mansbridge's article was well received by the leaders of the extension movement, who had often lamented their limited success with working-class groups, and welcomed the possibility of making new contacts, particularly with trade unions. No doubt also Mansbridge's doctrine of the infallibility of the truly educated mind appealed to university men. When Mansbridge wrote the article he had, in his own words, 'little or no idea of organising a movement'. He was, however, encouraged by Dr Holland Rose, then editing the *University Extension Journal*, to develop his ideas more fully in two further articles.[5]

For the second article of the series, subtitled 'A Plan of Action' (March 1903), Mansbridge found a topical illustration in the Taff Vale case. After a strike in 1900 on the Taff Vale Railway in South Wales. the company, which in common with most railway companies refused to recognize trade unions, sued the Amalgamated Society of Railway Servants for damages resulting from unlawful picketing and breach of contract. The unions thought that they were protected by the Trade Union Acts of 1871 and 1876 from being sued in a corporate capacity for a tort, but the House of Lords decided otherwise in July 1901. The ASRS had to pay £25,000 in damages, the total cost to the union amounting to £42,000. The moral which Mansbridge drew from the case, however, was the need to educate trade unionists so that they would not follow the wrong leaders. He quoted Richard Bell, general secretary of the ASRS and 'LibLab' MP for Derby, who complained about his members electing 'irresponsible' men to the executive committee, 'not the most thoughtful' but those 'who have become popular through the exercise of their oratorical power'.[6]

At this stage Albert Mansbridge's ideas on how best to develop his new initiative were still vague. He suggested renewed extension propaganda directed towards trade unions as well as Co-operative societies. They should try to involve representatives of both movements in the administration of suitable extension centres. Ultimately these activities should be co-ordinated by a national joint committee of extensionists, Co-operators and trade unionists.

Robert Halstead contributed an article to the April number of the *University Extension Journal*, warmly supporting Mansbridge and offering some practical advice about the approach to trade unionists. The main problem—of which Mansbridge was fully aware—was that trade unions, unlike Co-operative societies, had virtually no machinery or funds for educational work. Even if union activists could be persuaded of the value of workers' education, they would come up against 'the usual stone wall of a financial difficulty'. They would need either to alter their rules to allow part of the members' subscriptions to be used for education, or impose a special levy for the purpose. 'I am not at all sure that either of these proposals would be entertained by the rank and file of trade unionists.' In these circumstances the initial approach should be made to trades councils, some of which had proved responsive to Co-operative educational propaganda. Round-table talks with trades councils and Co-operative bodies should be followed by an exploration of needs and problems at a series of joint national conferences. Neither Mansbridge nor Halstead had any illusions about the difficulties lying ahead in this field, and they consoled themselves with the thought that 'when we are educating a co-operator, we are often educating a trade unionist at the same time'.

By May 1903, when his third and final article appeared in the *Journal*, Mansbridge had a much clearer idea of the way ahead. He proposed the formation of an association to penetrate working-class movements 'by securing entry to the very many Co-operative and Trade Union meetings … as well as permission to contribute articles to Co-operative Records and Trade Union Journals' in order to 'prepare the Democratic Mind for the ordinary operations of University Extension'. The association should be a self-governing body representing Co-operators, trade unionists and the university extension authorities, possibly with sympathetic extension lecturers as its working officials. An immediate start should be made by setting up a 'Pioneer Association' which could plan an inaugural conference.

Mansbridge looked around for support. He went to see Canon Barnett, warden of Toynbee Hall. Their meeting is presumably the one mentioned in the autobiography of William (later Lord) Beveridge, who was visiting Toynbee Hall in preparation for taking on the job of sub-warden. 'With the Canon I interviewed a wild-looking young man with a plan for getting workpeople to ask for education before it was given to them; when Albert Mansbridge had left us, the Canon turned to me and said, "That young man has fire in his belly".'[7]

Barnett thought that £50,000 would be needed to launch the new association. Mansbridge now showed the quality which turns ideas into movements. He and his wife launched the 'Association to Promote the Higher Education of Working Men' at 'a completely democratic meeting attended by both of us and no one else' in their own home. The initial funds amounted not to £50,000 but to a half crown from Frances Mansbridge's purse, and Albert Mansbridge was appointed honorary secretary, *pro tem*.[8]

Mansbridge made a rapid circuit of likely sympathizers, and received warm encouragement at every point. Holland Rose and Robert Halstead were enthusiastic. Mansbridge went to Oxford to see Marriott, who promised to help stage the inaugural conference in the following August, and secured for Mansbridge another valuable ally by sending him to St John's College to talk to Sidney Ball. Marriott and two other extension administrators, Cranage of Cambridge and Hartog of Victoria, met the cost of reprinting as a pamphlet the articles written for the *University Extension Journal* by Mansbridge and Halstead, and Roberts of London undertook to buy a number of copies. Holland Rose contributed a foreword, and the pamphlet was distributed as a propaganda document.[9]

Mansbridge now formed a 'Provisional Committee of Co-operators and Trade Unionists'. This was something of a stage army, consisting of personal friends, including his cousin, several of whom had been members of Mansbridge's Christian Economics Society. The committee sufficed, however, to draft a constitution and plan the conference at Oxford at which the association was to be formally established.[10]

The conference, held on 22 August during the Oxford summer meeting, was attended by a representative gathering of extensionists and Co-operators, with a sprinkling of trade unionists. The principals in the cast were in general the same as at the conference of 1899—Bishop Percival of Hereford, Marriott, Hudson Shaw, Halstead, Mansbridge—but the scripts were very different. The bishop and the university spokesmen confessed that extension work had largely failed with the workers. Marriott was reported as saying, 'They had begun at the wrong end. The initiative must come from the people themselves.' He gave Mansbridge all the credit for organizing the conference and for whatever it might achieve. Robert Halstead read a paper on 'The Working Classes and Higher Education: an Associated Effort' in which he put his finger upon the reasons for the limited success of attempts to build a higher education movement within organizations such as the Co-operatives.

> working-class organisations framed for other purposes are now so large, and their officials so preoccupied, that such a special subject as the higher education of their members inevitably finds a secondary place in their attention. Any individual efforts that may be made to promote the cause, though they should be encouraged to the end of time, are obviously fragmentary ... and too much at the mercy of personal contingencies to be adequate ...
>
> The promoters of this Conference in the light of these considerations believe that if the higher education of working men has to make desired progress, it will have to consolidate itself into a special movement, adopt a special organisation and frame special objects of propaganda, and appoint a properly equipped staff to carry out its purposes.

By an ironic reversal of fortune, Hudson Shaw, the most successful of the Oxford lecturers with working-class groups, contrived to strike the wrong note. He appeared to be claiming credit for many of the ideas put forward by Halstead, regretting the limited response of the Co-operative movement to extension opportunities, and applauding the virtues of the middle classes. His speech drew the comment, in the editorial column of the *Co-operative News*, that 'his open glorification of the middle classes ... of which he proudly confessed he was a member ... revealed just that lack of democratic inspiration which is the weakness of the University Extension lecturer'.

After a vigorous discussion Mansbridge rose, with the praise of his former critics ringing in his ears, to argue the need for a powerful association to act as a bridge between the universities and working-class movements. He moved the adoption of the constitution, in which the objects of the association were defined as the promotion of 'the Higher Education of Working Men primarily by the Extension of University Teaching, also (a) by the assistance of all working-class efforts of a specifically educational character, (b) by the development of an efficient School Continuation System'.

The constitution stated that all individuals and societies in sympathy with the objects of the association were to be eligible for membership. The executive committee was to consist of eight members directly elected, two representatives each from the Co-operative Union and the Trades Union Congress, and one each from the university extension authorities and the Association of Education Committees. The eight elected at the conference were two Co-operators — Halstead, who had been since 1900 the full-time secretary of the Co-operative Productive Federation, and Mansbridge, who was described as representing Battersea and Wandsworth Co-operative Society; two trade unionists—George Alcock of the Amalgamated Society of Railway Servants and George Dew, an official of the Amalgamated Society of Carpenters and Joiners, London County Council alderman, active Co-operator and old friend of the Mansbridge family; and four university men—Hudson Shaw (Oxford), Dr T. J. Lawrence (Cambridge), Dr J. Holland Rose (London) and Professor S. J. Chapman (Manchester). The constitution provided also for the appointment of an advisory council of educational experts and for the establishment of autonomous local committees representing university extension centres, Co-operative societies and other working-class organisations 'of standing in the locality'.

Mansbridge and Halstead suggested the appointment of 'a University man ... in sympathy with working class aspirations', possibly 'a Hughes or Neale scholar', as secretary of the association, but the idea met with resistance and was dropped. A delegate from the Southern Section of the Co-operative Union said, 'Instead of a university man being appointed, he would have preferred a working man who was closely in touch with the aspirations of his class.' Mansbridge retained the secretaryship.[11]

To launch the movement in London, a second conference, described as 'a large and representative gathering from co-operative societies, trade unions, workmen's clubs, University settlements and University Extension lecturers', was held at Toynbee Hall on 12 December 1903. The chair was taken by Cosmo Gordon Lang, now bishop of Stepney, who reminisced about the pioneering days of Oxford's mission to the Pennine Co-operative belt, and particularly his contacts with 'the heroic little company which was for so many years a witness to all that was truest and best in co-operation—

the fustian manufacturers of Hebden Bridge'. A resolution urging working-class organizations, and especially Co-operative societies, to affiliate to the association was carried unanimously. The only discordant note in what one correspondent called 'two hours of high thinking and keen talking' was sounded by 'a lady whose associations with Co-operation are rather more on the fringe than within'. The lady was Mrs Bridges Adams, who had played an active part in the 'great debate' on Balfour's Education Bill as a Labour member of the London School Board and secretary of the National Labour Education League. She was a political associate of Will Thorne, the socialist leader of the Gasworkers' Union. Mansbridge wrote of her,

> It became impossible to hold an advertised meeting anywhere without her intrusion or that of her commissioned friends ... She asserted that she had documentary evidence that I was paid by the universities to side-track the working classes from any participation in their benefits, or, as she termed them, their ill-gotten gains.[12]

For the next six months Mansbridge and his associates concentrated on problems of organization—some of which lingered on for a few years. The association wanted a working president who was at the same time a man of some standing in the educational world or the labour movement. Michael Sadler (now professor of education at Manchester University) and Sir Oliver Lodge (principal of Birmingham University) were both invited and declined. The post was in fact left unfilled until William Temple was appointed in 1908. In the absence of a president formal leadership devolved upon the chairman of the executive committee. Hudson Shaw was elected to this office in October 1903, but resigned in the summer of 1904 through ill-health. Dr Lawrence or Robert Halstead usually took the chair for the next few years, but neither was formally appointed as permanent chairman. In 1905 Richard Bell MP and David Shackleton, Labour MP for Clitheroe and a leading figure in the textile trade unions, were appointed to represent the TUC on the advisory council.[13]

From August 1904 the gospel of the association was spread by a series of carefully planned conferences in different parts of the country, at most of which a local committee was set up to develop the work. The style and conduct of these meetings set the tone of the movement for the next decade. Mansbridge brought together progressive ecclesiastics, university heads and professors, politicians of different persuasions, prominent Co-operators and, whenever possible, trade union leaders to declare their support for the aims of the association. He played a relatively minor part in the public proceedings, concentrating on the organizational work needed to set up the meetings, invite the speakers and persuade Co-operative and other working-class bodies to send delegates.

The first meeting of the series was held on 6 August 1904 at Exeter, where Cambridge was holding its summer meeting. Canon Barnett took the chair. Speakers included Professor J. H. B. Masterman of Birmingham University, Marriott, Cranage and four delegates from workers' organizations, including Halstead and W. H. Watkins, a veteran activist of Co-operative education in the south-west. A committee for the latter region was formed, including representatives of the University Colleges of Bristol and Exeter.[14]

In the following October and November similar meetings were organized in Manchester, Reading and Stratford (East London). At the first of these, held on 8 October, the vice-chancellor of Manchester University presided, and the principal speakers were Walter Nield, president of the North Western Association of Co-operative Educational Committees, J. Harker, president of the Manchester Trades Council, Mrs J. W. Bury, president of the Women's Co-operative Guild and Dr Dale vice-chancellor of Liverpool University. Dr Dale declared,

> Thirty years ago the universities of England were the universities of the few; today they were the universities of the many; tomorrow, he trusted, they would be the universities of all. The barrier of creed had practically gone, the barrier of sex was going, and now the task before them—the task to which many of them were addressing themselves—was to see that the social barrier should go as well (applause) and that the ... want of ... money should no longer stand in the way of getting a sound, solid and complete university education. He was convinced that this movement would never be what it ought to be unless the working men's societies took the work into their own hands ... The aim of the movement should be not to make more efficient workmen, but to make better men.

Mansbridge read letters of apology for non-attendance from several notables, to whom he had written in the hope of securing quotable replies. They included the prime minister, A. J. Balfour, and Winston Churchill. The latter wrote,

28

I need hardly say that I am in full sympathy and agreement with the objects of the association. It ought to be perfectly possible in this country for a man of high, if not necessarily extraordinary, intellectual capacity, to obtain with industry and perseverance the best education in the world, irrespective of his standing in life.

The conference resolved that a committee should be established, consisting of representatives of the universities of Oxford, Cambridge, Manchester, Liverpool and Leeds, the North-Western Section of the Co-operative Union, the North-Western Association of Co-operative Educational Committees, the Women's Co-operative Guild, the trades councils of Manchester, Liverpool and Leeds, the Manchester Ruskin Hall Committee, the National Union of Teachers and the National Conference of Friendly Societies. Its purpose was to enquire into the best methods of bringing the working classes of the north-west into closer touch with the universities. The inclusion of Leeds University and the West Riding reflected the facts of Co-operative geography, as 'the north-west' was in this case made to coincide with the territory of the North-Western Section of the Co-operative Union.[15]

The Reading conference was organized jointly by the Association to Promote the Higher Education of Working Men and Reading Co-operative Society. The speakers included R. F. Honter of the Bermondsey University Settlement (recently appointed treasurer of the APHEWM), who read a paper on 'Higher Education for Working Men'; W. M. Childs, principal (since 1903) of University College, Reading; Rufus Isaacs KC, recently returned at a by-election as Liberal MP for the borough; Henry Pugh, director of education for Reading; J. B. Johns, president of Reading Co-operative Society; J. A. R. Marriott; and Mansbridge. Marriott expressed his 'profound sympathy' with the efforts of the association to equip the citizens of the country for their responsibilities in 'one of the most interesting experiments in the whole history of political science, the experiment of ruling not merely a nation, but a vastly spreading Empire by means of democratic machinery'. Reading Trades Council and seventeen trade union branches were represented, and the local branch of the SDF sent two delegates, both of whom spoke in favour of the aims of the association. A local committee was set up, with H. C. Sanderson, secretary of Reading Co-operative Society Education Committee, as secretary.[16]

Childs and Pugh had already had discussions about the possible uses of the 1902 Education Act, which allowed LEAs to supply or support further education, including liberal adult education. The conference at Stratford (east London) in November 1904, called according to the now established form by the local Co-operative societies and the APHEWM, was dominated by this consideration. The two hundred delegates included representatives of five LEAs, trade union branches, over a dozen Co-operatives and twelve university settlements. Canon Barnett presided and repeated the now familiar argument that 'the working classes were becoming the governing classes, hence the need for higher education'. Mrs Bridges Adams also took part, 'occasioning some amusement by announcing herself as a representative of the Gasworkers' Union'.[17]

Two kinds of 'local committee' had emerged from these early conferences, covering respectively a region and a town. The north-western committee developed into the prototype district of the association, and even more quickly Reading emerged as the first branch. A second conference in the latter town, held on 18 October 1904, elected a committee to draw up a constitution, which was approved by a delegate conference on 15 November. The organization was called 'The Association for the Advancement of the Higher Education of the Working Classes in Reading'. Its objectives were to stimulate working-class interest in education and to satisfy that interest principally through evening classes provided by the Reading Education Committee and the university college. Membership was open to both individual members and affiliated societies. Provision was made for the representation of the latter on the governing council. The principal of the university college and the secretary of the LEA were to be ex-officio members of the executive committee. W. M. Childs emphasized, however, at a public meeting held on 30 November, that the new body was entirely under working-class control and was not an instrument of either the college or the LEA. The chairman and secretary were both Co-operators, and the executive committee included, as well as other Co-operators, and trade unionists, J. F. Hodgson, a working-class member of the SDF, who succeeded to the chairmanship in 1906. Rufus Isaacs guaranteed the expenditure of up to £75 to launch the branch.[18]

The example of Reading was quickly followed in several other towns, and by March 1905 branches had been established in Derby, Woolwich and

Ilford (where the Mansbridges were now living). In March and April conferences in Rochdale led to the formation of a branch which was to play a major part in the evolution of the association. The Rochdale story demonstrates the merits of the APHEWM as conceived by Mansbridge. It was federal at two levels. The districts and branches enjoyed a high degree of autonomy, and the branches were as much federations of interested organizations as collections of individual members. They tried to stimulate and co-ordinate all endeavours for workers' education (except those of a propagandist nature), but did not try to supplant any of them. Rochdale had a long tradition of university extension. In 1903 a new committee was set up to manage the evening extension lectures (lecture series were held in the afternoons under different auspices) with a view to attracting as many working people as possible. The committee persuaded the LEA to pay a tutor for a supplementary class which alternated with the fortnightly lecture provided by the Oxford Delegacy. Some of the extension students were also members of other classes—two Ruskin Hall correspondence classes meeting in the Toad Lane Co-operative Stores, and two classes organized by the Young Men's and Young Women's Classes of the Clover Street Unitarian Sunday School. One of the latter studied psychology under a Unitarian minister, and the other followed courses first on sociology and subsequently on economics under the leadership of T. W. Price, a warehouseman who was a member of the Social Democratic Federation. The combined membership of the Clover Street classes was about forty-five.

The Rochdale (Evening) Lectures Committee succeeded in attracting increased working-class support, but not on a scale to satisfy its own aspirations. The committee was therefore interested in Mansbridge's new association, and sent its joint secretaries, L. V. Gill and Alec Carter, to attend the conference held in Manchester on 8 October 1904. As a result of their report the committee decided to affiliate to the association. Both Mansbridge and Mr Y. Pickles, secretary of the North-Western Committee which was set up at the Manchester conference, followed up the affiliation with letters suggesting the formation of a local branch. A conference was held on 16 March 1905, at which Walter Nield and Professor S. J. Chapman and Sydney Waterlow of Manchester University spoke about the aims of the Association to Promote the Higher Education of Working Men. A resolution to form a branch, moved by the chairman of the evening lectures

31

committee and seconded by the secretary of Rochdale trades council, was carried unanimously. However, to quote T. W. Price, 'During the discussion … considerable criticism was levelled at the name of the Association, not only because it was too long, but also because many of the delegates considered that there was a suggestion of patronage in it.'

The provisional committee appointed by this conference was instructed to find a more suitable name, and its choice of 'Rochdale Education Guild' was accepted by a second conference held on 10 April. In the following month the evening extension lectures committee dissolved itself, and transferred its assets and responsibilities to the guild. L. V. Gill and Fred Greenwood became secretaries of the guild, and Alec Carter was appointed treasurer. The Co-operative society and trades council were amongst fifty local organizations—including the Clover Street and Ruskin classes—which had affiliated by the autumn of 1905.[19]

The APHEWM had included amongst its original objectives the development of a system of continuation schools for young people aged between thirteen and eighteen. At many of the early conferences the matter was raised, and the idea of compulsory attendance at evening schools received a good deal of support. The association was influenced by Michael Sadler's reports to the Board of Education on continuation-school systems in continental countries, but people like Robert Halstead drew also on their own experiences to urge the case for clearing young people off the streets and sending them to evening schools. Compulsory evening schooling, it was argued, would bring them to the age of eighteen both able and anxious to benefit from the provision of adult education. R. H. Tawney was in favour of compulsion. In his report on the first term's work of the Rochdale tutorial class (described in Chapter 3), he argued that it would both limit the working hours of young people and ensure that adult students were 'not handicapped by the mechanical difficulties of correct composition'.[20]

In August 1905 an impressive gathering of academics, politicians and labour representatives met in Oxford to consider the matter. Charles Gore, now bishop of Hereford, moved a resolution asking 'the Board of Education to ascertain from the local education authorities how far and under what conditions employers and employed, in their respective areas, would welcome legislation having for its ultimate object compulsory attendance at evening schools'. The resolution, supported by the Earl of Crewe, Michael

Sadler and Will Crooks, a Labour MP, was passed almost unanimously.[21]

A few months later a delegation of trade unionists and Co-operators, including Crooks, Shackleton and Mansbridge, waited on Sir William Anson MP, parliamentary secretary to the Board of Education, and Robert Morant, the permanent secretary, to ask for a 'scientific inquiry', not immediate compulsion. 'It is believed', wrote Mansbridge, 'to be the first deputation composed entirely of working-class representatives which has formally visited the Board of Education.' Morant subsequently expressed to Anson his doubts about the value of an inquiry, which was not likely to take the matter beyond a question of opinion.[22]

Mansbridge and his colleagues were criticized by some WEA groups, including the Reading branch, for pursuing the idea of compulsory evening classes which, it was feared, would delay the raising of the school leaving age. The matter was referred to the consultative committee of the Board of Education, whose members included Mansbridge, Shackleton, A. L. Smith and Sadler. Its report issued in July 1909 included several recommendations for improving the full-time and part-time educational provisions for young people. The report was pigeon-holed, although some of its proposals were incorporated in H. A. L. Fisher's Education Act of 1918.[23]

Meanwhile the association had acquired a new name and a full-time secretary. The title 'An Association to Promote the Higher Education of Working Men' was both cumbersome and needlessly offensive to the Women's Co-operative Guild. The central executive committee made the timid recommendation to the second annual meeting, held in Birmingham in October 1905, that 'to Promote' should be replaced by 'for', but it was overwhelmed by an onslaught led by women Co-operators and the delegates from the Rochdale Education Guild. The latter proposed the name 'The National Education Guild', but the title eventually agreed was 'The Workers' Educational Association'.[24]

The gathering at Birmingham was used also to launch what became the Midland District of the WEA. The usual representative assembly of Co-operators, trade unionists, adult school leaders and university men heard speeches from Sir Oliver Lodge, principal of the University; Richard Bell, MP for Derby and secretary of the ASRS; Charles Gore, now bishop of Birmingham; and others. A committee was set up with Professor J. H. B. Masterman of Birmingham University as chairman, and W. J. Sharkey, a brushmaker who had been at Ruskin Hall, Oxford, as honorary secretary.[25]

It was clear that the WEA could not continue to expand in this way without at least one full-time national officer. The financial position was extremely precarious, with an income in the second year of only £100. It was believed, however, that a full-time secretary could earn part of his own salary by increasing the income from membership subscriptions and affiliations. A central office appeal fund was opened, with the aim of guaranteeing an income of £250 a year for five years. In December 1905, when the appeal fund (the guarantors of which included Hudson Shaw, the Dean of Christ Church Oxford, the Earl of Crewe and the Marquis of Ripon) had reached nearly £70 a year, Mansbridge was offered and accepted the post of full-time secretary for a minimum period of five years.[26]

Mansbridge took up this position on 1 April 1906. Because of the financial difficulties of the WEA his salary was fixed at '£250 a year perhaps'. He received no more than £200 in his first year, and the finance committee resolved in 1908 that 'in the event of the funds of the W.E.A. ever rising to such a level as to make it possible, the General Secretary should be permitted to claim the difference between the salary received by him and the amount of his approved salary, £250 per annum'.[27]

With Mansbridge able to devote his whole time to the work, the expansion of the WEA accelerated, a process which will be discussed in Chapter 4. The number of branches rose from thirteen in June 1906 to forty-seven a year later. The healthy autonomy of these branches was reflected in the wide variety of activities in which they engaged in their early years: lectures and classes on historical, literary, social and political questions, reading circles, nature-study rambles, research into the local flora, art exhibitions, classes for other bodies especially church and chapel societies, and lectures on a wide range of domestic and practical arts, including gardening, first aid, 'The Care of Home and Children', and, for carters, 'The Care of the Horse'. The movement as a whole, however, was united in its commitment 'to educate Working Men to such a point as will enable them to take full advantage of the systematised teaching provided in a University Extension Centre or College, which it is intended to place in every town and district'.[28]

Several WEA branches, established in towns which already had well-organized extension centres, confined themselves to negotiating special terms for artisans. In 1906/07 the Portsmouth branch sold forty-four tickets for a lecture series at two shillings each instead of the normal charge of four shillings. Derby made a similar arrangement and also helped to organize a preparatory class. The numbers of working-class students drawn into extension work in this way were relatively small—at Oxford the attendance of workpeople was described as 'poor'—but the WEA had the consolation that its financial commitment was also limited.

A few branches, set up in close association with new universities or university colleges, were able to escape the financial straitjacket of traditional extension work because their academic partners were prepared to experiment without worrying too much about the income from students' fees. Two short courses provided by University College, Reading—the first by Principal Childs on local history and the second by A. L. Bowley on economic questions—had attendances of no more than twenty, but were regarded as academically successful. Eight lectures were given in Sheffield University on 'Reformers of the Nineteenth Century'. At Birmingham University, whose principal, Sir Oliver Lodge, was one of the WEA's strongest academic allies, five experimental courses of five lectures each were given on social and economic questions. The lecturers included Professors J. H. B. Masterman, W. J. Ashley and J. H. Muirhead. The average attendance was about 350, mainly trade unionists and adult school teachers in search of material for their Sunday morning lessons, and 'many essays' were handed in.[29]

The real test both of the WEA's ability to recruit working-class students for extension lectures, and of the suitability of extension methods for such students, came in the dozen or so towns where the WEA branch undertook the entire responsibility for extension courses. A few of these ventures were educational failures, with either low attendances or a poor response from the students. In most cases, however, an encouraging working-class response was secured at the expense of financial difficulties. Darwen Branch, established (as the Darwen Education Guild) in June 1905, quickly set to work to organize a series of six fortnightly extension lectures, alternating with six discussion classes, on 'Movements in Social Reform', for a fee of only one shilling. The resultant heavy deficit put the branch out of business within a year of its formation, and it was several years before WEA activity in the town resumed. At Ilford the WEA branch fared better. It revived a defunct extension centre in October 1905 by arranging a course on 'Social Teachers of the Nineteenth Century', taken by R. H. Tawney. Essex County Council refused to grant-aid the lectures but the branch managed to provide them with the help of a grant from the University of London Extension Board. The course was academically successful; eight students passed the examination, four with distinction. Michael Sadler praised Tawney's work in a report he was writing on higher education in Essex, and the county council was persuaded to underwrite the work from the following year.[30]

The educational and financial limitations of the extension system as a vehicle for workers' education were revealed most clearly by the experience of the Rochdale Education Guild. The guild, as already explained, owed its foundation partly to the initiative of the Rochdale (Evening) Extension Lectures Committee, the functions of which it immediately assumed. In its first year, 1905/06, the guild continued the policy of its predecessor in choosing literary subjects. Two six-lecture courses were provided by Oxford, John Cowper Powys on 'Six Selected Plays of Shakespeare' and Hudson Shaw on 'The Life and Teaching of John Ruskin'. Average attendances were between five and six hundred, which made the courses financially successful. According to the report in University Extension, the audiences included

> very large numbers of working men and women. "The world is bigger for us than it was before", declared one working man in proposing a vote of thanks to Mr. Powys, and Mr. Hudson Shaw has expressed his delight at the character of the audiences that assembled to hear him.[31]

For session 1906/07 the Guild planned a more varied programme, with courses by Powys on Shakespeare's historical plays, and E. L. S. Horsburgh on 'Political and Social Problems'. Both were preceded by summer discussion classes. Powys's course, held in the autumn term, attracted an average attendance of 550. When Horsburgh took over after Christmas, the attendance dropped to 220, causing the guild a serious financial loss. Ninety per cent of the students were said to be working people, and their thirst for knowledge was embarrassingly strong. According to T. W. Price,

> It had been usual in previous courses for a considerable portion of the audience to stay behind to put questions to the lecturer, and sometimes as many as 150 stayed; but in the case of Mr Horsburgh's course very few of

the audience left at the end of the lecture, and the questions were more numerous and insistent than in the literary courses, and invariably developed into a discussion. It was obvious to everyone that free, unrestricted discussion of economic subjects in a gathering of 200 persons, most of whom wished to speak, was an impossible proposition ...

Horsburgh reported that 'a larger number than ever before wrote papers'. The examiner's report was very favourable: 'some of the papers were of remarkable excellence'.[32]

This combination of financial and educational difficulties led the Rochdale people to 'inquire whether some better way could not be found of making University teaching in Economics and History available to working people than by University Extension courses'. The problem had been very much in Mansbridge's mind for some time. In an article published in the *University Review* in August 1905 he argued that the WEA would 'have failed unless intensive class teaching up to University standard is developed'. At the close of the five experimental courses mentioned above, the Birmingham branch urged the need for consecutive study over two or three years in smaller classes. In the WEA annual report for the same year, 1906/07, reference was made to the need for classes of not less than two years in length from which 'distinguished students' could go on to the university to read for a diploma. A conference held at London University in June 1906 set up a committee to consider the needs of the artisan-student, and it, too, reported in favour of tutorial teaching for small groups of students.[33]

The establishment of a system of university tutorial classes for small groups of working people, lasting for two or three years, and leading in some cases to full-time university study, would require either a greatly increased commitment on the part of the universities, or generous help from public funds, or both. It offered a greater challenge than had been involved in the foundation of the WEA, and provided at the same time a critical test of the value of the association. Some of its most important academic supporters had, in Mansbridge's words, 'made it clear that its success or failure ... would be estimated by the manner in which it promoted serious study on the part of small groups of working men and women'. Mansbridge chose his Rochdale colleagues, quite deliberately, as the group of workers whose hunger for learning could most powerfully be demonstrated, and proceeded to take up the challenge.[34]

# 3
## Oxford and Working-Class Education

'Labour has "arrived"', wrote J. A. R. Marriott in the *Fortnightly Review* in December 1906. Future historians would say 'that in that year a new force manifested itself for the first time in English politics'. The general election of January 1906 had resulted in an overwhelming Liberal victory, but Marriott's attention was focused on the fifty-three representatives of Labour elected to the House of Commons—twenty-nine members sponsored by the Labour Representation Committee and twenty-four 'Lib-Labs' in the ranks of the Liberal Party. Once the Taff Vale judgment had been reversed by the Trades Disputes Act of 1906, the Labour MPs became relatively docile allies of the Liberals. A few years later G. D. H. Cole wrote gloomily, 'The present Labour Party can never become a majority and would be sadly at a loss to know what to do if it became one … Trade Unionists as a whole have very little revolutionary spirit … they will lie down gladly in their thousands in the green pastures of Liberalism and Reform.' In 1906, however, the return of so many Labour MPs induced feelings approaching panic amongst some of the wealthier classes. 'The West End thinks its hour has come', commented Canon Barnett in a letter to his brother. Even some of the more radical Liberals were 'a bit awed about the power of Labour and wonder what it will do'.[1]

Marriott argued that the 1906 election signalled the transfer of 'a preponderating share of political control' to the common people.

> The British people have deliberately decided to try an experiment which is without precedent and without parallel in the history of the world. They have determined to attempt to rule, not merely a great kingdom, but a world-wide Empire by means of a democratic machinery.

Marriott had used the same argument, in almost exactly the same words, in addressing WEA meetings during the previous two years. Success or failure in the experiment was 'a matter of political life or death'. Marriott recalled warnings uttered during the previous thirty or forty years about the need to 'educate our masters' and the danger of teaching 'our democracy to read unless we also teach it to think'. Fortunately 'a new spirit [was] stirring among the working classes in regard to higher education'.

Marriott had a word of praise for Ruskin College and quoted with approval the observation of one of its students. 'It has come something in the nature of a shock to most of us that there are two sides to every question.' The WEA had achieved 'remarkable success' as a missionary organization and had 'worked wonders in bringing into closer and more sympathetic contact representatives of the Universities and of working-class organisations'.[2]

The political advance, and the educational demands, of labour interacted with a 'stirring of the spirit' which was taking place in, and about, the University of Oxford. A public debate on university reform was opened by eight articles on 'The University and the Nation' which appeared in the Westminster Gazette in February and March 1906 under the pen name 'Lambda'. Later in the same year similar ideas were ventilated by a young classics don from New College, Alfred Zimmern, in an article in the Independent Review entitled 'Oxford in the New Century'. In April and May 1907 'some Oxford Tutors' (a group of fellows and tutors from eight Oxford colleges) contributed a series of articles in The Times. The reformers' case was put before parliament by Charles Gore, then bishop of Birmingham, who opened a debate in the House of Lords on 24 July 1907.[3]

These initiatives were all part of a co-ordinated campaign. 'Lambda' was R. H. Tawney, who had been a student at Balliol College, Oxford from 1899 to 1903 and went after graduation to live at Toynbee Hall and do social work in East London. The 'Oxford Tutors' included William Temple (Balliol 1900–04), a close friend of Tawney who had been his contemporary at Rugby and became after graduation a fellow of Queen's College; Alfred Zimmern (Winchester, and New College 1898–1902), who was fellow and tutor of New College; Richard Livingstone (Winchester, New College 1899–1903), fellow and tutor of Corpus Christi; John L. Myers (Winchester, New College 1888–92), student (that is, member of the academic staff) of Christ Church; and William Beveridge (Charterhouse, Balliol 1897–1901) who held a prize fellowship at University College, had been sub-warden of Toynbee Hall in 1903/04, and became in November 1905 a leader writer on the Conservative *Morning Post*. The development of the campaign can be traced back to a discussion between Tawney, Temple and Zimmern in the summer of 1905 on the subject of Oxford reform. The discussions were resumed, at Tawney's suggestion, in November 1905. Temple could not take part as he had just left for a study visit to Germany, but he wrote from Jena on 5 November, 'I understand that a conspiracy meeting was held today under my mother's presidency.' Some of the 'conspirators' formed themselves into the Catiline Club, named after a man famous for conspiracies against the Roman state in the time of Cicero.[4]

Behind the activities of Tawney and his friends can be discerned the guiding influence of Canon Barnett, warden of Toynbee Hall. Barnett had been a warm supporter of the WEA since its foundation and was a member of its advisory council. He wrote an article for the second number of a monthly journal which began publication in May 1905, the *University Review*. In it he argued that

> Oxford and Cambridge need what workmen can give, and workmen have no less need of the Universities ... The Universities have the knowledge of human things ... They have followed the struggles of humanity towards its ideals ... Workmen have the strength of character which comes of daily contact with necessity, the discipline of labour ... If they had their share of the knowledge stored in the National Universities they would know better at what to aim, what to do, and how to do it. They, as it is, are often blind and unreasoning. If these National Universities ... were in touch with the industrial classes, they would adapt their teaching to the needs and understandings of men, struggling to secure their position in a changing industrial system and better acquainted with facts than with theories about facts.
>
> Workmen have the energy, the honesty, the fellow-feeling, the habit of sacrifice which are probably the best part of the national inheritance but as a class they have not ... the judgement which knows the value of evidence, the feeling which would guide them to distinguish idols from ideas ... The old Universities and industry must, if this analysis be near the truth, co-operate for social reform. There are many ways to bring them together. The University extension movement might be worked by the hands of the great labour organisations—legislation might adapt the constitution of the Universities to the coming days of labour ascendancy—workmen might be

brought up to graduate in colleges, and they might, as an experiment, be allowed to use existing colleges during vacations.[5]

Before this article appeared, Tawney had, at Barnett's suggestion, presented himself at the WEA office and been enrolled as a member. Mansbridge recognized that he had secured a most valuable ally, and at the annual general meeting of the WEA held in October 1905 Tawney was elected to the central executive committee. He and Beveridge had given lecture courses on industrial history and social problems at Toynbee Hall in 1904/05. As explained above in Chapter 2, Tawney began his career as a teacher under the auspices of the WEA by giving a course of extension lectures for the Ilford branch in the Lent term 1906. William Temple also joined the WEA in 1905, as a result, according to Mansbridge, of attending a WEA conference at Oxford in August 1905, on the subject of continuation schools.[6]

According to Tawney, his articles in the *Westminster Gazette* were 'inspired' by Barnett. It was certainly no coincidence that the editor of the *Gazette* was a close friend of the canon.[7] 'Lambda' demanded that academic standards at Oxford should be raised by having an entrance examination which was a proper test of aptitude and by the development of research; that the university should be strengthened by the diversion of some of the wealth of the colleges; and that the scholarship system should be reformed and living costs lowered to open Oxford to a wider social range. It would be necessary, however, 'to devise some expedient which will not end in making schoolmasters out of workmen, clergymen out of schoolmasters, and in sending as grist to the Civil Service mill men whose talents are needed elsewhere'. Artisans and elementary-school teachers should not be 'lost to the class from which they spring'. It was necessary

> in a democratic State that as many men as is possible should possess some knowledge of the corporate life of humanity which is expressed in literature, philosophy and history. Such knowledge it has always been the work of Oxford to impart ... Oxford has aimed primarily at the making of citizens ...

Oxford had been the foster-mother to the class which had been dominant in politics, education and business, training them in suppleness and moderation of intellect, in respect for the complexities of human affairs and in the ambition to offer a reasonable service to Church and State.

The spread of this teaching to new responsible groups would be no revolutionary departure. In his final article Tawney proposed the setting up of a royal commission to impose reforms in three areas: the system of government of the university, college revenues and scholarships.[8]

There were some spirited replies to 'Lambda' in various journals, especially the *Oxford Magazine*. Determined to keep up the momentum of the reformers' campaign, Barnett wrote to the editor of the *Independent Review*, Edward Jenks, asking if he would consider an article by either William Beveridge or Alfred Zimmern. Jenks preferred the latter as 'He must know more of the actual working of Oxford machinery.'[9]

While Zimmern was at work on this article, Mansbridge visited New College, accompanied by W. J. Sharkey, the secretary of the Birmingham WEA branch. It is probable that the visit was arranged through the good offices of either Marriott (another New College man) or Tawney. Mansbridge was seeking funds to enable Sharkey to become full-time secretary of the Midland committee of the WEA, and was also recruiting guarantors for the central office fund. Mansbridge wrote subsequently to Zimmern, thanking him for his 'generous guarantee' and for 'the kindly welcome' extended to Sharkey and himself. From this time Zimmern became one of Mansbridge's staunchest allies.[10]

Zimmern's article appeared in the *Independent Review* in October 1906. He reinforced and developed several of the points made by Tawney in the *Westminster Gazette*. He attacked the examination system, which discouraged original work, and the obstructive role of Convocation, the gathering of all the MAs, which was dominated by conservative-minded clergymen.[11]

The arguments of Tawney and Zimmern were elaborated in the articles in *The Times* in April and May 1907. The 'Oxford Tutors' were particularly severe on 'the idle pass men', who should be forced to make way for poorer but more deserving students, assisted by the provision of means-tested exhibitions. Some of the latter should be earmarked for school teachers. 'No duty of the University is more pressing than that of educating teachers.' Academic government of the university should be vested in a reformed Congregation controlled by the academic staff who held university appointments. The demand for a royal commission, unless Oxford speedily reformed itself from within, was repeated.

The next move was made by Bishop Gore, who was both a close friend of Barnett, and a father-figure to Mansbridge and the WEA. He asked the government, in the course of a debate in the House of Lords on 24 July 1907, to consider the establishment of a royal commission to inquire into the endowment, administration and teaching of Oxford and Cambridge, 'in order to secure the best use of their resources for the benefit of all classes of the community'. 'It had always been', he argued, 'the honour and the pride of the old Universities that they had trained the governing classes of the country', but they must realize that the term 'governing classes includes now the working classes'. After the now familiar criticisms of the idle pass men and the misuse of endowments and scholarships, Gore declared,

> The Workers' Educational Association and the Ruskin College at Oxford are signs and evidences that among the working classes there is a very considerable body of people who desire to be students and are capable of being students. What we want is that the Universities should be so reorganised and that their endowments should be so used as that whatever there is of real intellectual aspiration and real desire for knowledge, should find its home and instruction in Oxford and Cambridge; and that, and nothing else, should be the real object which the Universities manifestly exist to serve.[12]

The government decided to defer action on a royal commission to give the ancient universities the opportunity to consider what reforms were needed, and whether they could be achieved without legislation. The public discussions started by the Oxford reformers had, however, to quote Zimmern, turned university reform from 'a subject for academic debate' into 'one of the most urgent questions of national policy'.[13] They had, in particular, paved the way for Mansbridge's campaign, spear-headed from Rochdale, for the creation of a system of tutorial classes which would both satisfy the workers' appetite for sustained study in their home towns, and open the door, for some of them at least, to university residence.

Mansbridge decided not to wait for the establishment of such a system before satisfying the demand which had emerged in Rochdale in the spring of 1907. The WEA central executive committee promised, in Mansbridge's words, 'that if thirty working men and women would pledge themselves to study for two years, the Association would do what it could to secure the best possible tutor for the subject desired'. The Rochdale Education Guild soon found over forty recruits, and at a conference held on 18 July the subject of modern English History 'with special reference to the social, industrial and economic aspects' was chosen. To avoid interference from overtime, and to ensure that the students were fresh enough for 'serious and systematic study', it was decided that the class should if possible meet on Saturday afternoons. The Rochdale students attending the summer meeting at Oxford were appointed 'as a deputation to wait upon the Oxford authorities along with Mr. Mansbridge'.[14]

Two or three weeks later Mansbridge led this deputation to meet Dr T. B. Strong, dean of Christ Church, who was chairman of the Oxford extension delegacy. The dean was impressed by the fervour of the Rochdale men. When he raised the problem of finance, they told him that if he realized how hungry they were for knowledge, he would melt down the college plate to raise the money. Dr Strong preserved the plate, but promised active support. It was, however, Zimmern's college, New, which made a grant of £300 to allow experimental tutorial classes to proceed.[15]

The broader questions of what Oxford and workpeople could do for each other were made the subject of a conference held on Saturday 10 August, during the same summer meeting. Gore took the chair; 430 delegates from 210 organizations, most of them working-class and including many trades councils and trade union branches, attended. Sympathetic letters were received from the chancellor of the university, Lord Curzon, and the vice-chancellor, Dr Herbert Warren, both of whom were away from Oxford at the time of the conference. Warren wrote that he had very much in mind the question

> of how to make University teaching accessible in the most helpful form to working-men, either by taking it as far as it can be taken to them in their own places of abode, or by bringing those who can come for shorter or longer periods to Oxford.

Curzon told Mansbridge,

> I feel very great sympathy with your work … I cannot imagine any

endeavour of higher national importance than one to establish natural and living connections between the University of Oxford and the working classes.[16]

Marriott, in welcoming the delegates, spoke of the 'extraordinary progress' made in the four years of its existence by the WEA, which was the result of 'the enthusiasm, selfless devotion and organising skill of their General Secretary'. The university extension movement looked with pride on the achievements of its 'direct and legitimate offspring'. He hoped that further progress could be made towards making the universities national institutions, 'not by the exclusion of the rich but by the inclusion of the poor'.[17]

Two papers were read, by Walter Nield of Oldham, president of the North Western Co-operative Education Committees' Association, on 'What Workpeople want Oxford to do'; and by Sidney Ball, fellow of St John's College, on 'What Oxford can do for Workpeople'. Tawney, who was not present at the conference, had a hand in the drafting of both papers. Nield advocated the admission to Oxford of selected working-class students for periods of one or two years, to read for a diploma and then 'return as a matter of course to give the benefit of their experience to their fellows'. A 'union of labour and learning' in Oxford would also benefit the university, which needed 'a real living acquaintance with working-class conditions'.[18]

Ball quoted James Stuart, Arnold Toynbee, J. H. Seeley, Mark Pattison and T. H. Green (whose widow was present at the conference) to demonstrate that the 'ideal [that] a National University should be co-extensive with the nation' had often been put forward, but was not yet realized. He argued that educational and social reform must go hand in hand and went on to develop the familiar theme that the 'governing classes' traditionally educated by Oxford now included representatives of the workers.

> Changes in the structure of English society are throwing more and more responsibility on the shoulders of men who have had no opportunity of obtaining the 'synoptic mind' which, as Plato reminds successive generations of Oxford students, is desirable in 'governors' ... If working men, as Co-operators or Trade Unionists, as Local Councillors or Members of Parliament ... are to exercise rightly the unparalleled political power of which they have become possessed ... they must, as the wisest amongst them recognise, obtain a social and political education such as no other institution than a University is in a position to offer.

His practical suggestions included the development of systematic class teaching, organized locally by the WEA and staffed with graduates 'who have lived and are living in touch with workmen ... they must be prepared to meet working men on their own ground—to teach them from and through their own point of view'.

Both Nield and Ball laid great stress on the example of Ruskin College which, said Nield, 'must permeate the whole University'. Ball observed that the ideal of the college was 'not so much equality of opportunity as what I might describe as the solidarity of labour. The education it offers is one that will enable the workman to raise, not to rise out of, his class.' It was 'a model for imitation: what has been done on a small could and should be done on a large scale'.

The conference did not develop, after the papers and opening speeches, as Mansbridge and his associates had intended. The resolution which was to be put to the conference at the end of the debate had, in Mansbridge's words, been 'carefully prepared beforehand', but had not been circulated in advance of the meeting so as to allow delegates to take instructions from their own organizations. Some delegates from the Social Democratic Federation tried to move a resolution supporting the educational pro-gramme of the TUC (free and secular education from primary school to university, under public control). They were ruled out of order by Gore, on the ground that the motion, if adopted, would compromise the political neutrality of the WEA. It was a nice constitutional point, as the conference was an open one, and not a meeting of a WEA body.[19]

It was evident to Thomas Price, from the Rochdale WEA, that 'many of the delegates shared in the widespread working-class distrust of Universities ... It seemed as though the conference would fail of its purpose because of the impossibility of making contact between the two sections',[20] when J. M. Mactavish, a Portsmouth shipwright and Labour councillor, rose to his feet to declare, 'I am not here as a suppliant for my class ... I claim for my class all the best that Oxford has to give. I claim it as a right, wrongfully withheld.' Oxford needed workpeople more than they needed Oxford, because democracy would be achieved with or without its help. 'What is the true function of a University? Is it to train the nation's best men, or to sell its gifts to the rich?' Workpeople should go to Oxford to be trained not for self-advancement, but 'as missionaries ... for the great task of lifting their class'.

For this purpose they needed a new interpretation of history—'although we are supposed to have no recorded history, without us all history was and is impossible'—and economics—'You cannot expect the people to enthuse over a science which promises them no more than a life of precarious toil.' They also needed teachers sympathetic to the aspirations of the workers, not the typical extension lecturer who was 'decidedly middle and upper class in his outlook'.

Canon Barnett, who also spoke at the conference, may have recognized this speech as a working-class version of his arguments in the *University Review* two years earlier, but with the university, not the workers, depicted as 'blind and unreasoning'. Mactavish ended with the call, 'To Oxford I say: Open wide your doors and take us in; we need you; you need us.'

'At once', wrote Price, 'the spirit of the Conference was changed; the coldness and restlessness vanished as though by magic'. In Mansbridge's view 'no one but the speaker could perhaps approve every point in the speech', and Hudson Shaw, the veteran Oxford extension lecturer, 'protested against any suggestion that Oxford should "tune her pulpits" to suit any class'. However, Mansbridge was well satisfied with the results of his invitation to Mactavish to attend and speak at the conference. 'The day was won. Oxford and working people were swung together into line.'[21]

Mansbridge and Price exaggerated the importance of the mood of the conference. There was no serious danger that the prepared resolution would not be approved. The most important speech had much less impact on the delegates than Mactavish's stirring rhetoric. It was made by Sir Robert Morant, permanent secretary to the Board of Education, who declared that the Board was 'looking for guidance from such an Association as is represented here today to show us the way in which adult education can best be furthered. In particular we believe it is to small classes and solid, earnest work that we can give increasingly of the golden stream'. This offer of grant aid, without which the tutorial class movement could not have made much progress, did not come out of the blue. Mansbridge had been in close touch with Morant, who had recently brought him and David Shackleton MP on to the consultative committee of the Board of Education. Morant originally said that he would not be able to attend the conference, but because of its importance he would arrange for Dr H. F. Heath (Director of Special Inquiries at the Board of Education) to attend in his place. Heath wrote to

Mansbridge suggesting a meeting in Oxford before the conference to discuss tactics, but at the last moment Morant found it possible to attend in person.[22]

The conference resolution was carried with only four dissentient votes. It called for the appointment of a joint committee consisting of seven people nominated by the vice-chancellor of Oxford, and seven chosen by the executive committee of the WEA, 'with instructions to report before Easter next to the organisations here represented, as to the best means of carrying into effect the suggestions made in the two papers read before the conference'. The latter was wound up by Philip Snowden, Labour MP for Blackburn, on a less than inspiring note. 'The chief obstacle in the way of progress' was the 'ignorance and indifference of workpeople'. The WEA could do a useful job, said Snowden, in stimulating the demand of the workers for education, but could only partly satisfy it. The main provision must be the work of the state.[23]

The press reports of the conference—it was well covered in the serious journals—provided further material for the continuing debate. In articles published in October 1907 both W. W. Jackson, rector of Exeter College, and Marriott advocated limited reforms which would stop short of changing the character of the colleges. Intelligent boys from poorer homes should be helped to enter Oxford by better scholarship provision and by the dropping of compulsory Greek from the entrance examination. Adult working-class students should be admitted to Ruskin College, and similar institutions which might be financed by an appeal to labour organizations and 'great employers of labour', to read for university diplomas.[24]

Jackson was in favour of more generous financial support being given by the university to extension work. Marriott naturally took the same view. For the task of taking university education to the workers, he argued, the instrument was already to hand. The extension system had its defects but to describe it

as 'mere popular lecturing' is a flagrant misrepresentation … The tutorial class, the carefully selected library, the written essay, the testing examination are indispensable concomitants. So long as the system is compelled to be financially self-supporting, so long must the lecturer attract large audiences. Provided with adequate resources, the Extension system could adapt itself tomorrow to the demand recently formulated by the Bishop of Birmingham [Gore] and could furnish university teaching for the small classes of 'trained and sifted students' whom he has primarily in view. It is entirely a question of finance.

Marriott proposed that six colleges should each be asked to finance an 'Extension Fellow' to work for three years in a particular town and teach small classes. From the latter the best men should be sent to Oxford to take a diploma course.

The vice-chancellor of Oxford did not complete his nominations for the joint committee until nearly the end of the autumn term. The seven university representatives were:

Dr T. B. Strong, dean of Christ Church and chairman of the Extension Delegacy;

H. H. Turner, professor of astronomy and fellow of New College;

A. L. Smith, fellow and tutor of Balliol College;

Sidney Ball, fellow and tutor of St. John's College;

Alfred Zimmern, fellow and tutor of New College;

J. A. R. Marriott, secretary of the Extension Delegacy;

H. B. Lees Smith, professor of public administration and economics at University College, Bristol, chairman of the executive committee of Ruskin College, and lately vice-principal of Ruskin.

If Mansbridge had been asked to choose the university members, he could hardly have done better. They had nearly all declared their support for the WEA. Smith, Ball and particularly Zimmern were already close allies. Mansbridge wrote to the latter after the Oxford conference, 'What a blessing you are to causes', and since then Zimmern had been active in raising funds for the WEA. Lees Smith was a member of the WEA central executive committee.[25]

The WEA chose the following, by agreement with some of its affiliated bodies:

David Shackleton, Labour MP for Clitheroe and secretary of the Northern Counties Weavers' Association; and

C. W. Bowerman, Labour MP for Deptford and an official of the London Society of Compositors; both of whom represented the parliamentary committee of the TUC on the WEA Advisory Council

W. H. Berry, an official of the Working Men's Club and Institute Union, nominated by the educational committee of the Co-operative Union;

Richardson Campbell, nominated by the National Conference of Friendly Societies;

J. M. Mactavish of Portsmouth;

Alfred Wilkinson, a Labour member of Rochdale Town Council;

Albert Mansbridge.

Wilkinson took the place originally offered to Philip Snowden, who must have declined to serve. Mansbridge suggested the name of Berry, who was already a member of the WEA central executive, to the Co-operative Union, but there is no record of a similar approach to the other two bodies.[26]

Before the joint committee met, arrangements had been completed for the tutorial class at Rochdale. It had been agreed that the selection of the tutor could make or mar the experiment. He must be a man, said Mansbridge, 'of ready sympathy and intellectual power'. Tawney, who was currently assistant lecturer in Economics at Glasgow University, passed both tests with ease and agreed to take the class. It had been intended to start in the autumn of 1907, but negotiations with the Board of Education and the Rochdale LEA were not completed until the end of the year. An interesting by-product of the negotiations with the Board was an extension of the pioneer tutorial classes from two years to three (which would probably have happened later in any case). Under the existing regulations, a grant of eight shillings and sixpence per twenty hours' tuition was payable in respect of each effective student on a three-year course. For a two-year course the maximum was five shillings.[27]

Meanwhile a second request for a tutorial class had been received, from Longton in North Staffordshire. For several years extension lectures had been organized in Longton by a voluntary committee, generously assisted by the LEA. Hudson Shaw gave several courses of lectures, which attracted considerable numbers of both working people and elementary school teachers. Shaw's class work was particularly successful, and by the autumn of 1907 he had a nucleus of 'earnest students' who wanted 'more systematic and continuous study'. Some of them were members of the Social Demo-cratic Federation, under the auspices of which they were also studying economics. Shaw suggested that they should follow the example of Rochdale, and they were happy to choose the same subject and tutor. The LEA promised financial help, and the Oxford delegacy accepted the proposal. The Longton class met on Friday evenings. It began on 24 January 1908, the day before the first meeting of the Rochdale class. Each class had about forty students. The Longton tutorial class and the extension courses in the same place had as yet no connection with the WEA, and in April 1908 they formed the Longton University Extension Guild to provide the local organization and perform similar functions to those of a WEA branch.[28]

The Oxford joint committee met for the first time on 27 and 28 December 1907. Dr Strong was elected chairman with David Shackleton as vice-chairman; and Zimmern and Mansbridge were appointed joint secre-taries. At this and subsequent meetings the objectives were worked out: the establishment of a network of tutorial classes from which the ablest students would go on to full-time courses at Oxford; the adaptation of the Diploma in Economics to allow for a more thorough study of industrial problems; the creation of a parallel Diploma in Political Science; and an equal partnership between the university and the WEA in the administration of the new system.

Most of the discussions did not take the form of 'negotiations' between the two sides of the committee. Zimmern worked very closely not only with Mansbridge, but also with other members of the labour side. Mansbridge also corresponded with other university representatives. Most of the matters at variance were settled by compromise. For example the labour members were opposed to the idea of a written examination at the end of the course, but Marriott did not see how without one the university could grant a certificate. On the advice of Turner and Smith it was agreed that certificates could be awarded on the basis of the assessment of students' essays by two external examiners.[29]

The real issue was who would control the administration of tutorial classes and the admission of working-class students to Oxford. Here Mansbridge and his allies set out deliberately to isolate Marriott and manœuvre him into a position of impotence. Marriott had been a keen supporter of the WEA since its foundation, in word and deed, and had shown many kindnesses to Mansbridge. He was, however, a prominent Tory, and as he wrote many years later,

> it was perhaps not unnatural that some working-class students, themselves tending towards Socialiam, should come to regard me with suspicion as an obscurantist and reactionary. Our University Extension methods were not 'democratic' enough for them; they would fain, if not tune the pulpits, at least choose the preachers … above all, they revolted against what it became fashionable to describe as 'middle-class economics'.[30]

Mactavish was afraid that Marriott might take advantage of the proposed new system to send 'the wrong characters' from extension centres to Oxford. Mansbridge wrote reassuringly,

> we do not fear [Marriott] at all. He will not be allowed to even put his little finger in the new arrangements. We cannot, of course, help [that is, prevent] students going to Oxford other than [from] our centres, but you may depend upon it we shall take all the precautions that human wit can devise … We will not let any man go up unless he has passed the most complete system of selection that has ever been devised, and we will in the WEA hedge it about with rules that cannot be broken.

The committee received a very encouraging report from Zimmern on the first term's work of Tawney's class at Rochdale. 'The lecturer assumed a considerable level of knowledge and interest, with no attempt to play down.' The discussion was

> brisk, pointed and reasonable … I came away with a very high opinion of the grounding the students must have received from Mr. Horsburgh and other Extension lecturers before the Tutorial class was started, and I have not the least doubt that in two years' time several of the students will be more than fit for admission to a University course.

Zimmern wrote privately to Mansbridge,

> I was really impressed with the class. The men are much better than the Ruskin men, and Tawney's treatment of his subject is masterly. It was an Oxford lecture in conception and treatment, not a popular lecture at all.

As the committee had started work so late, and had such complex matters to consider, its report could not be ready by the target date of Easter 1908. To allow arrangements to be made for several new tutorial classes in the autumn of that year, an interim report was produced in May. It recommended the appointment of a standing joint committee of university and labour representatives to deal with both tutorial classes and other extension work in working-class centres. The local management of classes should be in the hands of representative committees of working-class organizations. Oxford should employ full-time tutors, who should have a recognized status in the university and some internal teaching, at a salary of £80 per class, therefore £400 for what was regarded as a full programme. Half of the cost should be met by Oxford, and half by WEA branches or other local centres. An important aspect of the latter arrangement was that grants from the Board of Education, the LEAs and bodies such as the Gilchrist Trust were to be credited to the WEA side of the partnership. It was recognized that the contributions from students could only be slight. There was thought to be enough work for six tutors in the near future, and the committee hoped that six colleges would each support one of them.[31]

In the autumn of 1908 new tutorial classes were started at Littleborough, Chesterfield, Wrexham, Glossop, Oldham (F. W. Kolthammer) and Swindon (R. V. Lennard). All were in Industrial History except for Swindon, which chose Economics. The first three classes were taken by Tawney in addition to Rochdale and Longton, making him the first full-time tutorial class tutor.[32]

The report of the committee, *Oxford and Working-Class Education*, was published on 28 November 1908. The final drafting was entrusted to Dr Strong, who, wrote Zimmern, was 'sure to phrase it rightly for Oxford reading'. Mactavish was more cautious on this point: 'I hope the Dean's patch will not spoil the original.'[33] The report has become a classic of adult education. Its theme is summed up in the following paragraph, which echoes the arguments of Barnett, Gore and Ball quoted above.

> It has always been the privilege of the older Universities (though, of course, not to the exclusion of the new) to train men for all departments of political life and public administration. Throughout the nineteenth century a considerable proportion of those who, as ministers or members of Parliament, or public officials, wielded great influence, have received their earliest education in political ideas at the hands of Oxford, and have acknowledged freely that they have learned through it to be more efficient servants of the community. The Trade Union secretary and the 'Labour member' need an Oxford education as much, and will use it to as good ends, as the civil servant or the barrister. It seems to us that it would involve a grave loss both to Oxford and to English political life were the close association which has existed between the University and the world of affairs to be broken or impaired on the accession of new classes to power.[34]

'The Report is ready at last', an anonymous writer commented in the December 1908 number of the WEA journal the *Highway*. 'We wondered what kind of a changeling would emerge from a Committee room, where the Dean of Christ Church sat at one end of the table and Mr. Shackleton at the other.' He need not have worried. Indeed, if the writer was Mansbridge himself—and the style fits—he was never worried. The report gave the WEA all it asked for, including the right of a WEA branch, or 'a representative body of workmen' to have 'a controlling voice in the selection of a teacher' for a tutorial class. 'The selection of curricula … must be the duty of the University acting in co-operation with workpeople.' Local control by the workers themselves would allay suspicion about 'unconscious class bias' in the teaching, and would guarantee that students secured the kind of education they wanted and not what the university thought they ought to want. Furthermore, because many of the worker-students would be members of several other working-class societies, created by 'the genius of English workmen for organisation', the influence of a class would filter 'through a hundred different channels and may leaven a whole town'.

The proposals in the interim report on the conditions of employment of tutors were endorsed, and the importance of their undertaking 'regular teaching in Oxford itself' was emphasized. This would bring knowledge of working-class thought and conditions into the university. At the same time, 'the critical atmosphere of Oxford' would save the tutor to a considerable extent from dropping into slipshod and unacademic habits of thought and expression. It is extremely difficult for a man who is engaged for half of the year in lecturing to an unacademic, often highly appreciative audience, to prevent himself from insensibly lowering his tone, dropping behind the work which is being done in his subject, and in short from losing the scholar in the lecturer. But the whole plan of these tutorial classes rests on the assumption that the teaching shall be of a University level ...

The 'main object' of the tutorial classes would be 'to prepare men for study in the University itself' mainly for the Diploma in Economics or the proposed Diploma in Political Science. 'The scholars may come up either as members of an ordinary college, or as Non-collegiate students, or as members of Ruskin College, according to the tastes of the individual and the advice given to him.' Non-collegiate entry, although cheap, might be unsuitable for working men whose 'strong ... corporate spirit' would fit them for college life.

> Though it is hard for a poor man to enter a College, he finds in it, once he has entered, a spirit of fellowship and equality and ... it seems to us that they would make very valuable contributions to the social life of Oxford, and that they would teach other undergraduates at least as much as they would learn from them.

Money to support these students should be sought from LEAs, from labour organizations, and from the colleges, which could be expected to divert part of their scholarship funds for the purpose.

It was recommended that the selection of tutorial class students to come up to Oxford should be in the hands of a committee consisting of two representatives of the university, the class tutor, and representatives of the WEA, 'the local organisation' (normally the WEA branch) and the class.[35]

On 27 October 1908, a month before the report appeared, a permanent joint committee was established, with equal university and WEA representation. It was to all intents and purposes independent of the extension delegacy, with its own officers and funds. It had originally been understood that the secretary to the delegacy would have 'a general supervision' of tutorial classes, but the WEA representatives had persuaded Dr Strong that there would be too much work for Marriott to be able to give it adequate attention. They even conveyed the impression that they had made a concession by agreeing to the Joint Tutorial Classes Committee being a standing committee of the delegacy instead of an entirely separate body.[36]

Mansbridge wrote to the labour members of the committee on 2 November that 'all is now in order at Oxford'. The powers given to the Joint Tutorial Classes Committee 'for a start appear to be eminently satisfactory'. He told the WEA central executive committee on 2 December that 'he had taken it upon himself' to nominate the seven WEA members of the temporary joint committee to serve on the new body. The committee confirmed his action. The university nominated Strong, Ball, Smith and Turner, together with Professor Michael Sadler; Langford Price, fellow and tutor of Oriel College, and an active supporter of both extension work and Co-operative education; and William Temple (Zimmern was planning to leave Oxford). Temple and Mansbridge became joint secretaries.[37]

The one member of the 1907/08 joint committee who regarded the outcome as far from being 'eminently satisfactory' was Marriott. He had been incensed by the attacks on Oxford's extension work which appeared in the first draft of the report. He complained to Dr Strong, 'It is altogether "superior", supercilious and patronising in tone ... it contains a repetition of many calumnies fully refuted by Sadler many years ago.' Marriott persuaded the committee to tone down some of this criticism. For example, the sentence

> Hitherto, in spite of the admirable efforts made by individual lecturers, University Extension work has been far too desultory and incoherent.

was replaced by

> Hitherto, in spite of efforts to the contrary, University Extension work has been far too discontinuous.

Later in the same paragraph, a discussion of the need for new financial arrangements so that centres would not have to make frequent changes of subject to attract large audiences ended with the words 'will in part obviate these defects', instead of the original expression 'will make any such mind-destroying versatility unnecessary'.[38]

These changes went some way towards meeting Marriott's objections, but he still resented the 'grudging and inadequate recognition of what has already been done by the University of Oxford for working-class education'. He wrote several drafts of a note of dissent to add to the report, pointing out that he had himself been advocating many of its educational recommendations for many years, but expressing serious reservations about the organizational changes. In one draft he argued that the latter should have been referred to a university committee or a royal commission. In the end he contented himself with a footnote to the report. 'Mr. Marriott cordially concurs in the educational recommendations of the above Report, but expresses no opinion on the administrative changes suggested in it.'[39]

It is not clear whether Marriott was sacrificed to appease the aggressive class consciousness of Mactavish, and anyone else on the labour side who shared the latter's view, or whether Marriott was being hopelessly obstructive. It is, however, of some significance that Mansbridge's letter to Mactavish promising that Marriott would be frozen out was written only a few days after the first meeting of the committee. His treatment of Marriott showed that Mansbridge was not the simple-minded evangelist depicted in his own writings, but a skilful manipulator with a subtle mind and a ruthless streak.

The report had said nothing about the 'idle pass-men' who had been frequently attacked earlier in the reform campaign. Gore and Mansbridge made it clear, however, that in their view the exclusion of the idle rich and the admission of the industrious poor were closely, if not inseparably, connected. Gore told a WEA rally at Toynbee Hall, just before the publication of the report, that he hoped for 'a great displacement of rich or well-to-do young men, who wanted to have a good time, by serious students, who would come equally from all classes but in large measure from among the workers'.[40] Mansbridge wrote a few months later,

A great national highway of education is necessary —so broad and free that none may fail to pass thereon because of lack of money. Brains and character are to be the only toll ... There are many workpeople in industrial centres who have been trained in the hard school of industry, and who have kept themselves responsive to the claims of their fellows, and to the claims of education alike. These men are ... far more worthy than a third of the undergraduates in many universities ... Workpeople hold that only the best students should work in the universities. They have no desire to oust those of the rich who work: their only desire is to replace the impotent rich who are idle, for many of whom Oxford and Cambridge both waste national endowments.[41]

According to the preface to the second edition of *Oxford and Working-Class Education*, dated August 1909,

> the reception of the Report by almost every section of English opinion has been so satisfactory that we feel justified in hoping that work of the character described in it may soon be regarded as part of the permanent educational machinery of the country.

It is true that there were many favourable comments in newspapers and periodicals, some of them being apparently written or inspired by Mansbridge's allies. For example, the laudatory article in the liberal weekly the *Nation* appears from internal evidence to have been written by either Tawney or Zimmern.[42] There was, however, some hostile criticism from defenders of the established order. The president of Corpus Christi objected to funds being spent 'on non-members and largely at the expense of undergraduates and their tutors who, on the faith that they will be fairly and properly treated, have joined the colleges'.[43] R. S. Rait, the dean of New College, argued that the character of Oxford would be destroyed if college expenses were curtailed sufficiently to allow for the admission of artisans. The latter should be catered for by institutions in the industrial towns.[44] Another critic saw the proposals of the report as 'destructive of progress in knowledge' because the workers wanted 'an education specifically adjusted to their needs ... conducted by teachers whom they have themselves selected for their willingness to teach what is wanted'.[45]

Perhaps the most comprehensive indictment of the proceedings at Oxford from the conservative side was the article by J. B. Rye, 'Oxford and the Working Classes', which appeared in the *Nineteenth Century* in March 1909. He pointed out that after the Oxford conference the vice-chancellor, Dr Warren, had appointed the university representatives on the joint committee without consulting either Congregation or Convocation. If the latter had wished 'to negotiate with the working-man organisations' they would probably have chosen men like Sir William Anson (warden of All Souls, formerly a junior education minister in the Conservative government, who was in fact a firm friend of Mansbridge and the WEA and had attended the Oxford conference) and Professor Dicey (the distinguished constitutional lawyer)

> or at any rate gentlemen less prejudiced in favour of Socialism than Mr Sidney Ball and Mr A. E. Zimmern, and of more experience than the latter, to represent them. The Chairman of the Executive Committee of Ruskin College [Lees Smith] would scarcely have been appointed.

Rye contended that the statute setting up the standing Joint Tutorial Classes Committee had been 'slipped through Convocation' a month before the publication of the Oxford Report, without which strategem it was unlikely that it would have passed unopposed. He attacked the idea of working-class control of the tutorial class organization, and the unsuitable character of parts of the suggested curricula. 'Some of the topics to be studied are distinctly dangerous. For instance, 'The Carbonari' and 'Bakounin and the Anarchist Parties' are scarcely edifying subjects to be taught to workmen.' Social differences would prevent working-class students benefiting from Oxford life. 'A mechanic in Magdalen or Christ Church would feel as out of place as he would at a dining table in the Carlton Hotel.' The university was one of the two chief finishing schools for politicians and civil servants, the sons of the rich, the landed gentry, the gentlemanly professions, Eastern princes and rich colonials—'what more ought to be expected from it?' It might be expedient, however, for Oxford to hand over some of its scholarship funds to the universities of London and Birmingham 'or to similar institutions more in touch with members of the working classes'.[46]

Mansbridge was no doubt gratified to learn that his cause had some support from the younger generation at Oxford. In a debate in the Union in February 1909 the motion that 'it is the duty of Oxford to take an increased part in the education of the democracy' was carried by 169 votes to 106. It was perhaps significant that two of the undergraduates who supported William Temple in speaking for the motion (Elliott Dodds and Nathaniel Micklem, both from the Liberal/Nonconformist tradition) came from Zimmern's college, New.[47] A few days later Professor Turner wrote in confidence to Zimmern asking him if he would like New College to elect him to a special fellowship for tutorial class work. Zimmern had made other plans, but accepted the position of HM Inspector for tutorial classes three years later.[48]

The Oxford Report was also assailed from the left, in the columns of *Clarion, Justice* and the *New Age*. Some of the attacks formed part of the long-running ideological struggle with some socialist opponents of the WEA, which will be discussed in Chapter 5. One of the milder criticisms was made by Ramsay MacDonald in the *Labour Leader*. The WEA, he warned, was in danger of letting Oxford views and social prejudice 'inoculate the more intelligent sections of the working classes'. He wrote to Mansbridge saying that he was in favour of the WEA and, with suitable safeguards, of tutorial class work. It was, however, a mistake to try to send workers to Oxford. 'Oxford is a poison ... You cannot recreate Oxford by an infusion of working men ... Oxford will assimilate them, not they Oxford.'[49]

Similar doubts were expressed right across the political spectrum. A writer in the *Socialist Review* did not think that 'young labour students would experience any outward social rebuffs at the hands of the ordinary undergraduate', but feared infection from 'the bacillus of the indolent, frivolous and selfish life' which was common in Oxford. W. A. Spooner observed in the *Church Quarterly Review* that 'the attraction to catch the tone and temper of a higher social grade with which they are habitually brought into familiar contact seems for most Englishmen almost irresistible'. An enlarged Ruskin College might safely be used, but otherwise it was better to take the university to the workers, rather than bring the workers to the university. The *Morning Post* commented, 'The atmosphere of Oxford transforms almost everything it touches, and it can hardly be supposed that a member of the working classes would go through the mill of the average college experience and remain completely sympathetic to his old associates.' It therefore preferred the provision of hostels.[50]

In the *Sociological Review* F. W. Kolthammer argued that these difficulties had been overstated. The Oxford undergraduates who were 'worth knowing will not patronise but welcome workpeople'. The 1907/08 joint committee had 'perhaps ... exaggerated' the danger that WEA students sent to Oxford, 'inspired by the will to serve', would forsake the 'highway' for the 'ladder'. He thought that the selection process envisaged by Mansbridge and his partners provided adequate safeguards.[51]

The Oxford Report made no reference to the question of a royal commission, which was outside the committee's terms of reference.

Mansbridge used the occasion of the publication of the report, however, to urge on Walter Runciman, president of the Board of Education, the case for an early establishment of a royal commission on Oxford and Cambridge. Runciman professed to agree in principle, but offered the not very convincing excuse that

> There are very few men who are capable at the same time of securing the confidence of Oxford and Cambridge and the world outside of them and are simultaneously endowed with the requisite spirit which I should regard of essential importance.

Runciman no doubt felt that he had enough on his plate with the royal commission on London University, for which, as he told Mansbridge privately in the same letter, he had secured the approval of Asquith, the prime minister.[52]

The campaign for a royal commission was kept up by Barnett, Zimmern, Graham Wallas, J. A. Spender and others. Mansbridge made it a major concern, despite all his other preoccupations. He was urged by Tawney to be more aggressive in demanding reform at Oxford, but maintained his own, more diplomatic, style. In November 1909, when a general election was pending, he wrote to Zimmern,

> I am arranging a purely Labour deputation to the new Prime Minister—Asquith rejuvenated or Balfour—to consist of five MPs and five rank and file to ask for a Royal Commission on University Education. Of course you shall have a hand in the manifesto which we will put into their hands.

In a pamphlet he wrote for delegates to a Co-operative educational conference in March 1910, Mansbridge urged them to put a resolution before the Co-operative Congress, demanding a royal commission.[53]

In the meantime the chancellor of Oxford University, Lord Curzon, had appointed himself as a one-man commission, with the idea of promoting reform from within the university so as to stave off the threat of reforms imposed from without. His report, over two hundred pages in length, appeared in the summer of 1909. He welcomed the 'singularly able and attractive report' of the Oxford joint committee, and took a similar line on the mutual benefits to be gained from close contact between Oxford and the emerging leaders of the workers.

It is well that, when the problems of labour and capital are being debated, or when a future Parliament is presented with a Socialist program, some at least of the working-men's representatives should speak with the advantage of a University training. It is well, too, when the educational appliances of the country are being overhauled, as must from time to time occur, that there should be spokesmen of the industrial classes, whether inside or outside the House of Commons, who will possess a first-hand knowledge of the conditions of Oxford.

Curzon's solution to the financial and psychological difficulties in the way of admitting workmen to Oxford was to propose the establishment of a 'University Working-Men's College', open both to workers and to other impoverished students, which would provide diploma courses lasting for one or two years.[54] Mansbridge wrote to the *Nation* emphatically rejecting Curzon's proposal, and asserting that workpeople had

an indefeasible right ... to use the existing colleges ... provided that they can do the high work which ought to be demanded ... they will never rest until they are assured that the best men, irrespective of wealth, birth or athletics, are working in them.

The disclosures in Curzon's report of Oxford's 'out-of-date and cumbrous machinery' would, in Mansbridge's view, strengthen the demand for a royal commission.[55]

Curzon's recommendation to establish a working-men's college was rejected by the Hebdomadal Council on the ground that there appeared to be no desire for it. The council's own proposals for modifications to the system of government in Oxford, dubbed by the *Nation* 'an essay in preventive reform', were sufficient to keep the spectre of a royal commission at bay until after the first world war.[56]

The great debate described above was concerned almost exclusively with the role of Oxford. Were there not other universities, including one at Cambridge? There are two explanations. In the first place the intellectual and religious movements which fed the zeal of the reformers (discussed in Chapter 5) developed in, or in close association with Oxford. Secondly, Cambridge pleaded not guilty to the charges laid against Oxford by its own radical sons. The *Cambridge Review* asserted, 'We have strained our re-sources to the utmost in opening new schools and new triposes, several colleges have made special efforts to attract the poorer class of men by reducing expenses to a minimum, we have lavished money on scientific apparatus, museums, workshops and the like, and at present we are reaping our reward.'[57]

In his paper to the Oxford conference of August 1907, Sidney Ball had spoken of the extension movement in terms of 'an experience, if not of disillusion, [at least] of failure and disappointment'.[58] Cambridge was well content with the standards of its extension work, which was based upon courses of twelve lectures, twice as long as the standard Oxford provision. A much higher proportion of Cambridge extension students passed the end-of-course examinations than was the case with Oxford. A four years' sequence of study was being followed (in 1907/08) at eight affiliated centres. New successes had recently been achieved in a few working-class centres.[59]

In the House of Lords debate initiated by Gore, Dr G. F. Browne, bishop of Bristol and formerly secretary to the Cambridge Syndicate for Local Lectures, asserted that

> we have our hands upon all the various classes of the community, so far as education is concerned … By means of affiliated colleges and local lectures … the local lectures were instituted by Cambridge for the special purpose of doing precisely what the Bishop of Birmingham has described—we send skilled men from Cambridge, accustomed to teach there, down to the great centres, and there students are collected to whom these men lecture exactly as they lecture in their own college or University rooms. That has had the most wonderful effect in drawing the University and various classes of the community together.

Bishop Browne asserted that Cambridge did not require 'one tenth part' of the reforms which were apparently needed at Oxford. While therefore some Oxford men were beating their breasts in contrition, pious Cambridge voices could be heard giving thanks that they were not as the rest of men.[60]

The only other base from which it might have been possible to launch the tutorial class movement was London. There were several reasons why this did not happen. The University of London had only recently (1902) taken over the responsibility for extension work from the London Society for the Extension of University Teaching, and its provision, unlike that of Oxford or Cambridge, was confined to the capital and its immediate environs. The working-class movement in London had not yet united for educational purposes to the degree which had been achieved in some industrial towns in the provinces. In June 1906 the London extension board organized the conference on working-class education mentioned above in Chapter 2, at which Tawney argued in favour of long courses catering for small groups of students. In the following session Dr R. D. Roberts, who had been since 1902 registrar of the extension board, offered the WEA a sum of money to start a pioneer tutorial class. However, the association was not yet ready for such an initiative in the capital. At that time only two branches in the London area were fully operational, at Ilford and Grays in Essex. The first branch in central London was South London, centred upon the Battersea–Southwark area, which was formed in the spring of 1907.[61]

If the Roberts offer had been taken up, the resultant class would not necessarily have robbed Longton and Rochdale of their distinctive place in WEA history. The term 'tutorial class' needs cautious handling. As a description of an interactive teaching method it is thousands of years old. Some scholars, in attempting to prove that 'tutorial classes' existed before Tawney, have failed to distinguish between the label and the substance. The label was used for the class meeting which followed extension lectures. Extension courses described as 'tutorial classes', lasting for at least two terms with lecture and class integrated, were provided in London from 1900/01. In 1907 a WEA 'tutorial class' on the subject of Civics was taught in Battersea, but it ran for only ten weeks and no written work was required. Within a short time the term 'tutorial class' came to be identified with a course under joint committee management, lasting for three years and requiring a substantial amount of student work. A joint committee providing this kind of class, on the new Oxford pattern, was formed in London in 1909.[62]

Had all the other omens been favourable, however, any major initiative on the scale of the Oxford conference and report would have foundered on the opposition of Dr Roberts. He supported the WEA but never developed much enthusiasm for it. He thought that the association should confine itself to missionary work as a junior partner of university extension. He urged it to concentrate upon schemes to raise funds to close the gap between the grants available from the Board of Education and the LEAs and the total cost of providing tutorial classes in working-class centres, instead of calling upon the universities to find up to half of the money.[63] Writing in 1913, two years after Roberts's death at the age of sixty, Mansbridge acknowledged the support which he had received from Roberts, but gently criticized his approach:

> it becomes clear that more credit is due to him than was ever accorded in his lifetime for helping to initiate the forces which produced the tutorial class, although he never appeared to realise that it was essentially different from the Extension course and that it demanded different treatment. It is not always wise to treat the son in the same way as the father...

Mansbridge showed his real feelings in letters to Zimmern, in which he fumed about the obstructive tactics of Roberts.[64]

The analogy of father and son was particularly appropriate. 'Mansbridge', writes Sir Ben Bowen Thomas, 'was a product of the movement to which [Roberts] had given his life.' The older man had done more for working-class adult education than any other extension administrator, and was reluctant in his later years to accept the need for a radically new approach. He expected the younger man to serve the extension movement, not to transform it. It required all Mansbridge's persistence and skill as a negotiator, and particularly the persuasive influence of Canon Barnett, for relations between the WEA and the London extension board to develop along normal lines.[65]

It was therefore the *Oxford Report* which laid the foundations for the development of joint committees and tutorial classes all over the country, and which stands as one of the great documents of liberal adult education. The report and the successful launching of the pioneer tutorial classes were collective achievements. Barnett, Gore, Tawney, Zimmern, Temple, Smith, Ball and Morant made up a very powerful team of allies, and Strong, Turner and even the discarded Marriott made valuable contributions. Mansbridge's combination of evangelical zeal and diplomatic skill had, however, been decisive in forging the alliance between the working-class students, the Oxford reformers and the Board of Education.

Professor Turner wrote to Mansbridge after the publication of *Oxford and Working-class Education*,

> The Report is a noble piece of work and I know how much of it is simply yourself. You will, I trust, do many more fine things, but I doubt if you will

do anything finer *or of more moment* than that Report.[66]

'Simply yourself' is itself too simple a statement, as the Mansbridge of 1908 was partly a product of his experiences during the momentous five years since the foundation of the WEA. The question why so many people of influence in national life were receptive to the pleading and dealing of Mansbridge forms the subject of Chapter 5.

# 4
## Mansbridge the Evangelist

The WEA branch as conceived by Mansbridge had three characteristics. First it had a high degree of autonomy, subject only to a commitment to the broadly-defined educational ideals of the Association and an avoidance of sectarian bias. Mansbridge's text for the work of evangelism was: 'Discover your own needs, organise in your own way … There are no two towns or villages alike.' Secondly, it was democratic, not just in terms of its constitutional machinery but through its assertion of the right of its members to decide 'how, why, what or when they wish to study'. Or as Tawney put it more poetically, 'To build from within, to help men to develop their own genius, their own education, their own culture, that is the secret.' Thirdly, it was federal. In describing the progress of branches in the early annual reports of the WEA, Mansbridge often used the expression 'a powerful federation' as though bestowing the highest accolade. The branches united working-class bodies in the pursuit of educational objectives, offered them a flexible service and support, but did not try to supplant or even compete with any of them. When the Torquay branch reported in 1907 that its work was handicapped by the existence locally of a large number of educational bodies, Mansbridge gently pointed out that a fundamental principle of the association had been misunderstood.[1]

Explaining the success of the WEA in its first decade, Alfred Zimmern pointed to the fact that it was not

> like most societies a collection of individual members … but … in the main a collection of affiliated societies. Unlike the middle class, the working class is habituated to corporate modes of life. The trade union, the club, the chapel, the co-operative society have kept alive for working people the instinct and habit of association … Hence to approach workpeople for any purpose is very different from approaching the scattered denizens of villadom.[2]

To develop and flourish, therefore, a WEA branch had both to reflect the character of the local working-class movement, and to strengthen, express and realize the educational aspirations of the latter. At the same time it sought the support of the LEA; the associated university, particularly if it was located in the same town or nearby; and as wide a spectrum of political opinion as possible. The notes on the formation of branches produced by the central executive committee recommended that all of the local working-class and educational associations should be invited to the formation conference. 'The Mayor is usually invited to preside, and care should be taken to secure that the platform reveals no undue sectarian or party bias.' Mansbridge's ideal WEA branch was an organization of the workers for the workers, but supported by all men of good will, who were won over by the non-party and unsectarian character of the WEA, and its commitment to education for social responsibility. The Bristol branch used language of which Mansbridge would have approved when it reported at the end of its first year, 1907/08, that it was supported by 'all classes … with no respect to creed or politics. The University Professor and student are fellow members with the men who labour with their hands, and distinctions of class are swallowed up in the propagation of a common ideal.'[3]

That it was possible for branches to develop quite different collective personalities and still conform to the Mansbridgean ideal is demonstrated by the early histories of the first and fourth local branches to be established, Reading and Rochdale. The pioneers of the latter disliked the original name of the WEA—the Association to Promote the Higher Education of Working Men—because it was clumsy and sexist, and chose instead 'Rochdale Education Guild', a style adopted by several branches in the Co-operative strongholds of Lancashire and Yorkshire, some of which were colonized from Rochdale.[4]

At the inaugural conference of the guild the mayor, Colonel H. Fishwick, a Conservative and a distinguished local historian, was elected president, an office he held until his death in 1914. The active vice-presidents included a local Conservative MP and two prominent Liberal aldermen, one of whom was elected MP for the borough in 1906. The working-class movement in Rochdale, based upon strong Co-operative and chapel organizations as well as trade unions, was mature and confident. Rochdale workers had pioneered the modern form of consumer Co-operation in

1844, and had helped and influenced James Stuart's extension enterprise in the late 1860s. In several of the textile towns of Lancashire and Yorkshire Co-operative/chapel activists had risen to positions of prominence in local public life, so that by the end of the nineteenth century power was often shared between Liberal Nonconformist manufacturers and Liberal Non-conformist Co-operators.

Despite the burden of so much social harmony, the key workers in the guild, and the students of the first two tutorial classes held in Rochdale, included a substantial proportion of committed socialists, members of the ILP or SDF. They were usually Co-operators and either Nonconformists or ex-Nonconformists, the latter carrying over into their socialist faith many of the values, certainly the idiom, of the chapel.[5]

The working-class movement in Reading operated in a rather different social climate, although the influence of Co-op and chapel was strong there also. Wages were low, trade unionism was weak and labour politics suffered from the stifling pressure of the leading employers, Huntley and Palmer. Although the Liberal MP for the borough—Rufus Isaacs, who had succeeded G. W. Palmer of the biscuit dynasty when the latter resigned in 1904—gave encouragement and financial support to the Reading WEA, and help was also forthcoming from the university college and the LEA, there was never any doubt that the WEA branch was a workers' organization, with a militant style. Middle class people were welcomed, but as supporters not beneficiaries.[6]

As explained in Chapter 2, the two organizations which provided the most active workers in the Reading branch in its first few years were the Co-operative society and the Social Democratic Federation. Prominent in the latter was J. F. Hodgson, a factory worker who was president of the WEA branch from 1906 to 1909. He was accused by some branch members of dominating the discussions which followed the weekly public lectures on controversial topics. Mansbridge tried to solve this problem in characteristic fashion by sending Bishop Gore to take tea with the atheist Hodgson, but without noticeable effect. Hodgson stood down in 1909, shortly before the Social Democratic Party (as the SDF had become) ordered its branches to disaffiliate from the WEA.[7]

From the foundation of the WEA until about the end of 1910, a considerable part of the total effort of developing a national movement was undertaken by Mansbridge himself. He set a cracking pace in his first week as full-time general secretary, in April 1906, addressing meetings at Darwen and Littleborough in support of recently formed branches and conferences called at York, Preston and Liverpool with a view to forming branches. In each case he gave a substantial address, tailored to the needs of the occasion. Later in the same month he visited South Wales and spoke to a conference at Newport.[8]

In the middle of September 1906 Mansbridge addressed a foundation conference in Darlington. As the new campaigning season opened, his diary of speaking engagements filled up. On Sunday, 23 September he 'gave an excellent address on education' to a meeting of railwaymen at St Pancras. The following Thursday saw him in Kettering, where he 'gave an eloquent address' at a meeting which set up a committee to draft a scheme for a local WEA branch. He went on to Sheffield where, to quote the local newspaper, 'a remarkable conference' was held on the afternoon of Saturday, 29 September, consisting of 'over 200 delegates from 90 societies, mainly working men, some of them still black with toil … The gathering was the outcome of a little pioneer work in the city by Mr. Albert Mansbridge'. After Mansbridge had followed up the local educational and political speakers by giving some practical advice, the usual resolution to form a branch was carried unanimously.[9]

On the following day Mansbridge was back in London to talk to his beloved railwaymen, this time at the Midland Railway Institute, Cricklewood. On Monday, 1 October he travelled to Ipswich, where 'an audience of about 350 people listened with eager attention to a most interesting and inspiring lecture on "The Education of Workpeople" illustrated by "a well-chosen series of lantern views".' The meeting was organized by the Ipswich Co-operative Society.[10]

The following Saturday saw Mansbridge in Cardiff, for a major conference to launch an area organization for South Wales and Monmouthshire. On 9 October he supported his old friend Dean Kitchen of Durham at the foundation conference of the Durham Branch. Later in the same month came the round of annual meetings. When Mansbridge reported to the central executive committee of the WEA in December 1906 on his activities during the preceding few months, he gave details of fourteen conferences addressed, and of visits to forty towns in England and Wales.[11]

By the end of 1907, when nearly fifty branches had been established, it was resolved to call a halt to further creations for the sake of consolidation. This decision may have been influenced by the failure of some of the early branches, including Darwen, Preston and Durham. A few new branches were set up in 1908, either as a result of regional initiatives—Rochdale was particularly active in colonizing neighbouring towns—or because earlier preparatory work had begun to bear fruit. Of the forty-eight branches regarded as functioning effectively at the end of the fifth year of operation (1 July 1908), twenty were the direct responsibility of the central WEA because there was no district operating in their region, a factor which added to the burdens of the central office.[12]

The new constitution adopted in October 1907 provided for the whole of England and Wales to be divided into districts, to form an intermediate layer between the branches and the centre. At that time only two districts were fully operational, Midland and North-West, which acquired full-time secretaries in 1906 and 1909 respectively. A new campaign to form branches began late in 1909, when two assistant secretaries were appointed, on modest salaries, to work in the central office. This allowed Mansbridge to spend more time on the road. He wrote to Alfred Zimmern, apparently in December 1909,

> Today I am on my way back from a periodical rush. I have visited Nelson, Colne, Burnley, Manchester, Liverpool, Bolton, Preston, Halifax, Sheffield, Accrington, given 4 lantern lectures, interviewed 2 Universities, met 5 tutorial class teachers, seen one class, attended one social, one WEA council meeting, helped to start one branch … I really am most atrociously tired …[13]

When Mansbridge was not talking, he was writing. On a four-day tour of South Wales, when he faced the hostility of the Plebs faction, he found time to write thirty-eight letters. In addition to his voluminous correspondence on WEA business—with branch secretaries, universities, the Board of Education, working-class organizations and sympathizers in all walks of life—he frequently wrote letters or articles for newspapers, periodicals, the organs of Co-operative, trade union and socialist bodies, wherever the gospel of the association could be preached or its critics answered. Many of his shorter articles were on the same general theme as his lectures, and would

71

not have taken much composition. For example, he contributed a monthly page to the *Co-operative News* under the heading 'Education and Co-operation'. He filled it with informed comment on current developments in adult and child education, interspersed with homilies on the nature of education and its importance to Co-operators. The sheer volume of such writings is, however, impressive and he found time for more substantial works. In the very hectic year 1906 he wrote a short biography of Arnold Toynbee and produced a 40,000-word 'Survey of Working-class Educational Movements in England and Scotland'. The latter, which was published in the *CWS Annual* and reprinted as a separate booklet, involved a considerable amount of research.[14]

In October 1908 Mansbridge received a double reinforcement in his task of spreading the gospel and holding the movement together. William Temple was elected president of the WEA, a position he was to hold until 1924. Temple took his presidential duties very seriously, and in speeches and writings offered the movement practical advice as well as inspiration. In the same month the first number of the *Highway*, the monthly journal of the association, appeared. It was edited by F. W. Kolthammer, an Oxford tutorial class tutor (who changed his name to Cuthbertson at the outbreak of the first world war). Mansbridge wrote a regular monthly column, headed 'Caravan', as well as other special articles, for example a very thoughtful series in 1912 on 'Tutorial Class Difficulties and Needs'. The opportunity to reach all the districts and branches regularly with information and guidance must have brought some economy of effort.

Always in the background during these formative years was the precarious financial position of the WEA, which regularly entered into commitments before the required resources had been secured. If Mansbridge himself worried about money, he never showed it. He ran the central organization in its early days on the assumption that the Lord would provide—or at least that some donation would arrive before matters became too desperate. As he wrote later,

> If an unexpected cheque came, enabling new work to be carried out, the typewriting machines hummed with triumph, whereas before such an arrival they contented themselves with tapping out confidence.[15]

Tawney, who was a member of the central executive committee, took the view that Mansbridge's optimism amounted to irresponsibility. In February 1907, shortly after the removal of the central office from Mansbridge's own home at Ilford to two small rooms rented in Buckingham Street, off the Strand, Tawney persuaded the committee to take financial decisions out of Mansbridge's hands. A finance committee was appointed, and the general secretary was forbidden to sign cheques for more than £2. This did not cure the problem. At the first meeting of the finance committee a deficit of £52 14s 10d was 'carefully noted'. Four months later the figure had risen to £79 6s 1d, which was 'seriously noted'.[16]

Tawney suffered from Mansbridge's financial methods when he became a full-time tutor for the Oxford joint tutorial classes committee. Mansbridge was joint secretary of the committee, first with William Temple and later with A. D. Lindsay. Mansbridge wrote to the latter in June 1911, 'I signed the cheques clearing all teachers' salaries. We will send them out as the bank allows or as the teachers press. You will remember we have got an overdraft allowance of £300.' When Tawney wrote a month later demanding his arrears of salary, Mansbridge was able to say that the request had been anticipated and the cheque already made out.[17]

The central office, and the offices of the Midland and North-West districts, were sustained by gifts from affluent sympathizers. Gore, Temple, Zimmern and T. Edmund Harvey (treasurer from 1908 to 1911) all dipped into their own pockets. In 1908/09 Harvey gave £40 and raised another £20 towards the fund for the employment of an assistant secretary. In the same year £500 was received from a legacy and a donation 'in memoriam', three members of the Cadbury family gave £30 to the Midland office, and Joseph Rowntree made the first of three annual payments of £50. These gifts made possible the appointment of two assistant secretaries, and the removal of the central office to two slightly larger rooms in Adam Street, Adelphi, rented for £42 a year. In November 1910 the office moved again to what Mansbridge called 'two rooms and an apology for one' at 14 Red Lion Square, where it remained for the rest of his period as general secretary.[18]

It was fortunate that Mansbridge was given some organizing help in the central office, because the rapid development of the tutorial class movement imposed new burdens. University joint tutorial classes committees increased from one in 1908/09 to seven in 1910/11, and the number of classes from eight to fifty-one in the same period. The setting up of the committees involved detailed correspondence and negotiations with universities, much of which work was undertaken by Mansbridge himself. He was a member of the joint committees at Sheffield and London, as well as being joint secretary of the committees at Oxford and (from 1913) Cambridge.

Mansbridge quickly realized that the universities and local WEAs involved in tutorial class work had many problems in common, and he proposed the establishment of a central advisory committee, representing both the academic and labour sides of the joint committees. The Oxford joint committee took the initiative at a conference on 'The University and Tutorial Classes in Industrial Centres' held in Oxford on 2 October 1909. The conference asked the joint secretaries (Mansbridge and Temple) to invite all the joint committees to send one representative from each side to an inaugural meeting. The vice-chancellor of Oxford, Dr Herbert Warren, agreed to convene the meeting, which took place in London on 26 February 1910. University representatives included Sir Oliver Lodge of Birmingham, the vice-chancellors of Durham and Liverpool, and the principal of University College, Southampton. Mansbridge was elected honorary secretary.[19]

On the face of it, the creation of the Central Joint Advisory Committee for Tutorial Classes was a remarkable and effortless achievement by Mansbridge. At the second meeting Dr Henry Miers, principal of London University, was elected chairman, with David Shackleton MP, as vice-chairman and Temple as treasurer. The universities' side of the CJAC was always high-powered in the early years, with vice-chancellors or principals normally in attendance. Temple commented a few years later,

> I wonder if nowadays it is realised how great an achievement was the founding of this Central Joint Advisory Committee. The Board of Education had been struggling for years to persuade the universities and university colleges of England to come together in one body for any purpose ... Then Mansbridge persuaded the Oxford Joint Committee to invite the other universities and the university colleges to join in forming the C.J.A.C. The thing was immediately done. As far as I know there was no hesitation in any quarter; what had been impossible to the concentrated efforts of the British State was immediately achieved when Mansbridge flourished his wand.[20]

The true story is a little different. Mansbridge was, as usual, careful to prepare the ground with the universities, but received a chilly reception from D. H. S. Cranage, secretary of the Cambridge Syndicate for Local

Lectures, and Dr R. D. Roberts of London. Cambridge had been extremely cool about the whole tutorial class movement. The Syndicate agreed in 1909 to provide tutorial classes, which must be in Economics or Political Science, in three centres only. Cranage allowed one centre, Wellingborough, to switch to Literature as there were no ordinary extension courses provided in that town, but he assured the local extension secretary at Portsmouth that the tutorial class there would not clash with extension lectures because it was in 'Economics ... a subject which has hardly been taken at all by any University Extension centre for many years'. Cranage told Mansbridge that he was 'especially instructed to emphasize the experimental and temporary character of the scheme', and repeated this point with no lack of emphasis on several occasions.

As late as October 1911, Cranage was expressing his reluctance to form a joint tutorial classes committee at Cambridge, and had voiced his opposition to the idea of the CJAC to the other disgruntled extension veterans, Marriott and Roberts.[21] Mansbridge had some idea of what the three witches were brewing in their cauldron. He wrote to Zimmern in October 1909, 'M[arriott] is undermining. Temple doesn't believe it, but he never could see down cracks.' After the first meeting of the CJAC he told Zimmern,

> Last Saturday all the Universities came together and it was a muddle. It made me very ill. Anyway I was elected to be Secretary, and there is a fighting chance of bringing the day through, but that is all. Cambridge is perturbed because I am not a 'Varsity man. Well, well. I'll do my best ... Dr. Roberts ... tried to oust me out of the Universities Committee Secretariat but the forces were against him.

Mansbridge's concern about the prospects for the CJAC merged into a greater anxiety about the future of the tutorial class movement. The Board of Education had recently asked J. W. Headlam HMI, and Professor L. T. Hobhouse to undertake a major inspection of tutorial classes. Mansbridge confided to Zimmern,

> My heart is in my mouth. If they report adversely, Tutorial classes on the present plan are at an end. If they report well—I hardly dare imagine the prospect. Its the work of Tawney, You and I in the main. May it last.[22]

The Headlam–Hobhouse Report was published towards the end of 1910. It was, wrote Mansbridge, 'a complete vindication of the tutorial class theory' and 'the most complete justification of the claim of the W.E.A. to help to establish educational institutions in accordance with the workmen's needs'. The report, which was based upon visits to fourteen classes, has become a minor classic of adult education. It contained an eloquent exposition of a 'University standard' of teaching which complements and reinforces the concept of a liberal university education put forward in the Oxford Report.

> We may assume that University teaching is teaching suited to adults; that it is scientific, detached, and impartial in character; that it aims not so much at filling the mind of the student with facts or theories as at calling forth his own individuality, and stimulating him to mental effort; that it accustoms him to the critical study of the leading authorities, and that it implants in his mind a standard of thoroughness, and gives him a sense of the difficulty as well as of the value of truth. The student so trained learns to distinguish between what may fairly be called matter of fact and what is certainly mere matter of opinion, to look at separate questions each on its own merits and without an eye to their bearing on some cherished theory. He learns to state fairly, and even sympathetically, the position of those to whose practical conclusions he is most stoutly opposed ... Finally, without necessarily becoming an original student, he gains an insight into the conditions under which original research is carried on. He is able to weigh evidence, to follow and criticize argument, and put his own value on authorities.

Headlam and Hobhouse took the view that a direct comparison with undergraduate work at Oxford or Cambridge would be

> of doubtful value. The conditions differ, and the product is in some respects better and in others not so good. There is more maturity of mind and more grip of reality [but] less of the qualities arising out of a general literary education.

The inspectors found that the quality of teaching conformed 'to the best standard of University work'. The essays varied considerably in standard, but showed considerable progress and included some which compared 'favourably with the best academic work'. In their conclusion they wrote, no one could attend these classes without being struck by the zeal and earnestness of the students, their happy relations with the lecturer, the general atmosphere of comradeship and good feeling in the classes and the strong appreciation by the students of the benefit which they are deriving from the work ... The experiment of the Association has, in fact, revealed the existence of a very widespread demand for serious teaching of the best and most thorough kind on matters standing in an intelligible relation to the life interests of the workmen ... we have no hesitation in saying that the money contributed by the Board for the support of these classes is being put to thoroughly good use. They are establishing in a number of great industrial towns centres of genuinely educated thought on social and industrial problems ... Its effects are ... likely to be permanent and to spread from the actual members of the class to those who come into contact with them.[23]

The judgment, in a thorough and cautious report, that tutorial class work was, with a few exceptions, of university standard, conferred a double blessing on the WEA. Universities were encouraged to develop class provision, and an important requirement of the Board of Education grant regulations was fulfilled. At the commencement of the tutorial class movement, Mansbridge and officials at the Board looked through the grant regulations for technical classes to find ways of drawing on Morant's 'golden stream'. The normal maximum grant for 'advanced instruction' was five shillings for every twenty student-hours of the course, subject to conditions for regularity of attendance. For a three-year course in commercial subjects the grant went up to eight shillings and six pence. From session 1908/09 the Board agreed to waive the 'commercial subjects' requirement 'if the course as actually carried out by the students is of a standard corresponding with that required for an Honours degree'. The length of tutorial classes, originally planned by Oxford to last for two years, had to be extended to conform to the regulations but many, if not most, of the early tutorial classes would have continued into a third year in any case.

New regulations, specifically for tutorial classes, were introduced on 1 August 1913, after lengthy negotiations between the Board and the Central Joint Advisory Committee. Classes were to last for not less than three sessions, each of twenty-four two-hour meetings, with half of the latter devoted to class work. The maximum number of students was fixed at thirty-two, but the Board was empowered to reduce the limit to twenty-four. A grant of £30, or half of the tutor's fee if that was less, was payable in respect of each class, provided that the number of 'qualifying' students was not less than two-thirds of the original enrolment, with a minimum of twelve in the first year; a half and nine in the second year; and one-third and six in the third year. To qualify, a student had to attend two-thirds of the meetings and to do 'such written work as may be required by the tutor'. Students admitted after the third meeting of the course were not counted for grant. It was laid down that 'The instruction must aim at reaching, within the limits of the subject covered, the standard of University work in Honours.'[24]

At no stage did the Board of Education specify the number of essays to be written, taking the view that this was a matter for the university joint committees. The Oxford requirement of twelve essays per session was derived from the extension practice of encouraging committed students to write an essay for each fortnightly lecture. Other joint committees adopted the twelve-essay provision, although some regarded it a target rather than an obligation. Manchester, for example, demanded a minimum of eighteen essays in a three-year course for the issue of its certificate of satisfactory attendance and work. Only a minority of students in the early tutorial classes managed to write as many as twelve essays every year, although many produced what by any standards was an impressive amount of written work.[25]

Mansbridge was concerned administratively with the question of essay-writing for two reasons. If a student wrote no essays, or so few that the joint committee concerned could not regard him or her as 'effective', no grant was earned in respect of that person under the 1908 regulations, and the payment of the full grant under the 1913 regulations was threatened. Secondly the Gilchrist Trust made supplementary grants to some of the early tutorial classes, amounting to £1 per session for each working-class student who attended regularly and wrote twelve essays. Mansbridge therefore found himself writing to tutors, class secretaries, and even individual defaulters, about the importance of keeping up the flow of essays. He confided to R. V. Lennard, an Oxford tutor, 'Essays get on my nerves a little bit because failure of essays means financial loss.'[26]

Mansbridge was, however, a good listener and reader as well as a fluent talker and writer. He gained valuable insights into the problems of tutorial class students, particularly with regard to written work. Some of the most able and successful tutors took the view that a requirement of twelve essays per year was not so much an unreasonable load—although it became so for students burdened with long hours of compulsory overtime—as undesirable on academic grounds. When students moved out of topics to which their experience of life and work directly related into the more theoretical aspects of the subject, they needed more time to read and think before productive written work could be done. Some students wrote long and substantial papers. Sam Moore, a member of Henry Clay's tutorial class in Hebden Bridge, had a 5,000-word article on local economic history published in the *Economic Journal*. It was a shortened version of a carefully-researched paper of 15,000 words, yet another contribution to knowledge from a worker in the Fustian Co-operative Manufacturing Society.[27]

From class secretaries Mansbridge learned not only about the general problems of persuading students to commit themselves to three years' study and regular essay-writing, but also about the difficulties of individual students. Some of them had to wait until the rest of the family had retired to bed before they could find peace and quiet for study. E. S. Cartwright, who spent one evening a week with the aid of two other members of the Longton tutorial class coaching several recent recruits to the class, explained to Mansbridge that students' difficulties with written work were not only intellectual and psychological. 'One thing this has brought home to me, personally—how very difficult and distasteful the mere physical act of writing is to a miner or a potter.'[28]

Mansbridge tried to lay the 'essay bogey' in the first of a series of articles about tutorial class work published in the *Highway* in 1912. He began by denying very firmly that the WEA existed solely to develop tutorial classes. These classes represented the highest academic level of WEA work, but

> the Association exists for the working men and women who have the least pretensions to scholarship—for men and women who are simply interested in the simple things of life. It is not possible for all men and women to be scholars.

Prospective students, he argued, misunderstood the nature of essays and the purpose of essay writing.

> No tutor expects finished articles … students have the idea that they are

called upon to produce something in the style of Charles Lamb at the first effort ... an essay is what its name implies—an attempt to place upon paper the things which one knows about the subject under consideration [so that] the tutor is able to see exactly what the student knows and what his point of view is.

Working people should not worry if their spelling was inaccurate (a common fault amongst undergraduates), their handwriting deficient (that of some tutors was quite indecipherable) or their grammar weak. These skills would improve through practice. 'Bad writing, bad spelling, bad grammar never yet did any damage to the community, but bad thinking has done much.' Tutorial classes were designed not for people who knew, but for people who wanted to know, and wanted to help each other to learn.

> A tutorial class needs keenness, enthusiasm, interest and a readiness to put the interests of the whole class before one's own. It is not a place of competition. It is a place of comradeship.[29]

The subtlety of mind which had helped Mansbridge to create the tutorial class movement stood him in good stead in administering it. In January 1912 he wrote, as joint secretary to the Oxford tutorial classes committee, to one of the full-time tutors, F. W. Kolthammer, asking whether it would not be possible for him to reduce the expense of travelling to classes by staying with some of his students instead of returning home every night.

> We hoped when we started the work the tutors would stay with their students as far as possible. Some Oxford tutors do it every week, and, as one said to me, a man cannot very well leave your class when you have stayed with him.

On another occasion Mansbridge asked Tawney whether any of his students' essays could be counted as two to satisfy the conditions of the Gilchrist grant. He played down the difficulties of assimilating students added in the third year of a tutorial class as long as the grant regulations made this policy financially desirable. 'The third year is sure to be a special division of the subject' and although carefully selected 'new students will not be up to those who have studied for the two years in the class, yet they will be well up in the subject'. As soon as the 1913 regulations were introduced, however, Mansbridge warned against admitting 'students who had not been thoroughly tested as to their determination to attend the class for three years' as defecting students could be a cause of financial loss.[30]

Mansbridge had every right to be proud of the tutorial class movement. When he received the reports from tutors and class secretaries at the end of the 1909/10 session he told Zimmern, 'The Oxford classes are a glorious triumph ... Each class has been a success and the Tutors are all splendid. Was there ever such a good piece of educational work.'[31] Mansbridge delighted in reports which testified to the great enthusiasm of many of the students— classes which carried on working if the tutor was delayed, women students wading through deep snow to reach a class, an unemployed man from Glossop who went to Sheffield looking for work but walked back twenty-four miles across the Pennines to attend his class meeting. The testimony of scholars of great ability about what they had learned from their students confirmed Mansbridge's faith in the benefits of the dialogue on equal terms between labour and learning. Tawney paid tribute to the contributions of his students to his first major work, *The Agrarian Problem in the Sixteenth Century*, which was dedicated to Temple and Mansbridge. In reviewing the book Professor W. J. Ashley expressed his pleasure that Tawney's intense 'sympathy with the underdog' had not distorted his academic judgment. 'It is reassuring to be presented with a book like this, which has come out of a WEA atmosphere, tingling with feeling, it is true, and yet on the whole so balanced and fair-minded.' Henry Clay praised the quality of discussion in his second-year Economics class in Halifax, which had made him 'even more dissatisfied than I was before with the treatment of those problems in the ordinary economic text book'. This concern moved Clay to write *Economics for the General Reader*, published in 1916.[32]

At the same time, Mansbridge was candid about the failings of the tutorial class system. Oxford paid its tutors £80 a class (which meant a salary of £400 a year for someone doing a full programme of five classes), Cambridge £72 and London £60. The rates at other universities were lower, usually £50 a class but sometimes even less, until the 1913 grant regulations caused a general increase to £60. The result was a rapid turnover of lecturers, as they moved to more secure and better-paid posts, sometimes in mid-session.[33]

Book supply was a serious problem. Most universities supplied book boxes to their classes, but a few left the students to rely on their local public libraries. Mansbridge criticized 'inexperienced and ill-advised tutors' who did not realize the importance of books, including one who 'had taken his class for two years in Economic Theory with only one textbook and no books of reference'. There could be no proper study of economics unless the students had access to the full range of academic opinion on the subject. 'No class, for example, can afford to disregard either Marshall or Marx.'[34]

To ease the problem of book supply, the WEA arranged for the publication of cheap editions of books in great demand, including Sidney and Beatrice Webb's *Industrial Democracy* and *History of Trade Unionism*. The idea of a central library service was considered in the summer of 1910, when Canon Barnett offered to place a room at Toynbee Hall, and a stock of books, at the disposal of the CJAC. The offer was not taken up until 1912, when the WEA raised a special fund for the purpose. Mansbridge and Barnett arranged for the Central Library for Tutorial Classes to be established at Toynbee Hall, managed by a joint committee of the Hall and the WEA. Barnett provided accommodation and the loan of some books belonging to Toynbee Hall. A librarian paid out of the special fund was appointed by the joint committee, and additional books acquired. When Mansbridge wrote *University Tutorial Classes* in the early months of 1913, he was already thinking of the possibility that, with the aid of substantial state grants, the Central Library for Tutorial Classes might become a National Central Library, catering for the needs of all studious readers.[35]

Mansbridge considered that 'by far the most serious internal problem of the classes' was the great difficulty of giving 'the individual tuition outside the class hours which the whole system implies'. In support Tawney argued that full-time tutors should take fewer classes, and use the time saved to give individual tuition.[36] The need for additional personal tuition was met in part by the development of WEA summer schools. By 1909 the number of WEA students attending part of the extension summer meeting, held in alternate years in Oxford and Cambridge, had risen to two hundred. In the following year the WEA began to hold its own annual school in Oxford, with the support of A. L. Smith, who offered Balliol College as a base. The school, which provided small-group seminars and individual tuition as well as lectures, ran for eight weeks. The Bangor (North Wales) school, started in 1913 by the universities of Liverpool and Manchester and University

College, Bangor in co-operation with the North-West District of the WEA, lasted for six weeks. Schools of such length catered for students from northern industrial towns, which had annual summer holidays in different weeks. It was also possible for some textile workers to take extra holidays without pay if scholarships were provided for their maintenance. Several more joint committees began schools of two weeks' duration. The Oxford school made heavy demands on Mansbridge and his tiny band of professional organizers.[37]

It seemed to be agreed in the WEA that the tutorial class movement would have failed unless substantial numbers of students found their way into full-time courses leading to a diploma if not to a degree. In the absence of a royal commission on Oxford and Cambridge, which, Mansbridge hoped, might tap the wealth of the colleges for the benefit of the poor scholar, adequate funds for this purpose were not forthcoming. It was difficult enough to find enough money for the expanding needs of the WEA and the provision of tutorial classes. In these circumstances Mansbridge did not argue—although Tawney did—when tutorial classes began to have ideological doubts about the selection of a few students from each to go to the university.[38]

University scholarships were provided for a handful of tutorial class students, but increasingly the class members and WEA branches took the view that it was better to use any available funds to give summer-school scholarships to the many rather than full-time places to the few. A special WEA conference on this issue, held in May 1914, adopted resolutions which discouraged, without forbidding, further full-time admissions: 'no movement for the admission of students to the Universities should be permitted to hinder the growth and efficiency of the Tutorial Class Movement'.[39]

With so many matters to occupy his attention, it was fortunate that Mansbridge was both able and willing to devolve responsibility for important areas of work. This was particularly the case with women's education. Although middle-class women had been taking advantage of university extension lectures since the 1870s, working-class women, and particularly housewives, had few opportunities for adult education until the WEA was founded. In 1907 the association convened a group of women which developed into the Women's Advisory Committee. The leading lights were

Frances Mansbridge, Maude Royden, Miss E. M. Zimmern (sister of Alfred), Margaret McMillan and two leading Co-operators, Julia Madams and Catherine Webb. Margaret MacDonald, wife of the Labour leader, was a member until her death in 1911. By 1910 enough money had been raised to appoint a national organizer. Large numbers of classes for women were formed, both in domestic subjects and in liberal studies, especially literature. The proportion of women, both workers and housewives, in tutorial classes increased steadily, and by 1914 the WEA was making an important contribution to the intellectual emancipation of working-class women. Although Mansbridge sympathized with this movement, he saw no need to interfere with the successful endeavours of such a formidable team of ladies.[40]

He played a more active part in another crusade on behalf of the disadvantaged—the promotion of rural work, and particularly of classes for agricultural labourers. His approach was influenced by his admiration for the Danish folk high schools, residential centres catering mainly for young adults from peasant families and teaching both technical and liberal subjects. The interest in their work taken by the Quaker leaders of the Adult School movement led to the foundation of Fircroft College, Birmingham, in 1909. Mansbridge and Margaret McMillan, who visited folk high schools in Denmark, hoped to establish similar institutions in England, partly because they were uncertain about the suitability of normal WEA organization and teaching for rural communities. The English folk high schools never materialized, but the issue was settled by the colonizing efforts of the Swindon and Bristol branches, forming branches in surrounding villages, with classes taught by voluntary tutors from the urban centres.[41]

Mansbridge made a distinctive personal contribution to this work in 1911, when he addressed a meeting in the picturesque Oxfordshire village of Ascott under Wychwood, attended mainly by farm workers and their wives. When asked what they would like to study, four men, after a long silence, said 'shorthand'. Mansbridge was staggered, but 'perhaps through a knowledge of the workings of the rural mind, which is not given to revealing its secrets or desires in public, I divined that they wished to study history' and a class in that subject was formed successfully.[42]

The early history of rural WEA work offers a useful reminder of a truth that Mansbridge himself was fond of enunciating—nothing could be achieved which was not in harmony with the needs and wants of the working people of the country. As a firm believer in democracy and decentralization, Mansbridge was in general content to let the waters of local initiative flow where they would. On two issues, however, he tried to give firm leadership, class administration and the maintenance of the non-party and unsectarian character of the association.

Mansbridge recognized the significance of the system which was emerging, whereby branches not only promoted tutorial classes, but organized other classes which were either provided by the LEA at the request of the WEA, or put on by the branch itself with the aid of whatever grants could be secured from the Board of Education and the LEA. It meant that WEA branches were becoming part of the public education service. This was a heavy responsibility for voluntary officers, and Mansbridge used the *Highway* to offer appropriate guidance.

> From all sides applications for classes pour in. On no account must a WEA branch ask an Education Authority to set on foot a class unless a sufficient number of its members have pledged themselves to make the attendances at it.

It was not important to have a lot of classes, but each application should be sound. '"WEA" and "Thorough" should be synonymous terms.' (*Highway*, June 1910.)

> The Board of Education asks of W.E.A. secretaries just the same fitness and efficiency as it asks of local Education Authorities, and so it often happens that we have to give the advice: 'Just do a few things and do them well, and wait for the time when expansion comes of itself.' But the real thing is to let all W.E.A. members do their best to help their branch. Don't let them go to sleep and let the secretary do it all. (*Highway*, April 1911.)

The 'non-party and unsectarian' character of the WEA was emphasized on every possible occasion. Mansbridge believed that the identification of the movement with any political party or religious sect would 'stultify its utility or even render its existence altogether impossible'.[43] The unity of an association drawn from all sections of the working-class movement, the maintenance of objectivity and thoroughness in teaching, the co-operation of the universities, the support of 'all men of good will', and access to public funds, all depended upon the WEA's ideological independence. At successive annual demonstrations the same resolution was carried,

> That this National Demonstration, representing Labour and Education, expresses its confidence in the unsectarian, non-party, democratic character of the W.E.A., in attempting alike to stimulate and to satisfy the demand among working men and working women for education, and affirms its belief that in the continuance of such activity lies one of the chief hopes for the development of a national system of Education ensuring to every child, adolescent and adult, that Education which is essential for the complete development of their individual and corporate capacities.

In 1909 the above resolution was moved by the archbishop of York, Cosmo Gordon Lang, and seconded by David Shackleton MP. In 1910, it was moved by Joseph Pointer, Labour MP for Sheffield Attercliffe (trade unionist, Methodist local preacher, ex-Ruskin College), and seconded by Professor Gilbert Murray. The proposer and seconder in the following year were Bishop Gore and Margaret McMillan. The involvement of churchmen was appropriate, as the resolution was the WEA's version of the Creed.[44]

Mansbridge emphasized his own detachment from party. He told *Highway* readers that he took a Conservative, a Liberal and a Labour journal—the *Morning Post*, *Manchester Guardian* and *Labour Leader*. He made strenuous efforts to maintain all-party support for the association, both locally and nationally. He had, for example, some difficulty in securing Conservative support for the formation of the Wrexham branch, which he blamed in correspondence with Zimmern on 'the political indiscretions of My Lord Tawney', who was the tutor of a tutorial class already established in the Welsh town. He wrote to the acting branch secretary,

> It must be quite understood that Mr. and Mrs. Tawney are not to be asked to take part in politics, or their names used. Neither is any partisan literature to be issued by the Class. I write this to you quite privately. We must work to cover up the mistakes of the past.[45]

Mansbridge's attitude to Tawney's political activities was ambivalent. When it suited him to do so, he paraded Tawney's socialist credentials. Mansbridge responded to attacks on the WEA in the socialist press by arranging for activists in the movement, including Tawney, to write letters of refutation with their political affiliations—ILP, Fabian Society, and so on—appended to the signatures. In 1911 Mansbridge asked Tawney confidentially to prepare a statement about university reform for the Labour party. Yet in writing to Zimmern, Mansbridge complained about the effect of Tawney's political activities. For example,

> Yesterday I stayed with the Tawneys—the R.H.T. is getting more and more revolutionary and will infallibly land the tutorial classes in some muddle. Well, we'll forgive him for he has done more than much.[46]

Mansbridge's public response to left-wing attacks was to argue that they were based upon misconceptions about the position of the WEA. He told the annual meeting in 1908,

> there had really been no attack upon the Association. It was true that there had appeared in one of the Labour papers misrepresentations concerning the Association, but those had been entirely due to misapprehension ... the critics would see that it was non-party, non-political and non-sectarian, and that it was governed almost entirely by labour.[47]

Mansbridge tried to explain away the one major defeat which he suffered at the hands of his left-wing enemies, when at a meeting in Poplar, east London, the resolution calling for the establishment of a WEA branch was lost. He claimed that Temple, speaking for the WEA, had won the argument, but lost the vote because delegates were mandated in advance. In private Mansbridge was less restrained. 'The Bridges–Adams opposition is more furious than ever—lies, misrepresentations, the devilments of the pit—are all brought to bear.'[48]

It was important to Mansbridge that he should give the wisest guidance to activists in the WEA. They were repeatedly told, by Temple and Gore as well as Mansbridge, that knowledge was power. Temple declared, in his presidential address to the 1910 annual meeting, 'Army of labour, advance and occupy the citadels of that knowledge which is at once the source of power and the guarantee that the power shall be beneficent.' The most famous of all of Gore's speeches to the WEA, delivered later in the meeting, centred on the same idea. Lawrence Goldman notes the conflict of evidence about the date of this speech, the 1909 annual meeting according to Mary Stocks and 1910 in other accounts. In fact Gore made a similar speech in 1909 and virtually the same speech in 1911. At this period a flood of oratory was sustained by a trickle of composition though the addiction to repetition and plagiarism, with not only the same ideas, but the same words, surfacing repeatedly. The address at Reading in 1910 burned into the memories of those who heard it because of a particular circumstance. Proceedings were running late, and Gore rose to speak, not a little frustrated, only a few minutes before ten in the evening, when the meeting was scheduled to end. He concentrated his oratory into a short, powerful, rhythmic declaration:

> all this passion for justice will accomplish nothing, believe me, unless you get knowledge. You may become strong and clamorous, you may win a victory, you may effect a revolution, but you will be trodden down under the feet of knowledge unless you get it for yourselves; even if you win that victory, you will be trodden down again under the feet of knowledge if you leave knowledge in the hands of privilege, because knowledge will always win over ignorance.[49]

Speeches such as this contained two messages. The first was 'study before you act'. But what about the implications for the WEA of the second, 'Act after you have studied'? Mansbridge had a ready answer. WEA members must pursue political objectives though the organizations affiliated to the WEA, especially trade unions and political parties, not through the Association itself.[50]

Mansbridge did not, however, apply this 'self-denying ordinance' to matters of educational policy. In speeches and articles he called for 'one system of schools unified upon a great highway in which there were no class distinctions whatever', and specifically for secondary education for all, with maintenance allowances for needy families. Supporting Margaret McMillan's campaign for school clinics and nursery schools, he proposed a national system of crèches, provided by LEAs. He even demanded paid holidays for all workers, so that they would be refreshed to enjoy opportunities for learning.

Mansbridge applauded the resolutions of WEA branches, calling for the raising of the school-leaving age to sixteen and the reduction of class sizes to thirty. The Colne branch pointed out that some LEAs were counting against the statutory minimum of twenty-five per cent free places in grant-aided secondary schools, scholarships provided by other bodies, for example Co-operative societies. Mansbridge and Shackleton went to see Walter Runciman, president of the Board of Education, and persuaded him to alter the regulations to prevent this abuse. Mansbridge asked trades councils to take issue with LEAs which refused to admit children under five (the commencing age for compulsory education) if they lived in slum dwellings. Other targets for his indignation were child labour, including the delivery of newspapers and milk, and the 'half-time system', which allowed children at the age of twelve to start work for half of the day in textile mills. In 'these days of unemployment' child labour was 'utter foolishness'.[51]

In October 1912 Mansbridge was invited to give a paper on 'The Education of the People' to a sectional meeting at the Church Congress in Middlesbrough. The delegates were used to hearing criticisms of the capitalist system from members of the Christian Socialist movement, then at the height of its influence, but they can rarely have heard a stronger attack than Mansbridge's:

> many working men and women are bitter beyond bitterness because the Church has acquiesced in the existing economic order, the materialisation of our mental condition which spoils their lives, damages their children, throws up slums, produces starvation at one end of the scale and gross luxury at the other, and hating, as they must hate, the existing state of affairs, they hate the Church and reject the gospel of our Lord.

The remedy, argued Mansbridge, was for the Church to work for 'the fullest and freest opportunities of education for all'. He was caustic about the current claim 'that the way to the University is now open to any poor boy of parts'.

> The construction of ladders has been a cherished feature of English educational administration during the last twenty years ... In many parts of England they do not rest upon the earth; when they do, the rungs are not infrequently missing.[52]

Mansbridge repeated his demands for a school-leaving age of sixteen, with maintenance allowances where needed; and a radical reform of Oxford and Cambridge to make them accessible to the poor as well as the rich.

Mansbridge never faced up to the basic contradiction between his commitment to political neutrality and his advocacy of any changes necessary to achieve equality of educational opportunity for all children, adolescents and adults. It is unlikely that he admitted the contradiction even to himself, shielded as he was by the belief that no intelligent and civilized person, of whatever political persuasion, could actually be in favour of the evil conditions which he attacked, or opposed to a general extension of the benefits of education. It was therefore possible for the same paragraph, in the annual report for 1909/10, to contain both the assertion that 'any nation which believes in education as the fundamental source of its true power will arrange its material resources so as to administer to educational needs' and the usual declaration that 'The W.E.A. is steadfastly determined to keep to its own work and leave to other bodies the alteration of the law'.

There was, however, a rough logic in the ideological line followed by Mansbridge and the WEA—no holds barred on educational questions, except for the avoidance of sectarian controversy, and neutrality on other political matters, give or take a few ambiguities. Radical educational policies offered a safety valve for pressures in the WEA which might otherwise have built up out of the fear that objectivity could induce passivity. Expounded with obvious enthusiasm by Mansbridge, the same policies guaranteed his *bona fides* as a committed member of the working-class movement. His educational radicalism and his burning zeal made many converts and to most, although not all, of the people who met him they gave the lie to the accusation that his purpose was to draw the teeth of the workers and preserve the existing structure of class privilege.[53]

'Burning' was the word often used in the WEA to describe Mansbridge's infectious zeal. W. H. Hosford, who began work as an office boy in the WEA central office in January 1909, saw people leaving Mansbridge's office obviously inspired, 'as if they had seen a vision'.

The word 'burning' was also appropriate in the sense that the sun warms the earth by consuming part of its substance in the fire. Mansbridge persistently drove himself to the point of exhaustion. He confessed in a letter in October 1908, 'I find difficulty in doing even my letters because I have broken down a little.' In May 1910 he wrote to Zimmern, to whom he was always prepared to unburden himself,

I am tired and overdone—almost too weary for letters. If only we could charge our spirits and send them out—perhaps we do … You will say I am depressed. Well I do feel played out, but I'll get up tomorrow morning feeling fresh and strong …

Later in the same year his friends became increasingly concerned about his health. In July Dr John Brown Paton, the veteran Congregationalist who was a close personal friend, told Mansbridge that his 'enormous activities' had 'seriously weakened' him, and urged him to take more rest.[54]

In September the Mansbridge family was sent off on a long sea voyage. Readers of the *Highway* were assured that 'The General Secretary is going not because he is in ill-health, but because he wants to gain strength for the arduous work of the next few years', but in truth his friends feared that he was close to a nervous breakdown. The sea trip was arranged through the good offices of Dr Tom Jones, who had been a member of the WEA central executive committee until 1909, when he had become professor of economics at Queen's University, Belfast. The Mansbridges shipped in a small tramp steamer sailing to Mediterranean ports, Mansbridge as purser, Mrs Mansbridge as stewardess, and their son John, aged nine, as assistant purser. The discharge certificates of Albert and John, testifying to their good character, are preserved in the Mansbridge MSS. The trip lasted about seven weeks.[55]

At the end of the year Dr J. B. Paton took the trouble, on the day after the funeral of his wife who had died after a long illness, to write to Frances Mansbridge urging her to persuade her husband to rest more.

> He has what has been a splendid fault, and no doubt it has given him the success he has so wonderfully achieved, but he is a little too earnest, a little too emphatic now that he has won his cause, and I think he spends too much strength now in emphasising his work, and seeking to convert men who are already on his side … Ask him to be calm and thank God that his emphasis and driving force are not now needed, save very occasionally.[56]

In December 1911 Sir Robert Morant, in a letter written as he was about to leave the Board of Education, expressed similar anxieties,

> that you were giving too much and not reserving enough of your strength to face the strain which is going to continue a long time yet. May I, as my last word to you from this official Chair, though (I hope) by no means my

> last word to you as a friend, sincerely and gravely beg of you to give determined attention to thinking out ... ways in which you can somewhat diminish the strain on your strength ... for a very great deal indeed depends upon your being strong enough to bear it.[57]

The gradual build-up of professional staff in the districts and the central office offered the prospect that Mansbridge might be able to devote himself to propaganda, public meetings and fund-raising without being burdened at the same time by routine administrative duties. In 1911 L. V. Gill, a pioneer member of the Rochdale WEA who had been North-Western district secretary, moved to London as central organizing secretary at a salary of £250 a year. Mansbridge's salary was increased to £300, a sum which was covered by private donations and grants from the Gilchrist Trust. He enjoyed in addition a small income from the directorship of the Co-operative Permanent Building Society to which he had been appointed in the previous year. Mansbridge was also given a personal secretary, and he appointed Dorothy Jones who was to work with him, except for a short break, for the rest of his life. E. S. Cartwright, who had been a local-government officer and one of the leading lights of the tutorial class movement in North Staffordshire, became organizing secretary to the Oxford joint committee, and took on most of the work previously undertaken for that committee by Mansbridge himself.[58]

The translation of Gill to London did not work. He fell ill almost immediately—he too had been overworking—and was on sick leave for about eight months. He returned to work, but never recovered his full vigour, and he left the service of the WEA in March 1913. The central office staff was strengthened by the appointment of Ernest Wimble in September 1912, and Bill Lowth in the following year, both destined to give a lifetime of service to the WEA and its associated organizations.[59]

In 1910 the South Wales district, three years old, was extended to cover the whole of Wales. Mansbridge's main contributions to developments in Wales were his lecture tours in South Wales, where he encountered the opposition from the Labour College movement which is described in Chapter 5, and negotiations to establish joint tutorial classes committees in the constituent colleges of the University of Wales, Aberystwyth, Bangor and Cardiff. In 1911–13 four new districts were formed, and three additional full-time appointments made, making a national total, excluding clerical staff, of thirteen, still very modest for an expanding national organization. At the end of 1912 Mansbridge's achievements were recognized by the award of an honorary MA by the University of Oxford.[60]

In January 1913 Mansbridge began what was intended to be a year's sabbatical from the central office, although he remained an officer of the Oxford and Cambridge joint committees and the CJAC. Within a matter of weeks, however, he was invited to visit Australia. T. E. Harvey, the Liberal MP and former national treasurer of the WEA, and Henry Clay, an Oxford tutorial class tutor, set to work to raise a special fund, a substantial part of which came from the Joseph Rowntree Trust, to staff the central office adequately during Mansbridge's absence. Sir Henry Miers, the principal of London University, proposed that on Mansbridge's return from Australia he should be offered a new post, that of national organizer of tutorial classes. His function would be to develop and standardize tutorial class work across the country. He would be employed by the WEA through a fund of £500 a year to which all of the universities providing tutorial classes would contribute. The London and Oxford joint committees readily agreed to pay £60 each, but the response elsewhere was not sufficient to make the scheme possible. There seems to have been, however, a general understanding that the great pioneering effort of establishing the WEA was over, and that Mansbridge's talents should be used for new creative work rather than absorbed in heavy administrative routine, provided, of course, that he could be persuaded not to burn himself out.[61]

Henry Clay put this point to Mansbridge in a letter written on the eve of his departure for Australia. The constant effort and worry of the past ten years had, he suggested, been both a strain and an education to Mansbridge, 'if you don't mind my saying so, you seem to me much more mature, with a surer and firmer grasp of men and situations, than when I first came to you four years ago'. Both the movement and Mansbridge's friends would miss him very much,

> But I still think you ought to go. It is not only that you *need* a rest, and Mrs. Mansbridge still more; but I feel that if you can only get three months' 'Sabbath' your spiritual and intellectual forces will consolidate and make a bigger man of you ... your health and spirit are *far more important to the movement* than the organisation ... of W.E.A. work ... I think the W.E.A., as it is, is only a miserable beginning, compared with what you will make it when you come back.[62]

To wish the Mansbridges *bon voyage*, a dinner was held at the Working Men's College in London. There were six toasts, and a remarkable succession of speeches. One was made by the lord chancellor, Lord Haldane, who described the efforts made by Sir Robert Morant and himself to secure a place for WEA work in the recent report of the royal commission on the University of London. He summed up the achievement of 'my friend Mr. Mansbridge' in these words.

> Latent in everybody, reachable in very many, is a spark of idealism which you can touch, be he rural labourer, or be he professor. You can rouse it, and you can get it to flame up. If you do that you have a great moving force in the individual, and if you can get it in many individuals you have a great moving force in the nation. Now that has been the secret of Mr. Mansbridge's ideals: he believes in his fellow creatures, he is an optimist, and he is not afraid to ask the highest and nothing but the highest. That is the secret of success ...[63]

# 5
## Friends and Enemies

By 1908 Mansbridge had travelled a long way from the kitchen in which his association had been launched five years earlier with two members and two shillings and sixpence in funds. The WEA had become firmly established and the tutorial class movement launched; both were to go from strength to strength during the next few years. The indispensable grant-aid from the Board of Education had been secured. It had been agreed in principle that special arrangements should be made to admit worker-students to Oxford. Mansbridge had gained the sympathy, and often the practical support, of many influential people, in the universities, in the Church of England and in political life. To quote H. P. Smith, an administrator for the Oxford delegacy who was an assiduous historian in his spare time, 'Mansbridge stood out in his generation as an original force, attracting all sorts and conditions of people to adult education.' It would be wrong to underestimate the power of this 'original force', of Mansbridge's fervour, eloquence and magnetism. On the other hand these personal qualities would have counted for little if important sections of Edwardian society had not been so well tuned to the wavelength on which Mansbridge, after his early struggles, learned to transmit.[1]

In exploring this subject, that is, the relations between Mansbridge's own input, the influences upon him, and the social and political forces which proved to be favourable, one consideration must be emphasized. Although throughout his adult life Mansbridge waxed eloquent about the 'glory of education'—the value of learning for its own sake—he reinforced this belief in the period 1906–14 with specific demands for far-reaching reforms in educational provision for both children and adults. It was not the muddled youth or the dreamy sage who achieved at least partial victory in the campaign to harness the universities in the service of workers' education, but an advocate of radical educational policies.

95

Some of the men of influence who supported Mansbridge's efforts in the first ten years of the WEA performed a limited role because that was all they were asked to do (Dr Strong and Professor Turner), all they wished to do (Dr Roberts), or all they were allowed to do (Marriott). Those whose support or influence was greater were well represented at the May 1913 dinner at the Working Men's College. The speakers (there were more toasts than courses) included Mansbridge himself, who presented his vision of an educated democracy; the Revd William Temple, then headmaster of Repton School and president of the WEA 1908–24; Charles Gore, bishop of Oxford since 1911; A. L. Smith, fellow, later master, of Balliol College; Sir Henry Miers, principal of London University; Sir Charles Lucas, principal of the Working Men's College; Philip Snowden, Labour MP; J. M. Mactavish, destined to succeed Mansbridge as general secretary of the WEA; two representatives of the trade union movement and one of the Women's Co-operative Guild; Sir Robert Morant, permanent secretary of the Board of Education; and Viscount Haldane, lord chancellor. Also present were Christopher Turnor, a landowner who later supported more than one of Mansbridge's organizations, and Geoffrey Dawson, editor of *The Times*. According to Turnor, Dawson was impressed by Mansbridge's speech to the point of being 'overwhelmed'. He turned to his neighbour and said, 'Twelve such men and England would be saved.'[2]

The schools of thought represented at the dinner ranged from Christian Socialism, through ethical socialism, the active citizenship/public service ethos, and New Liberalism to the cult of national efficiency. Morant and Haldane, together with Rosebery, Alfred Milner and the Webbs, were prominently identified with the last named. The movement had its roots in the humiliations of the Boer War, and particularly in concern about the loss of Britain's lead over its industrial rivals which was attributed in part to the inadequacy of scientific research and technical education. At first sight there was little common ground on questions of working-class education between the efficiency group, which thought in terms of ladders to be climbed by intelligent working-class boys, and Mansbridge, with his 'free and open highway upon which the only tolls are to be mental equipment and high character'. However, their advocacy of a 'national minimum' of nourishment, health and education, which was seen as essential for national efficiency and social harmony, fitted in well with the WEA objective of 'the elevation of the whole body of workers … not raising people out of their class, but raising them and their class at the same time'.[3]

This 'elevation' involved not only improving the education, housing and health of the workers, but also eradicating their moral weaknesses. Mansbridge observed that 'the class has not shown itself backward in adopting the vices of leisured people with less time to accomplish them'. Charles Masterman, although a sympathetic reformer, considered that the average working man was restrained from behaving like the sport-loving, self-indulgent occupants of the Conservative back benches in the House of Commons only by lack of opportunity.[4] Something of the same attitude is expressed in a passage from a speech by Haldane, part of which was quoted approvingly by Mansbridge in one of the articles which launched the WEA.

> to me … education … appears the most important, without exception, of the great social reforms which await treatment at the beginning of the twentieth century. Educate your people, and you have reduced to comparatively insignificant dimensions the problems of temperance, of housing, and of raising the condition of your masses. These things solve themselves if you only get the right spirit into your people.[5]

The reference to temperance is the key to understanding this passage. Haldane did not mean that the workers would use their education to seize political control and solve the social problems of the day by a redistribution of wealth. He meant that educated people did not have social problems.

Education was Haldane's favoured instrument for breaking down class barriers and encouraging moderation in the labour movement, and so reinforcing both social cohesion and national strength. In 1899 he had advocated means-tested student grants, to give equal access to the universities 'to the son of the duke and the son of the working man'. According to Mansbridge, Haldane 'helped and encouraged me in all my work from 1905', when they first met. A close partnership seems to have developed out of discussions about the adult education role of the University of London during Haldane's chairmanship of the royal commission on the university, 1909–13.[6]

Mansbridge met Morant in 1905, when a WEA deputation went to the Board of Education to ask for an inquiry into the possibility of making attendance at continuation schools compulsory for 14–17 year olds.

Morant sent for him in February 1907. The Consultative Committee of the Board, and by implication the Board itself, had recently been attacked by the National Union of Teachers as being 'permeated with a caste feeling and ... endeavouring to limit the educational opportunities of the working class'. According to the NUT, the committee was 'entirely estranged from working class needs'. Morant was anxious to disabuse the public of 'this very false idea', and it was decided to enlarge the committee. The name of a woman from Sheffield was suggested as an additional representative from the teaching profession. The permanent secretary was warned that she was something of a firebrand—exactly what we need, he replied. Morant told Mansbridge that two representatives of the labour movement were to be invited to join the committee. One was to be David Shackleton, 'probably the best of the Labour Members for educational purposes and likely in himself to be a very valuable Member of the Committee for general purposes'. Morant asked Mansbridge to suggest another, preferably not a trade union official. Mansbridge wrote putting forward eight names, nearly all Co-operators and/or trade unionists, and including, despite Morant's advice, some trade union officials. 'Trade Unionists should be able to recognise the person appointed as one of themselves.' Mansbridge emphasized, however, that he had 'purposely avoided extreme men'.

Mansbridge's letter crossed with one from Morant, saying that Reginald McKenna, president of the Board of Education, had agreed that

> the best thing we can do is at once to offer a place on the Consultative Committee both to Mr Shackleton and to yourself ... I have to thank you for a most interesting talk today, which is, I hope, only the first of many later talks on the same subject.[7]

After this Morant was always accessible to Mansbridge, and some of the 'later talks' produced the offer of grant aid for tutorial classes. The two men became firm friends. Morant wrote to Mansbridge on his departure from the Board of Education in 1911:

> I look back to my relations with you as one of the most delightful and fruitful of many of the myriad happenings in my work here. What led up to the Oxford meeting, and the Oxford meeting which I had the pleasure of attending, seemed to me at the time quite one of the largest matters to

which we could put our hand at this Board. But let me assure you that what has really helped to inspire one to effort in that particular direction has been the feeling of the intense enthusiasm and devotion that you yourself have given throughout.[8]

The 'elevation of the whole body of workers', incorporating moral as well as material improvement, presented no threat to enlightened members of the 'Establishment' such as Morant and Haldane. Charles Masterman depicted the privileged class as fearing 'an uprising of the uneducated, suddenly breaking into its houses: their clumsy feet on the mantelpiece, their clumsy hands seizing and destroying all beautiful and pleasant things. So it lies awake at night, listening fearfully to the tramp of the rising host.' Much less anxiety was caused by a reformist educational movement, committed to thoroughness and objectivity in study, whose founder regarded Oxford and Cambridge as holy cities.[9]

Mansbridge's relationship with Gore and Barnett, as father figures, and with Temple, Tawney, Zimmern, Ball and A. L. Smith as reformist allies at Oxford, has already been discussed. Mansbridge sometimes said that Charles Gore was the real founder of his movements, a devotional observation which need not be taken too seriously. Gore was, however, a key figure in a network of influence and ideas which helped to smooth Mansbridge's path. He was one of the founders of the Christian Social Union (1889) and together with Henry Scott Holland its principal ideologue on social and economic issues. Gore and Holland emphasized the incompatibility between contemporary business morality and the spirit of Christ.[10] As William Temple argued, in a CSU journal in 1908, the 'great sins' of the age were 'sins not of the individual but of the citizen', resulting from connivance at 'a vast organisation of wickedness for which no individual is altogether responsible'.

> Competition is inherently a principle of selfishness and, indeed, of hatred. It sets the interest of every man against that of his fellows ... If the doctrine of the Brotherhood of Man is to be worked out in the economic sphere, we must substitute a co-operative basis for the existing competitive basis of society ... It is urged that Socialism is too ideal ... 'If you want to get the best out of a man, you must appeal to his self-interest.' Now if that is true, Christ was wrong.[11]

One of the roots of Tawney's political philosophy was a similar concept of sin. He criticized sociologists for substituting

> inexpediency for sin and social welfare for conscience … economic privi-leges must be abolished, not primarily because they hinder the production of wealth, but because they produce wickedness … To preach in public that Christianity is absurd is legally blasphemy. To state that the social ethics of the New Testament are obligatory upon men in … business affairs is to preach revolution.[12]

In his book about Tawney, Ross Terrill observes, 'Life in the WEA made him a socialist; work in the WEA made him an economic historian.' Tawney's socialism was rooted in the Christian Socialism of Gore and Temple and the ethical socialism propounded by Sidney Ball, the principal founder (1895) of the Oxford Fabian Society. In an article on 'The Moral Aspects of Socialism', Ball argued that a reform of the industrial structure without a spiritual change would bring no benefit.

> just as Democracy is the most difficult form of government, Socialism is the most difficult form of industry because [of] the amount of education—in ideas and character—that is required before any sensible advance can be made in the direction of co-operative industry …[13]

Another ally of Mansbridge was L. T. Hobhouse, whose joint report with J. W. Headlam HMI on the pioneer tutorial classes became a minor classic of liberal adult education. He was not intimate with Mansbridge, but was a close friend of Sidney Ball, who may have recruited him to the cause. In 1907 he became the first professor of sociology in the University of London. He and J. A. Hobson had become the leading intellectual spokesmen of what came to be called 'New Liberalism'. The 'new' dimension was a recognition that the distribution of economic power had become so unequal that the state had to redress the balance through its social policy if the freedom of the individual which was the bedrock of Liberal faith was to become a reality for society as a whole. Hobhouse argued that 'The "right to work" and the right to a "living wage" are just as valid as the right of person or property. That is to say, they are integral conditions of a good social order.'[14]

Christian socialism, ethical socialism and New Liberalism clearly had much in common, in both ideas and applications. A major cause was their shared inheritance of the theories of Thomas Hill Green (1836–82), whose influence was still strongly and consciously felt throughout the Edwardian period. For example, the *Nation* quoted Green in its comments on the Oxford conference of 1907. In the following year a retiring branch secretary of the Postal Clerks Association in Liverpool received as a valedictory present a copy of Green's *Prolegomena to Ethics*.[15]

In 1860 Green became the first layman to be elected as fellow of Balliol College, and in 1878 he was appointed Whyte's Professor of Moral Philosophy in the university. His lasting contribution to the development of philosophy may have been limited, but he had a major influence on the evolution of religious and political thought. He integrated metaphysics, ethics and theology to provide practical programmes for both socially-conscious churchmen and the radical wing of the Liberal party.[16] Green provided the political philosophy and, subject to important revisions, major elements of the theology, of the socially-conscious leaders of the Church of England. The revisions, involving the restoration of the transcendental elements of the Christian faith, were undertaken by Gore, Holland and others in a volume of essays entitled *Lux Mundi* (1889). Some of the same group were involved, in the same year, in the formation of the strongly Greenite Christian Social Union.[17]

Two aspects of the Greenite scene, one general and one particular, helped to smooth the path of the Mansbridgean WEA. The first combined a faith in the ability of 'the industrious workman' to build a better society from the bottom upwards through Co-operation, friendly societies, trade unions and adult education, with a reluctance to create an over-powerful state apparatus. In Hobhouse's words, 'democratic collectivism' was greatly to be preferred to 'benevolent officialism'. A voluntary organization, receiving state support for its mission to democratize learning fitted in well with the Greenite value system. Jose Harris has pointed out that Greenite idealism 'was for a time as popular and persuasive among the socially active middle classes as evangelicalism or utilitarianism had been in the nineteenth century'.[18]

The second factor was the feeling of frustration in the Christian Social Union at their failure to reform a capitalist society by means of preaching and pamphlets. Their sense of impotence was gently satirized in a poem by G. K. Chesterton.

> The Christian Social Union here Was very much annoyed;
> It seems there is some duty Which we never should avoid,
> And so they sang a lot of hymns To help the unemployed.[19]

Nor had the CSU penetrated the working-class movement, apart from giving moral support to Co-operation. There was little more than rhetoric in William Temple's declaration, 'The Church is called then—called by the Labour movement—to a new effort for the regeneration of mankind.' The 'call' that the Church heard was the echo of its own voice, crying in the wilderness.[20]

Turning from friends to enemies, although the WEA tutorial class movement came in for some right-wing criticism, as described in Chapter 3, the only enemies which Mansbridge and his allies needed to take seriously were the advocates and practitioners of a committed socialist education for the workers. The Social Democratic Federation had been running classes in economics in London, Glasgow and other towns from about 1900. One of the students in London was Tommy Jackson, who went on to become a very popular freelance socialist lecturer. In his engaging autobiography, he describes how he gave a 'sermon' in a Methodist chapel in Chopwell, County Durham, on the text 'Isaiah was a Bolshevik'. This aroused so much interest that he was invited by the local Labour College to give a series of lectures on the Principles of Socialism. The audience grew week by week until it filled every seat, gangway, staircase and windowsill in the Co-operative Hall.[21]

In 1903 nearly all of the SDF branches in Scotland seceded to form the Socialist Labour Party, taking most of the educational work with them. One of the students involved was Thomas Bell, who graduated to become a class tutor. His method was to direct the study, paragraph by paragraph, of key Marxist texts, so that after six months each conscientious student became a potential tutor. In 1903 John Maclean, a schoolteacher who completed a part-time degree in the following year, joined a surviving SDF branch in Glasgow and began taking classes in Marxist economics and industrial history. One of the most remarkable figures in British workers' education in the twentieth century, Maclean attracted a devoted following. Several of his courses recruited over a hundred members, and as many as five hundred attended his main class in economics and industrial history.[22]

Neither Maclean's nor Bell's methods would be strange to Scottish learners. Maclean was the evangelical preacher, Bell the catechist. Maclean gave the Sunday sermon, Bell took the weekly bible class. The religious analogy is appropriate, not just because socialist fervour at this time had the overtones of a revivalist crusade. Both Calvinism and Marxism dealt in doctrinal absolutes. In terms of the triangular relationship of tutor, students and source materials, there was a world of difference between the methods used by either Maclean or Bell, and those adopted in the WEA tutorial classes.

The Labour College mentioned by Tommy Jackson was not a building but an association, a product of a secession from Ruskin College in 1909. A detailed analysis of the latter affair is outside the scope of this book, but as interpretations of it have strongly influenced perceptions of Mansbridge's role, some consideration of it is necessary. The foundation of Ruskin Hall (the name college was adopted in 1907) has been described in Chapter 2. The founders were the Americans Walter Vrooman, whose wealthy wife Amne paid most of the early costs, and Charles Beard, who concentrated on setting up an extramural programme under the title the Ruskin Hall Educational League.

Vrooman was named principal of the Oxford Hall. His educational and social ideas were expounded in the journal *Young Oxford*.

> Young men who before were mere critics are turned by Ruskin Hall into builders ... The only struggle that is necessary is that of the mass of the people, rich and poor, wishing to organise life intelligently against such as seek to stop them ... We have no definite scheme to propose for the reorganisation of society, but we hold definite moral convictions on social problems: whatever is can be improved.

Vrooman scoffed at academics, declaring that most of their knowledge was useless. The elimination of the 'speculative element' in education would bring a university training within the reach of everyone, even 'the seemingly duller lads'.[23]

The Vroomans and Beard returned to the USA in 1902. Dennis Hird, who had been warden of the Hall, was re-designated principal in 1903. He was a former Anglican clergyman, who had found that the life of a country parson was not ideal for a free-thinking socialist. Hird was an easy-going, genial character, the author of, *inter alia*, a book on evolution, a topic which formed a major component of his lectures on sociology. The vice-principal, H. B. Lees Smith, was regarded by friends and critics alike as an exceptionally able teacher of economics. He was a dedicated follower of current free-market theories, arguing for example that the worker always received the net product of his labour.[24]

Ruskin Hall affiliated to the WEA soon after its foundation, appointing Lees Smith as its representative on the central executive committee. Most of the branches of the Ruskin Hall Educational League merged happily with the WEA. The two organizations were regarded as belonging to the same broad movement. Partly as a result of the departure of Vrooman and the demise of *Young Oxford*, relations between Ruskin and the University of Oxford improved. Sidney Ball and the bursar of Balliol College joined the council of the hall. In June 1906 a meeting at Balliol attended by A. L. Smith, Bishop Gore, Hudson Shaw and Mansbridge discussed the idea of closer links between Ruskin and the university.[25]

By 1906/07 Ruskin had about fifty students, all studying for at least a year, in contrast to an earlier period when some had stayed for as little as a month. Lees Smith began a campaign to raise academic standards, arguing that the lectures covered too much ground and that the students did insufficient written work. He was opposed by Hird, but gradually gained in influence partly because Hird had competing interests. He had a small farm at Bletchley in Buckinghamshire, which was presumably the source of the foodstuffs which he sold to Ruskin. He was a county magistrate in Buckinghamshire, and went away frequently to address socialist meetings.[26]

Socialist students were in a minority in the early days of Ruskin. By about 1907 the position had changed. Many students arrived with some kind of socialist affiliation, mainly ILP, SDF or Clarionite, and others were converted by the fervour of their fellows. They found Lees Smith's lectures on economics quite unpalatable, and therefore organized their own study groups to work on *Capital* and other key Marxist texts. They found reinforcement in Hird's lectures on evolution. According to one of them, William Craik, the combination of Marxist and Darwinian theories gave them 'a glowing feeling of immense liberation'.[27]

The students who embraced these doctrines proceeded to proclaim their faith outside Ruskin, at socialist meetings in Oxford and elsewhere, and to practise it inside. They behaved as though they were trade unionists and the college authorities were their employers. A good deal of time was consumed in meetings, deputations and sometimes strikes about details of the curriculum and the domestic arrangements, particularly the food.[28]

In 1907 Lees Smith was appointed professor of economics at University College, Bristol, but far from bowing out of Ruskin affairs he used his change of status to strengthen his grip upon the college. He became a member of the college council, and was appointed chairman of the executive committee and also to a post variously described in the Ruskin records as 'Director of Studies' and 'Advisor on Studies'. In September 1907 he tried to marginalize Dennis Hird even further by proposing that his teaching subjects should be changed from sociology and evolution to literature, rhetoric and temperance. The students protested, and the executive committee rejected the proposal. Approval was given, however, to the introduction of a programme of regular essays and quarterly revision papers.[29]

To replace himself on the Ruskin staff Lees Smith had arranged— apparently without involving Hird—for two appointments to be made. Charles Buxton, twenty-three years old, a product of Eton and Balliol, son of a cabinet minister in the Liberal government, became vice-principal. Henry Sanderson Furniss, aged thirty-nine but with virtually no teaching experience because he was nearly blind, lectured in economics. They were intended to carry on Lees Smith's campaign against Dennis Hird, but were ill equipped to do so, knowing little about teaching and less about industrial conditions, trade unions or Co-operation. Furniss later admitted that his ignorance of Marxist theories had not prevented him from attacking them. The militant students, who wanted only Marxist economics taught, asked Hird to excuse them from attendance at the lectures of Buxton and Furniss, but he replied that he had no power to do so.[30]

The part that Ruskin College might play in bringing working-class students to the university was briefly touched upon at the conference on Oxford and working-class education held in August 1907. Noah Ablett, a young South Wales miner who had gone to Ruskin at the beginning of 1907 as a promising local preacher but was by now a fervent socialist, addressed the conference as a representative of the Ruskin students' Marxist society. The joint committee appointed as a result of the conference included five members of the Ruskin council—Bowerman, Berry, Shackleton, Ball and

Lees Smith. Before it began work another member, A. L. Smith, visited Ruskin to sound the students out about the possibility of some kind of loose affiliation with the university. The committee discussed the possibility that new lectureships in applied economics and politics might be established in the university, and the lectures opened free of charge to Ruskin students; and that second-year Ruskin students might be allowed, and helped by scholarships, to take university diplomas. It was apparently agreed, however, that Ruskin existed primarily to train men who would return to their former occupations and take part in trade union and local government work, and could not therefore be turned into a hostel for a general university education.[31]

Meanwhile Ruskin College was visited first by the chancellor of Oxford University, Lord Curzon, and later by the vice-chancellor, Dr T. H. Warren. In Sanderson Furniss's version of events, Curzon toured the college with the students, and then made 'a most charming and tactful speech with which everybody was delighted'. According to the militants, in their pamphlet *The Burning Question of Education*, the students were offended by the chancellor's autocratic manner and supported Hird when he rebuked Curzon. The 'loyalist' students labelled this 'sheer invention'. In fact the recorded statements of Hird and Curzon were not very different, and could have been woven into the same speech by Mansbridge or Gore.

> To ask Ruskin College to come into closer contact with the University is to ask the great democracy whose foundation is the Labour movement, a democracy that in the near future will come into its own, and, when it does will bring great changes in its wake. (Hird)

> The men I see before me represent the class to whom has been given the vote, and who, because of their numbers, are the ruling power in the nation. It is supremely important that having the power they should also have the education. (Curzon)[32]

Tension inside Ruskin mounted during 1908. Only a minority of students took the revision papers when they were introduced in April. Matters came to a head when, on 9 October 1908, the militants, in alliance with Hird and another member of staff Alfred Hacking, resolved at a meeting held in Oxford to form a league of past and present resident and correspondence students and sympathizers. The object of what was soon named the Plebs League was to bring the college closer to the labour movement by means of a magazine (to be edited by Hird), annual gatherings and the formation of local branches.[33]

The executive committee of Ruskin responded by appointing a sub-committee to examine the state of the college, and asked its officers in the meantime not to associate with either the league or its journal. The report of the sub-committee, issued apparently in February 1909, criticized Hird for not supporting executive committee decisions, but rejected the charge that he had deliberately identified the college with the promotion of socialism, presumably through his political speeches. He had been guilty only of 'some indiscretion' in this matter. Sanderson Furniss's teaching of economics was 'one-sided and mainly critical of socialism'. To redress the balance another lecturer, 'more familiar with economics from the standpoint of the Labour Movement' should be employed. The sub-committee further proposed that one or two former students should be appointed to the executive committee, and that Dennis Hird should stop selling kitchen garden produce, provisions and books to the college.[34]

The relative mildness of the criticisms made by the sub-committee implies a belief that reconciliation was possible. However, what Sidney Ball described as the 'continued agitation' of the Plebs students inside the college, and the activities of the Plebs League outside (an Oxford branch was formed on 4 December 1908), convinced the executive committee when it met on 6 March 1909 that the only solution was to dismiss either Hird or his opponents on the academic staff. The axe fell on Hird. He was given six months' salary (£180) in lieu of notice, and a pension of £150 a year for life. The decision was confirmed by the college council on 31 March, but in the meantime a majority of the students had voted for a boycott of lectures until Hird was reinstated and Buxton and the college secretary, Bertram Wilson, dismissed.[35]

The Ruskin authorities decided to close the college for a fortnight, and then re-admit any students who would sign an undertaking to observe the rules. Forty-four of the fifty-four students did so, and re-assembled on 20 April. They included several members of the Plebs League—the militants seem to have numbered about twenty before the closure. Clashes continued between the Plebs group and the 'loyalists' who published a pamphlet attacking the rebels.[36]

On 2 August 1909 a meeting of the Plebs League held in Oxford launched the Central Labour College, which occupied two rented houses in the town. (It moved to London in 1911.) Dennis Hird became warden, without salary as he had his pension, Hacking a tutor and George Sims secretary.[37] The foundation of the new college intensified the battle which had been going on since the 'strike' at Ruskin for the support, moral and especially financial, of the labour movement. An early casualty was the truth. The Plebs students, and some of the journals which sympathized with them, put about the story that Hird had been dismissed because he refused to stop teaching sociology, which had to be removed from the curriculum to allow closer links to be established with the university. One version of this story blamed the WEA and/or Oxford Joint Tutorial Classes Committee for engineering Hird's dismissal. The *Clarion* declared,

> The Oxford and Working Class Education Committee, which has the support of some of the more amenable Labour members, has forced Dennis Hird to resign the Wardenship of Ruskin Hall because he would not substitute 'English Literature and Temperance' for 'Sociology and Logic'.

This proposal had, of course, been rejected by the college authorities in 1907. William Seed missed a chance to put the record straight in an article he wrote for the next issue of the journal, and so the denials sent in by Mansbridge, Temple and the executive committee of Ruskin may have been disbelieved.[38]

Albert Mansbridge and his associates declared publicly that neither the WEA nor the Oxford joint committee had anything to do with the internal affairs of Ruskin College. Privately they argued that the main cause of the trouble was Hird's preaching of socialism, or as Mansbridge put it rather less charitably in a letter to a French friend, 'the low-down practice of Dennis Hird in playing upon the class consciousness of swollen-headed students embittered by the gorgeous panorama ever before them of an Oxford in which they have no part'. On the evidence available there is no reason to believe that Hird's teaching was more biased than that of Lees Smith or Furniss. Nor was Hird as consistent in his opposition to association with the university as Craik has suggested. He co-operated with A. L. Smith in making plans for Jack Lawson, who was a Ruskin student in 1907 and 1908, to become an undergraduate. Hird offered to coach him for the entrance examination, but Lawson decided that his vocation was to return to the coal mines.[39]

The Plebs leaders recognized the danger that they might be thought to be indulging in 'a purely emotional act of personality worship'. Sims told a meeting of the Oxford branch of the league on 1 April 1909, that they had 'set out a few months ago with the object of altering Ruskin College, of changing its control … Their regard for Mr Hird was quite a secondary matter.' According to Craik, the Plebs League 'was already an accomplished fact before Dennis Hird ever knew of it'. Hird seems to have been as much the victim as the hero of the militants' campaign.[40]

The Plebs League concentrated much of its attention on winning the support of the Amalgamated Society of Railway Servants and the South Wales Miners' Federation, from whose ranks several of the Plebs leaders had come. These unions were keener than most on education. A considerable number of WEA branches had secured the affiliation of the local ASRS branch, although the long hours and awkward shifts worked by the railwaymen made it difficult for them to take advantage of class provision. The Plebs League sent speakers to several ASRS branches, but some of the latter wanted to hear both sides. The discussions in the Barry (South Wales) branch demonstrate the seriousness with which the railwaymen approached the questions raised by the Oxford Report and the Ruskin dispute. The branch sent a delegate, J. Murgatroyd, to the 1907 Oxford conference. His report, which was critical of the proceedings, was discussed at three meetings, as a result of which the branch resolved that the working classes should avoid contact with Oxford until it taught 'a truer view of social questions'. Mansbridge was asked to report this resolution to the WEA central executive committee, which he did. Mansbridge seems to have sent a copy of the Oxford Report to Murgatroyd, who promised to read it carefully and impartially. In the summer of 1909 the Barry railwaymen discussed the Ruskin dispute, and resolved to invite Noah Ablett and Mansbridge to address separate meetings.[41]

Mansbridge accepted the invitation. He prepared the ground with an article in the *Railway Review* of 2 July 1909, in which he ignored Ruskin College but argued that 'no body of working men' had given greater support to the WEA than the railwaymen. A letter in the next number of the *Review* from Charles Watkins, a Plebs leader and former Ruskin student, denounced

Mansbridge's 'flattery' and 'special pleading' and claimed that the 'real nature' of the WEA, as a body outside working-class control, had been revealed by the Ruskin dispute. Mansbridge replied with a long letter giving details of affiliations to the WEA which, he argued, showed that it was a democratic body, overwhelmingly working-class in character.[42]

No record of Mansbridge's talk at Barry, scheduled for 25 July, appeared in either the *Railway Review* or the local press, but if he made the visit he was no more successful than on a tour in South Wales a few months earlier, when he met 'bitter and implacable opposition' from the Plebs faction. Barry came down on the Plebs side, and shortly afterwards the indefatigable Murgatroyd gave a 'very able report' on the inaugural conference of the Central Labour College. In October 1909 the annual general meeting of the ASRS transferred its two scholarships from Ruskin to the CLC. The South Wales Miners Federation made a similar decision.[43]

Ruskin College was quick to learn the lessons of the dispute. A new constitution was adopted in 1909, vesting the government of the college in a council consisting of representatives of trade unions, the Co-operative movement and other working-class organizations. An organizer-agent was appointed to argue the case for Ruskin within the labour movement. The new principal of the college, Dr Gilbert Slater, had impeccable credentials. His book *The English Peasantry and the Enclosure of the Common Fields* had made his name as a social historian. He had been Labour mayor of Woolwich and was well acquainted with working-class conditions and aspirations.[44]

The Ruskin dispute and its aftermath put pressure upon the WEA in two ways. First, left-wing critics declared that the true nature of the association as a tool of the governing classes had been exposed, and some of them blamed the WEA for the dispute. Secondly, the Plebs League and the Labour College started extramural classes, particularly in association with ASRS branches in Lancashire and miners' lodges in South Wales. With an impudence bordering on blasphemy the spiritual home of the tutorial class movement was invaded, and a Rochdale and District Labour College formed. To rub salt in the wound the organizer was Harold Kershaw, who had been sent to Ruskin in January 1909 on a WEA scholarship. William Craik took Labour College classes in Rochdale, Bury, Bacup and Preston. His subjects were economics, history and philosophy.[45]

110

The developments of the period 1907–09—the Oxford conference, the 1908 Oxford Report, the tutorial classes and the joint committee system, the Ruskin dispute and its aftermath—have been regarded as the defining episodes in the interpretation of the history of workers' education in the first half of the twentieth century. Some historians have relied too much on partisan or defective sources. For example, Tommy Jackson's account of the Ruskin crisis, in a book which he describes as 'a bona fide recollection, either of actual experience or hearsay', has Hird introducing Marxist economics to the college curriculum in response to student demand; refusing an instruction from the governors to exclude it; refusing to resign and being sacked out of hand; with the students refusing to attend classes conducted by his successor as principal. It would be difficult to squeeze more errors of fact into so short a space.[46]

Brian Simon cites Jackson as one of his sources, and otherwise relies heavily on Craik and Sims, with predictable results. He gives the impression that the decision to form the Plebs League was taken after, and partly as a result of, the publication of the Oxford Report, when in fact the first public meeting was held six weeks earlier. He quotes *The Burning Question of Education* account of Curzon's visit without referring to the conflicting evidence of Sanderson Furniss and the Ruskin 'loyalists'. The petition against the proposed changes in Hird's teaching subjects is mentioned, but not the rejection of the proposal by the executive committee. The termination of Hird's appointment is described without any reference to the compensation and pension.[47]

Some of the brief references to these controversial developments beg a few questions. For example, John Saville:

> What we have in these years is both the attempt to channel working-class education into the safe and liberal outlets of the Workers' Educational Association and Ruskin College, and the development of working-class initiatives from below; and it is the latter only which made its contribution to the socialist movement—and a considerable contribution it was.[48]

There is no doubt that the 'Establishment' preferred the 'safe and liberal outlets' to the Labour College movement, a fact exploited by the WEA in the 1920s. Temple, Tawney and A. D. Lindsay all warned the Board of Education and the LEAs that if they withdrew their financial support or infringed the academic freedom of the WEA they would have delivered the working-class movement into the hands of the association's Marxist enemies.[49] However, most of the WEA branches in industrial towns were formed as a result of 'working-class initiatives from below', if we include, in addition to trade union branches and trades councils, the Co-operatives and chapel societies which were mainly, but not exclusively, working class in composition. The claim that the WEA and Ruskin made no contribution to the socialist movement is valid only on the assumption that the socialism espoused by WEA activists, mainly within the Labour Party, was not socialism at all.

Carolyn Steedman, in her book about the life and work of Margaret McMillan, comments, 'In 1909 McMillan provided Mansbridge with public support over the Ruskin College crisis, when claims for a worker-directed education came into sharp conflict with the WEA brand of education.' The WEA could, and did, claim that through the joint committee system, the tutorial classes were subject to a significant measure of 'workers' control'.[50] Carolyn Steedman's source is Jonathan Rée's *Proletarian Philosophers*. According to his account, the 1908 Oxford Report was produced jointly by the university, Ruskin College and the WEA; and 'nearly all of the Ruskin students went on strike, and after a fortnight seceded from the college'. As explained above, 'after a fortnight', only ten of the fifty-four students failed to return to the college. On the broader issue, Rée explains, 'The aim of the WEA was to direct the aspirations of proletarian autodidacts towards a Green-tinged corporate state', the Green being of course T. H. Green. Unless tutorial class members became 'autodidacts' by reading and writing essays at home there were very few such people amongst the serious WEA students. Mansbridge was 'himself a lower-middle-class autodidact'—he was presumably elevated from the working class when he became a boy clerk at the age of fourteen—'always tormented by the consciousness that he never had the opportunity of a university education'. Tormented? Always? Even the middle-aged sage, with his North American lecture tours, who had served on the royal commission on Oxford and Cambridge and the statutory commission on Oxford, was a member of Oxbridge common rooms and received five honorary degrees?[51]

Anne Phillips and Tim Putnam correctly attribute the authorship of the

Oxford Report to the university and the WEA, but give the date of publication as 1907. They refer to 'state initiatives in working-class political education, such as represented by the WEA'. Argue if you will that the state welcomed, or suborned, the WEA; to describe it as a state *initiative* is nonsense. The authors explain that the reluctance of the staff of Ruskin College to meet the demands of the militant students was due in part to their concern for the endowments, built up by selling the idea of safe education, which had reached £265,000 by 1907. No source is given for this figure, which is described by Harold Pollins in his history of the college as 'ridiculous'. He explains that by 1914 the endowments amounted to £1,221.[52]

That it was possible to be committed supporters of the Plebs/Labour College cause and write an objective, accurate and fair-minded account of the clash of ideologies is demonstrated by Frank and Winifred Horrabin in their book *Working-class Education* (1924). (Frank's brilliant cartoons enliven the covers of the magazine *Plebs*.) The book gives a balanced account of the Ruskin dispute, and recognizes the sincerity of the left-wing activists of the WEA. The authors looked forward, however, to the day when 'not a few of the many able and sincere supporters of the "extension" idea', that is to say the WEA–University partnership, 'will finally cut free from their old associations and come over to work in Labour's own educational movement'.[53]

Another prominent member of the labour college camp willing to be fair to Mansbridge and the WEA was John Maclean. In 1909 he was elected to the provisional committee of a WEA initiative for workers' education in Scotland, although nothing came of it in the short term. In an article published in 1917, Maclean argued in favour of all kinds of educational advance.

> We, as socialists, must be intensely interested in improved education along technical and commercial lines, and it is our special business to see that all public educational institutions be used for the creation of intelligent, class-conscious workers. In this respect we differ from the WEA, which simply has for its object the creation of intelligent workers. Personally I wish to see all opportunities for self-development opened to the working class. But I am specially interested in such education as will make revolutionists.[54]

Bias and a lack of charity have not been monopolized by the pro-Plebs writers. To quote from the jubilee history of the WEA by Mary Stocks:

> There is no doubt that Marx's Das Capital was, and still is, an exceedingly impressive book especially to those who are not able fully to understand it, or having understood it, are not able to relate it to its historical background. At any rate this was the kind of teaching demanded by an ardent group of Ruskin College students.[55]

One result of the errors and distortions of some of the pro-Plebs writers has been to associate the WEA and the Oxford reformers with the disorganized pre-strike regime at Ruskin College. The Marx-hungry militants were not challenging tutors of the calibre of Tawney, Henry Clay and W. T. Layton, but the ill-equipped pair of Furniss and Buxton, with the easy-going Hird, having been marginalized by Lees Smith, unable to control the situation. The doctrine 'those who are not with us are against us' too readily becomes 'those who are against us are much of a muchness'. Such writers disregard, or deny, the radical nature of the Oxford Report and its implementation, particularly the joint committee system. There were members of the WEA, as fully committed to socialism as the labour college activists, who argued that without access to the universities the workers would receive an inferior education, and that the joint committee system guaranteed them control over their own learning.

Frank Pickstock, who was for many years the officer in charge of joint committee work at the Oxford delegacy and was active in Labour politics in the city of Oxford, commented on the developments discussed in Chapter 3:

> it is clear that by-passing Marriott meant that Mansbridge was opting for a Labour alliance, not a Liberal one. Yet later Mansbridge obviously did not like the Labour alliance, and the only conclusion one can draw is that in 1908 Mansbridge did not realise the full implications of what he was doing.
>
> The enormity of the innovation which the Tutorial Classes Committee represented is too often little understood—democratic power to working class students in sharing in (with an effective power of veto) planning the syllabus, selecting the tutor, managing the classes and equal sharing in the governing committee. This was democracy with a vengeance, and when you realise how doubtful and equivocal the Oxford reformers were about democracy, the more you realise what a momentous step 1908 was.
>
> Once the classes were in being, the students, the working men, took over.

They were without any doubt Labour (in the general sense as it was then known) many of them socialist, and this was reflected in all sorts of ways … above all their influence on tutors … I have little doubt that it was contact with students of tutorial classes that resulted in tutors making the transition from liberalism to labour.[56]

The transition is, of course, less significant if the Labour party is seen as a device to contain, and not promote, the development of socialism. This is the thesis advanced by Ralph Miliband and applied to the present matter by Roger Fieldhouse in his paper 'The 1908 Report: Antidote to Class Struggle'. The WEA/tutorial class movement

was welcomed by the establishment as a bulwark against revolutionism, a moderating influence and a form of social control. It helped to channel and reduce pressures and conflict, neutralise class antagonism and integrate the working class into British society—just like its 'partner' the Labour Party.[57]

A clear distinction must be drawn between adherents of the Miliband thesis who are scrupulous in their scholarship, and those left-wing critics of the WEA and Ruskin who have an unconscious affinity with the authors of medieval monastic chronicles whose motto seemed to be 'never let the facts spoil a good moral tale'. In fact monastic history offers a closer parallel, in what might be called the Gasquet Syndrome. The books of abbot Francis Gasquet were criticized for bias in the selection of evidence and numerous technical errors in the transcription of documents. But those who walk in the path of righteousness need fear no criticism, and to prove the point Gasquet was made a cardinal.

As a postscript to the great ideological battles of the Edwardian period, the National Council of Labour Colleges rejoiced in 1945 when large numbers of its tutors and students were elected as Labour MPs. Nine became ministers, alongside fourteen WEA tutors and students. In the words of Chushichi Tsuzuki, 'The NCLC Marxists … searched for a British way to socialism and found it in the Labour Party and trade unions'. The antidote to class struggle had been swallowed once more.[58]

# 6
## Expanding the WEA

The favourable conjunction of socio-political structures and attitudes discussed in the first section of Chapter 5 underpinned Mansbridge's achievements in three areas: the creation of autonomous local branches, normally based upon a range of predominantly working-class organizations; the alliance with the universities which produced the tutorial class system; and the securing of central government grants in support of tutorial classes. When Mansbridge and his associates turned their attention to the colonization of Ireland and Scotland, they were aware that they faced different circumstances and attitudes. For example, Morant's 'golden stream' could not flow in Ireland or Scotland, which had separate educational systems for which the Board of Education was not responsible.

The English WEA was, in its early days, rooted in industrial society. Although it soon surprised itself by its rural successes, most of the evangelization of the villages was undertaken by nearby urban branches. In Ireland an obvious target area was the industrial north-east where, however, the development of a strong working-class movement had been hampered by sectarian divisions. The principal supporters of the WEA/tutorial class idea were the Belfast Trades Council and the city's main Co-operative society. When Queen's College Belfast became Queen's University in 1908, it was urged by the trades council to make provision for workers' education on the lines of the WEA/Oxford partnership. The request was repeated in 1910, by a deputation from the trades council and the Independent Labour Party. At about the same time a WEA branch was formed. By the end of its first year it had recruited eleven affiliated societies and fifty-four individual members.[1]

Tutorial classes began in session 1910/11, and by 1912/13 three classes were in progress, two studying the Economic History of Ireland and one Political Science. Manual workers were only just in a majority. Nearly twenty per cent of the students belonged to the 'clerks and telegraphists' category and fourteen per cent were teachers. A joint tutorial classes committee was not established, however, and Queen's was not represented on the Central Joint Advisory Committee for Tutorial Classes. No national or local authority grants were provided, but the classes received some financial support from the Belfast Co-operative Society. Mansbridge and Margaret McMillan visited the Belfast branch in April 1911, and addressed meetings including one large public gathering. The *Highway* reported optimistically, 'All sections of the community came together and composed their differences for the time being.'[2]

About Scotland Mansbridge had written in 1906, 'The need is there, the apathy was there, the opportunities are there.' He considered that the Scottish and English Co-operative movements had similar strengths and weaknesses. He recognized, however, that because the Scottish higher education system was much more democratic, in terms of both attitudes and opportunities, than was the case in England, it would be more difficult to stimulate a distinctly working-class demand for a new partnership with the universities.[3]

In the 1860s about a fifth of the university students in Scotland came from working-class homes, and the proportion of the population attending university was six times as great as in England. As early as 1727 some lecture courses at the University of Glasgow were open to the public. In the early nineteenth century university classrooms contained sizeable numbers of what would be called in North American terms 'non-credit' students. Partly because university teaching in Scotland relied upon the formal lecture rather than a tutorial system, it was possible to combine work in some professions with attendance as a notionally full-time student. In 1892 the Scottish universities were opened to women on the same terms as men.

Against this background the launch of an organized system of extension lectures, on the lines of that created in England by a Scotsman, James Stuart, who was shocked by contact with a class-ridden system of higher education, achieved little. The pioneering work of St Andrews University led to the establishment of a university college in Dundee in 1883. The universities of Edinburgh and Glasgow provided a few courses of extension lectures, but by 1895 all such activity had ceased.[4]

A WEA branch was formed at Springburn, on the north side of Glasgow, in August 1905. It achieved some initial successes, but had closed within three years. Mansbridge visited Glasgow in May 1909 and addressed a gathering of social workers presided over by the principal of Glasgow University. At a meeting afterwards a provisional committee was formed to develop WEA work in Glasgow, but it achieved nothing. In October of the same year a well-attended conference in Glasgow appointed a provisional committee, representing trade unions, socialist parties, Co-operatives, friendly societies and other groups, to plan a 'Glasgow and West of Scotland WEA'. John Maclean was a member. This initiative also failed.[5]

When Tawney, an assistant lecturer at Glasgow University who was travelling at weekends to take the pioneer tutorial classes in Longton and Rochdale, tried to interest his university colleagues in the idea behind the venture, he was told that what he was doing in England was not needed north of the border. By 1913 WEA branches had been formed in Glasgow, Edinburgh and Aberdeen. They were not securely based, however, and did not long survive the outbreak of war. Glasgow branch was re-formed in 1916/17, but the WEA did not become firmly established in Scotland until the 1920s.[6]

It turned out to be easier to transplant the WEA to Australia than to Scotland. After the valedictory dinner at the Working Men's College, described at the end of Chapter 4, Albert and Frances Mansbridge set sail for Australia, where they spent four months. This visit and the developments to which it contributed make up an important chapter in the history of adult education in Australia. They also help in the evaluation of Mansbridge's achievements in his own country, as the purpose of his mission was to try to repeat those achievements in a social and political context by no means identical with that of Britain. Australia in 1913 was still heavily dependent for its ideas and models on the home country. It had, however, a more open and democratic society, with a labour movement already in power in some states and challenging for power in others. The state governments wielded greater power over the universities than did the government in Britain, mainly through the conditions attached to the grants which made up a larger proportion of the income of the Australian than the British universities.[7]

In the late nineteenth century university extension courses on the English model had been established by the three universities then in existence: Sydney (New South Wales), Melbourne (Victoria) and Adelaide (South Australia). They seem to have made even less impact on manual workers than in England, although this was not for want of effort.[8]

Australian university men who were concerned either about the failure of university extension to reach the workers, or more generally about the relations between the university and the community, could not fail to be interested in the launching of the tutorial class movement in England, and the principles and proposals set out in *Oxford and Working-class Education*. These ideas were given wide publicity through a visit made to Australia in 1910 by William Temple. who had been elected national president of the WEA two years earlier. He was invited to undertake a lecture tour by the Student Christian Movement of Australasia, and arranged to give several public lectures on the theme of 'Education and Democracy'. These talks attracted large audiences in Adelaide, Sydney and Melbourne. On Temple's return Mansbridge wrote to the universities of these three cities inviting them to affiliate to the WEA. They did so. Temple's propaganda had moved the Labour government of South Australia to increase its grant to the University of Adelaide by £4,000.[9]

Meanwhile the University of Sydney extension board had appointed a committee to study *Oxford and Working-class Education*. A scheme for tutorial classes on the Oxford model was considered. The representatives of the trades hall (a more influential version of the British trades council) were interested in classes in economics and politics, but the university had no teaching staff in these subjects. The renewed interest in adult education was reflected, however, in a big expansion of extension lectures, including some short courses provided in Sydney trades hall.[10]

At Mansbridge's suggestion the Australian universities proposed 'University Tutorial Classes for Working People' as an item for consideration at the first Congress of the Universities of the Empire, held in London in July 1912. Cranage, Marriott, Temple and Mansbridge all contributed to the discussion. One of the Australian delegates was Dr (later Sir) James Barrett, a member of the council of Melbourne University. Invited to Oxford by A. L. Smith, he was greatly impressed by the quality of the essays written by tutorial class students, and became convinced that the WEA could meet Australian needs. He invited the Mansbridges to make a missionary visit—Tawney had been his first choice, but he was not available—and underwrote their expenses.[11]

Albert and Frances Mansbridge visited all six Australian states. Albert spoke at university and labour meetings, addressed other bodies such as teachers' unions, and preached from both Anglican and Nonconformist pulpits. In all he made over a hundred speeches. Frances gave about thirty talks, mainly to gatherings of women at universities, trades halls and other locations. The notes and reports of his speeches indicate that Mansbridge gave enthusiastic accounts of the achievements of the WEA and tutorial class movement in England, and argued that their successes could and should be repeated in Australia. He was inclined to overstate both the spontaneity of the workers' demand for higher education and the universities' eagerness to respond, and gave no hint of the great diplomatic skill and persuasive powers which he had brought to bear to help create the tutorial class system.[12]

A detailed account of the work of the Mansbridges in Australia, with due attention to chronology, is given in *The WEA in Australia: the Pioneering Years*, by the present writer, published by the WEA in Sydney in 1998. Here the achievements of the visit are considered briefly, state by state. The least successful effort was in Western Australia, despite the fact that the recently formed University of Western Australia had grown out of extension courses provided by the three oldest Australian universities and required its academic staff to engage in extramural as well as internal teaching. Mansbridge made an unfavourable impression when he spoke at a trade union conference in Perth in July, being regarded, as he wrote many years later, 'as but a globe-trotter with a gold brick for sale'. The damage was repaired by Gilbert Foxcroft, a schoolteacher, and Professor Edward Shann, who had both been involved with the WEA in England. On his return on 1 October, Mansbridge was welcomed by both the university and the trades hall, and plans were made for the establishment of a WEA. Shann took the first tutorial class in 1914, and three more were formed later. The work was hampered from the start by financial difficulties, mainly because the Labour government, in power from 1911 to 1916, refused to make a grant. By 1918 the WEA of Western Australia was moribund.[13]

Albert and Frances Mansbridge spent a week in Tasmania, staying for most of the time in Hobart as guests of the governor, who was an Oxford graduate. The ground had been prepared by some members of the council of the University of Tasmania, one of whom, an archdeacon, had asked

Bishop Gore for information about the WEA. The University Progress Association was formed to promote university adult education. The association sponsored a public lecture given by Mansbridge, with the prime minister and leader of the opposition speaking in support. The prime minister later arranged for a grant of £500 a year to be provided, to support a new department of university extension. After Mansbridge's return to England he, Zimmern and the Tasmanian agent-general in London were empowered to appoint to the university staff a man who would divide his time between extension work and internal teaching in history and economics. They chose Herbert Heaton, then teaching both undergraduates and tutorial classes for Birmingham University, who became recognized as a distinguished economic historian.

The Trades and Labour Council in Hobart voted to support the establishment of a WEA, but union branches were reluctant to affiliate. The Tasmanian WEA was formed nevertheless, and its general secretary was appointed as one of the five external members of the twelve-strong university extension board.[14]

The University of Queensland, founded in Brisbane in 1910, was initially reluctant to receive Mansbridge, believing that the WEA/tutorial class system would not suit a state with such a scattered population. At this point the long arm of Oxford reached out to save the day. The vice-chancellor, R. H. Roe, who was a Balliol man, received a letter from his old college friend A. L. Smith, praising Mansbridge and the WEA. The Mansbridges were invited to Brisbane, and stayed as the guests of Archbishop Donaldson, whose brother was vice-chancellor of Cambridge and a supporter of the WEA.[15]

In Queensland Albert Mansbridge swept all before him, winning the support of the political leaders, the university and the trades hall. A newspaper report described him as 'one of the most remarkable personalities and most eloquent speakers who have visited our metropolis in recent years'. The secretary of the Queensland Parliamentary Labour party wrote shortly afterwards to Mansbridge conveying 'our sincere thanks and appreciation for the very instructive address' he had given, and endorsing his efforts for 'the social, moral and political education of the workers'. The Queensland WEA was formed, and the first tutorial class recruited, during Mansbridge's visit. The new movement was insecure until the Labour government, elected in 1915, promised in the following year an annual grant of £1,000 to be shared between the university and the WEA.[16]

Mansbridge's prospects in Victoria were greatly enhanced by the enthusiastic support of Dr James Barrett, and by a current review of the state's annual grant of £20,000 to the university. In May 1913 the university extension board asked for the resources for a considerable expansion of its programme, to include tutorial classes for workers. After Mansbridge had spoken at the trades hall, delegates from the latter and the university agreed on a scheme for tutorial classes. The trades hall decided, however, 'for the present' to keep control of the organization of the classes instead of establishing a WEA. This may have been a pragmatic decision, but 'certain Left Wing enemies in England' had warned the Melbourne trade unions to beware of Mansbridge. The University of Melbourne, reluctant to confine its contribution to workers' education to a partnership with the trades hall, decided to form joint committees with any bodies interested in establishing tutorial classes.[17]

The WEA of Victoria was formed, independently of the trades hall, by four recent immigrants who had been members of the British WEA. Mansbridge commented in an article sent from Australia to the *Highway*, 'But what a lot of tutorial class students there are in Australia! Almost at every meeting one turned up and on one occasion three … They are all anxious to get to work again out here and we are looking for Australian editions of their former tutors. Emigration has made bigger inroads on our classes than we thought—but this country can do with our students.' The four men wrote separately to Mansbridge on his arrival in Melbourne, and were invited with their wives to take tea in a café with Albert and Frances. One of the four was a young carpenter, L. T. Leathley, a former member of a tutorial class in Leeds, who had been in Australia for only six months. Fifty years later he described a typical Mansbridgean operation in the café:

> after tea Mansbridge told us of what had been decided at the University. He then proposed we form a WEA in Melbourne. This meeting with approval, he asked me if I was prepared to do the secretarial work at the centre while the others worked in their respective suburbs. Fred Milnes was successful in getting a group together at Footscray, and there the first WEA tutorial class was held in Economics …

Leathley became honorary general secretary of the Victorian WEA when it was formally established in September 1913.[18]

For the visit of the Mansbridges to South Australia some measure of support from both the University of Adelaide and the Trades and Labour Council was already assured. Temple had gained the sympathy of both in 1910. The university affiliated to the British WEA in the following year, and sent Professor Darnley Naylor to the Congress of the Universities of the Empire in 1912. Naylor was impressed both by Mansbridge and the WEA/ tutorial class idea. Another natural ally was Professor Henderson, chairman of the extension board, who had studied at Balliol under A. L. Smith and had lectured for the Oxford Extension Delegacy between 1897 and 1902.

The president of the trades and labour council was Thomas Ryan, a railway worker elected a few years earlier to the state parliament. In 1910 he had used the Oxford Report as a text for his motion calling for the appointment of a select committee on the role of the university. He argued the need for workers to have a university education to help them to solve their problems as workers and not to secure personal advancement—the Mansbridgean 'highway' as opposed to the 'ladder'.

Mansbridge was warmly received in Adelaide. He addressed meetings at the university, the School of Mines and Adelaide High School, being accompanied on the latter occasion by the prime minister of South Australia and the state director of education. On 26 September he spoke on 'The Workers' Educational Association' to a meeting in the trades hall convened by the trades and labour council. It was attended by representatives of trade unions, the university, the school of mines, the state education department and both houses of the state legislature (including members of the governing Labour party and the opposition Liberals). The gathering of such an assembly was in itself a considerable achievement, and when Thomas Ryan, who was in the chair, successfully moved a resolution requesting the Labour Council to establish a WEA in South Australia, Mansbridge must have been delighted at the outcome of his five days in Adelaide. Unfortunately the audience seems to have contained far more chiefs than Indians. Only fourteen unions had affiliated by the time the WEA was officially inaugurated in April 1914. Surprisingly the Labour government refused to make a grant towards the cost of providing tutorial classes, pleading the financial difficulties resulting from the severe drought of late 1914. The movement languished until 1917, when Herbert Heaton was appointed director of tutorial classes at the University of Adelaide. In the following year the government offered an annual grant of £1,300.[19]

Mansbridge's aim in each state was to promote a partnership between the university and the labour movement, and secure at least some modest financial support from the state government. In New South Wales Mansbridge was able to concentrate on winning over the university, because the commitment of the labour movement and the state government had already been secured by the work of two men, Peter Board and David Stewart. Board, state director of education since 1905, had visited Britain and the USA and had been impressed both by the WEA tutorial class system and by the Wisconsin scheme of university extension. He carried on a campaign to make the University of Sydney more responsive to community needs, and his opportunity came when the first Labour government of New South Wales was elected in 1910. He drafted a bill which changed the constitution of the university, established two hundred free scholarships for full-time students, and provided for 'the establishment and maintenance of evening tutorial classes in science, economics, ancient and modern history and sociology'. Opposition within the university was disarmed by a doubling of the government grant, from £20,000 to £40,000 a year. The bill became law in December 1912.[20]

David Stewart was a carpenter who had emigrated from his native Scotland in 1908. After two years in New Zealand he moved to Sydney, and in 1911 he was elected by the Amalgamated Society of Carpenters and Joiners as a delegate to the Trades and Labour Council of New South Wales. Meanwhile his brother Alex had spent a month at an Oxford summer school where he had met Mansbridge. He wrote enthusiastically about his experiences to David Stewart. In 1912 Alex suggested to Mansbridge, who was then planning his visit to Australia, that his brother would be a useful ally. Mansbridge wrote to David Stewart asking him to try to establish a branch of the WEA in New South Wales. Stewart commented later, 'Why he should have picked on me I have never been able to understand. As a working carpenter I had neither position nor influence, nor did I have the personality which I thought necessary for such a task. I did, however, possess enthusiasm.'

David Stewart proved to be one of the most effective of Mansbridge's many disciples. He persuaded the labour council to appoint an education committee, with himself as convenor, to consider a scheme for workers' education. Its report, adopted by the labour council in February 1913, advocated a WEA tutorial class system. A conference held at the end of April endorsed these proposals and appointed a provisional committee, with Stewart again as convenor, to draw up a constitution and plan an inaugural meeting to be addressed by Mansbridge.[21]

Stewart found Board very supportive, but the university authorities were reluctant to accept the Oxford model of a joint committee controlling the tutorial classes and appointing tutors. It was pointed out that the state government, although doubling the grant to the university as part of an 'access' strategy which included tutorial classes, had not earmarked any of the grant for adult education. Board arranged for £1,000 a year to be allocated to tutorial classes.[22]

When Mansbridge arrived in Sydney on 29 July 1913 the only major question still unresolved was the administration of the tutorial classes. He spoke at public meetings in Sydney, Newcastle, Wollongong and elsewhere in the state. His speech at Sydney University Club was followed by one from Sir Edmund Barton, who had been the first prime minister of the Commonwealth of Australia, which, wrote Mansbridge, 'stated the case for the WEA in words which surpassed almost any I have heard'. At some meetings W. A. Holman, the state premier, took the chair. Mansbridge found this a mixed blessing 'as his [Holman's] political enemies threw questions at us which were really designed for Holman as Premier'. Under the railway arches in Sydney Mansbridge addressed a meeting consisting, he wrote, 'entirely of "Industrial Workers of the World", some seventy or eighty of them becoming keen to join Tutorial Classes. This created a difficult position. Even we had not envisaged Tutorial Classes consisting entirely of the most extreme "Left Wingers".' The 'wobblies' were advised to apply to the joint committee then in process of formation. Both Mansbridge and the university were no doubt relieved when they did not do so. From this meeting Mansbridge went straight to speak to the Sydney Club. 'the members of which were orthodox and conventional'.[23]

Much more important than Mansbridge's public speaking was the diplomatic skill used in negotiations with the senate and professorial board of the university, the trades and labour council and the department of public instruction, as a result of which a joint committee for tutorial classes was established, consisting of three representatives each of the university and the WEA. The university established a department of tutorial classes and, at Mansbridge's suggestion, Meredith Atkinson, a young Oxford graduate who was then a tutorial class tutor for Durham University, was appointed to head it as lecturer/organizer.[24]

After visiting other states Mansbridge returned to Sydney to preside over a conference held in the trades hall at which the WEA of New South Wales was inaugurated, with 'a constitution embodying the essential characteristics of the English movement'. Mansbridge commented in his autobiography that this was 'the first and only occasion upon which I have taken the chair at a WEA public meeting of any kind'. Many trade unions were represented, and twenty-eight had already affiliated, a tribute to Stewart's work behind the scenes as well as to the persuasiveness of Mansbridge. Peter Board sat on the platform. He had done all that Morant had done in England and more. Stewart wrote later that 'we have every reason to regard Mr Board as the real parent of the WEA in the Southern Hemisphere ... and the best friend the Association has had in this State'.[25]

Albert and Frances Mansbridge had hoped to spend two weeks in New Zealand, but only a two-day visit to Auckland was possible. The missionary tour of New Zealand was undertaken instead, early in 1915, by Meredith Atkinson and David Stewart. Both were enthusiastic disciples of Mansbridge. Stewart developed a Mansbridgean style of expression, and Atkinson commented, 'Everywhere I find Mansbridge a name to conjure with. I use no other introduction.' The two men established branches of the WEA in five cities, secured the co-operation of all four university colleges, and, despite some sniping from the Marxist left, won support from organized labour. The University of New Zealand (not itself a teaching body) made a grant of £300 to each university college for tutorial classes or extension courses.[26]

In an unpublished account written, apparently, in 1918, Mansbridge described his antipodean journey in characteristic style. He exaggerated the extent, and the spontaneity, of the response to his message and understated his diplomatic achievements:

everyone we met and many whom we did not meet in Australia were eager

to help us. The various Governments gave us free railway passes. The
Universities gave us generous hospitality. The Directors of Education put
all their machinery at our disposal. Trades Halls made us feel that labour
rejoiced in our visit. Mayors gave us official receptions. But, best of all,
working men and women heard our message gladly and became eager to
study.

In the same account Mansbridge admitted, however, that 'The strain did
not lie so much in the speaking as in the unceasing work of organisation,
negotiation and correspondence.'[27]

F. A. Bland, a lecturer at Sydney University, attempted a more sober
appraisal in an article published in 1918. About thirty-five tutorial classes
were running in Australia—nearly all in capital cities, and twenty-one of
them in New South Wales—and a further fifteen in New Zealand. In
addition there were many shorter courses, study circles and lectures in both
countries. The WEA, wrote Bland, had brought the universities and the
trade unions closer together, and had caused a curricular revolution.
Previously the main energies of the universities were concentrated on the
professional schools of medicine, engineering and law. There was no
systematic study of economics, and very limited provision for the teaching
of history and sociology. 'The university was quite out of touch with the
great bulk of the citizens, and the academic was an object of suspicion in the
industrial and commercial world.' As a result, in part at least, of the
promptings of the WEA and the demand for tutorial classes in economics
and industrial history, 'almost all Governments have proved willing to
provide an increasing endowment, for Chairs of Economics, Education,
History, as well as Applied Science'.

Society would benefit also, in Bland's view, from closer contact between
trade unionists and other sections of the community, and from 'the process
of enlightenment' which had led the trade unionist 'to examine the
foundations of his beliefs and the reactions of [sic] his policy'. Tutorial
classes and lectures, conferences and meetings with non-unionists and
academics had all 'contributed to destroying complacency and self-satisfac-
tion and to awakening a spirit of inquiry'. An effective alliance between
labour and learning had been created, despite misconceptions about the
nature and purpose of the WEA arising both within and outside the labour
movement. One of the largest trade union federations had offered to

subsidize WEA classes 'provided that they had the choice of tutors and textbooks'.[28]

Although some of these successes were short-lived, Mansbridge's achievements in Australia were outstanding. In the hierarchy of his creative works they are outranked only by the establishment of the WEA and the tutorial class movement in Britain. As in his own country he needed the support of allies in positions of power or influence, particularly Barrett, Board and Stewart. Much less progress would have been made, however, without Mansbridge's remarkable combination of talents—his organizing and diplomatic skills, and the ability to appeal simultaneously to organized labour and the universities.

# 7
## Many More Fine Things

Mansbridge returned to the WEA central office in January 1914, after an absence of seven and a half months. The movement was still growing steadily, as the following figures show.

|  | July 1911 | July 1912 | July 1913 | July 1914 |
|---|---|---|---|---|
| Branches | 86 | 110 | 158 | 179 |
| Affilliated societies | 1541 | 1879 | 2164 | 2555 |
| Individual members | 5345 | 7011 | 8723 | 11430 |
| University joint committees | 8 | 8 | 13 | 14 |
| Tutorial classes | 72 | 101 | 117 | 145 |
| Tutorial class students | 1829 | 2780 | 3158 | 3343 |

The number of tutorial classes in 1913/14 would have been significantly higher if money had been available to meet all the demands from WEA centres. Mansbridge took up once again the pressing problem of fund raising. He arranged a meeting of the Labour representatives on the Oxford joint committee, which planned a comprehensive campaign. Tawney, Mactavish and Mansbridge were to approach MPs. The WEA was asked to make a national appeal for funds to provide more tutorial classes. Trade unions affiliated to the centre were to be invited to Oxford during the 1914 summer school, to see the latter at work and to be infected with enthusiasm for working-class education. Finally a national conference of trade union representatives was to be held in Oxford in the following year to consider again the implications of the report *Oxford and Working-Class Education*.[1]

The emphasis upon approaching trade unions is significant. Although trade union branches and trades councils made up the largest single category of affiliated societies, the support for the WEA from the trade union movement was still very patchy. Shortly before Mansbridge's return, a WEA deputation had met the Parliamentary Committee of the Trade Union Congress (the forerunner of the General Council of the TUC) to ask for financial support. The TUC had been represented on the WEA advisory council a few years earlier, but did not become properly affiliated until 1915. Bill Lowth was given the task of carrying the message of the WEA to labour organizations, especially trade unions. Three enemies had to be fought— apathy, parsimony and the ideological hostility fomented by the Labour College movement.[2]

To strengthen the financial management of the central WEA, Ernest Wimble was appointed financial secretary in April 1914. He continued to act, in addition, as South-Eastern district secretary. Dorothy Jones was promoted from the position of Mansbridge's private secretary to be assistant secretary. The district organization was strengthened by hiving off a new Yorkshire District from the North-Western District. George Thompson, who had been appointed Yorkshire organizer in the previous year, became secretary of the new district. A carpenter by trade, he had attracted attention as an outstanding member of Henry Clay's tutorial class in Halifax.[3]

Mansbridge took on other responsibilities, including membership of the Selborne Committee on the relations between Church and State. This body, appointed by the archbishops of Canterbury and York, had a distinguished membership, including leading politicians—A. J. Balfour, Lord Hugh Cecil, Edward Wood (later Earl of Halifax) and the Duke of Devonshire— and several friends of Mansbridge—Gore, Temple, Dr T. B. Strong, A. L. Smith and Sir William Anson, a Conservative MP and warden of All Souls College, Oxford.[4]

Mansbridge showed no signs of having taken the advice of many friends that he should slow the pace of his working life and conserve his strength. At a meeting of the Selborne committee in June 1914 he collapsed and was rushed to hospital. At first his illness was thought to be, in the words of Dorothy Jones, 'a severe nervous breakdown', and Mansbridge was sent home for what was expected to be a long period of complete rest. Miss Jones wrote to Professor J. A. Dale,

> The doctors tell us that it will be many months before he is fit for any kind of work again. He is not allowed to see either friends or letters, although he occasionally asks for people and we have to satisfy him. The absolutely important thing to be done now is to keep his mind free from worry.[5]

Mrs Mansbridge had some doubts about the doctor's diagnosis, and called in Dr W. E. Gye, who found that Mansbridge was suffering from cerebro-spinal meningitis. Some years earlier Gye, an ardent young socialist, had been so persuaded by Mrs Bridges Adams of the iniquity of Mansbridge and the WEA that he had joined in the pamphlet war against them. Eventually he met Mansbridge, realized, in the latter's words, 'that he had been skilfully duped', and became a firm friend. It was partly as a result of the encouragement of Mansbridge and Tawney that Gye went on to Edinburgh to study for his MD. Mansbridge believed that without Gye's intervention he might have died, and the whole episode provided him with a romantic story, rich in biblical allusions, which he never tired of telling in later years.[6]

T. W. Price agreed to act as general secretary during Mansbridge's illness, and was soon faced with the problems caused by the outbreak of the first world war. In November 1914 the central council was told that Mansbridge was making steady progress, but would probably suffer from neurasthenia for some time. His doctor, probably Gye, was reported as saying 'that unless Mr Mansbridge is kept entirely free from all news with regard to the WEA, a further and more serious breakdown may occur, the ill-effects of which will probably be permanent'. No-one, therefore, was to see or write to him.[7]

By the middle of February 1915, Mansbridge felt well enough to attend a meeting of the Cambridge joint committee. At the central executive committee on 6 March 1915 he brought forward proposals, which were accepted, for a re-organization of the central office. He explained that he would have proposed a move to new premises, to relieve serious overcrowding, were it not that a sub-committee, appointed in January, was considering changes in the constitution. Mansbridge told the central council on the same day that his health was improving, but that he would have to consider whether he could best serve the movement by continuing as general secretary or in other ways. He attended a conference of labour members of joint committees and other representatives of the labour movement which was held at Oxford on 8 May 1915, to plan fresh appeals for support for tutorial classes, and for new trade union affiliations. On 15 May, however, he told the central executive committee that he could no longer cope with the administrative work of the central office. At his request, his salary was reduced from £300 to £156 a year while he considered his position.[8]

In September 1915, fifteen months after his collapse, Mansbridge resigned as general secretary. In his letter to the executive committee he gave two reasons for his decision, his continued physical weakness, and his disinclination to hold 'that high office for too great a time ... New times will demand new methods. The Association has anticipated this in part by taking steps to develop its constitution.' The new constitution, formally adopted later in the year, vested the management of the central body in the central council, to consist of the national officers, one representative of each centrally-affiliated society and six representatives of each district, with the district secretaries attending but not voting.

The ambiguities over the standing of the annual meeting were resolved by turning it into an Annual Convention, without any power to determine the association's policy. Mansbridge considered that the running-in of the new constitution should be the responsibility of his successor, and therefore the best time for his resignation to take effect was 'at once'.[9]

Under the new constitution, there were no longer any individual members attached to the centre. According to Dorothy Jones, Mansbridge disliked this provision, although he did not fight it, because it threatened the loss of famous supporters who would subscribe to the WEA nationally, but could not be bothered to associate with a district or a branch. The transfer of individual members had, however, been anticipated in the review of the constitution in 1907, and can hardly have had any influence on Mansbridge's decision to resign.[10]

In accepting Mansbridge's resignation, the executive committee recorded its

> profound sense of the wholly inestimable services which he had rendered to the Association, its earnest hope that he will soon be restored to complete

health and vigour, and its delight in knowing that in spite of relinquishing his office he will still devote his great gifts and his labours to the Association and the cause for which it stands.

An address containing this message was inscribed on vellum and presented to Mansbridge at the meeting of the central council in November 1915.[11] Mansbridge replied with a lengthy speech, in which he reviewed the history of his creation from his first faltering efforts at the Co-operative Congress of 1898 to the point, seventeen years later, at which the WEA

> stands higher than I could possibly express in the estimation of all that counts in England ... I feel the pain of leaving an unfinished work but I believe I shall have the pleasure, which is the highest a man can have, of seeing it steadily proceed through the years which are to come ... as one whose life as far as possible will be devoted to the cause of the education of working people right to the end, I will help it as much as I am able.

The council asked that that the speech might be printed, although this was never done.[12]

Mansbridge was relieved of financial worries after his resignation by the action of influential friends who created educational trusts to which he acted as consultant; through his income from the Co-operative Permanent Building Society; and through the award, in 1917, of a Civil List pension, initially worth £70 a year. J. M. Mactavish was appointed general secretary of the WEA, taking up his duties in March 1916. Mansbridge tried to carry on with his offices in the tutorial class movement—joint secretary at Oxford and Cambridge and honorary secretary of the CJAC—but was compelled to give them up during the course of 1917. Before long he was elected to the less onerous office of vice-chairman of each body. In 1918 Mansbridge accepted an invitation to become vice-president of the WEA.[13]

Mansbridge hoped to serve the WEA as a free-lance propagandist. In February 1916 the central executive committee accepted with gratitude his offer to prepare a WEA handbook and to raise part of the publication costs himself. The production of this work was, however, prevented by the ill health which troubled Mansbridge for two full years after his resignation. He had to limit his activities and take long periods of rest. The Mansbridges spent part of 1916 as guests of Christopher Turnor at Stoke Rochford, the

133

latter's country house near Grantham in Lincolnshire. Turnor was a wealthy landowner who had met Mansbridge when they were both serving on the consultative committee of the Board of Education. They became close personal friends, and Stoke Rochford was to become, in effect, an informal conference centre for Mansbridge's movements. 'There we remained for many months, benefiting greatly', wrote Mansbridge in his autobiography. During 1917 he spent a month at Nayland sanatorium in Suffolk, then a convalescent home for soldiers, as the guest of its founder Dr Jane Walker.[14]

Mansbridge's principal achievement during his convalescent years was the conversion of the WEA's small Central Library for Tutorial Classes into the Central Library for Students. He approached the Carnegie United Kingdom Trust in 1915, and secured an offer of initial grants totalling £2,600 and an annual grant of £400, on two conditions. The application had to be made by an appropriate organization, and £320 a year was to be raised by voluntary subscriptions. Mansbridge arranged for the CJAC, of which he was still honorary secretary, to make the formal approach to the trust, and was able to tell the committee in January 1916 that he had secured a private guarantee of £320 a year for five years.

Mansbridge's belief that the guarantee would not be needed proved to be correct, and voluntary contributions rose quickly to the level of £1,000 a year. The new library, located in Tavistock Square, was put in the charge of H. A. Twort, who had been the librarian of the WEA central library. Mansbridge became chairman of the executive committee, and gave this project a good deal of his time for several years.[15]

The private guarantor was George Drummond, a member of a wealthy banking family, who was recovering from wounds received at Ypres in May 1915. He invited Mansbridge to join the management committee of a weekly journal, *New Days*, sub-titled 'the journal of new conditions', which was launched in September 1915. The committee included John Buchan, later Lord Tweedsmuir, and Philip Kerr, later Marquess of Lothian. Kerr was a graduate of New College, Oxford, who had spent several years in South Africa as one of Lord Milner's bright young men. Returning to England in 1909, he joined with some friends in the following year to found a quarterly journal, the *Round Table*, which concentrated on Imperial affairs. He became the first editor. In 1914 Kerr published an article on the WEA, unsigned but written by Alfred Zimmern, whom he had known at New

College. The most likely sequence of events is that Zimmern introduced Mansbridge to Kerr, who put him in touch with Drummond. Such networks of social communication gave Mansbridge the chance to impress and persuade an ever-widening circle of influential acquaintances.[16]

*New Days* survived for only seven months, but Mansbridge gained an unexpected bonus from the venture. Drummond gave him the rent-free use of the journal's rooms on the first floor of 13 John Street, WC2. From this convenient office, Mansbridge ran several organizations which he founded in the years 1917–21, with the help of Dorothy Jones, who rejoined him as his devoted assistant.[17]

Mansbridge had come to be regarded as a versatile educational expert, useful in a consultancy role not only for his personal qualities but also because of his wide connections, especially in the Church, the universities and the labour movement. In August 1916, he was appointed to the prime minister's Committee on the Teaching of Modern Languages, and in the following May he was included in a delegation from the Classical Association which met the president of the Board of Education to argue the case for the provision of classical studies in secondary schools. He was a natural choice for membership of the Adult Education Committee of the Ministry of Reconstruction, which began work under A. L. Smith, master of Balliol College, in July 1917.[18]

During his long periods of enforced rest, Mansbridge had time to ponder upon the directions which his life and work might follow. He had reached the age of forty in 1916, and with normal expectations had half of his working life left. The security and emotional comfort of a routine administrative job had no appeal for him. He was recognized by his friends, and seems to have regarded himself, as essentially an innovator.

In his search for 'fresh woods and pastures new', Mansbridge naturally turned his mind back to his original vocation, for the Anglican priesthood. His income, although modest, would sustain him and his family if he chose to study for holy orders. He began to consider this idea seriously, but was dissuaded by Gore. His old mentor thought that he could do more for the Church as a layman than as a cleric. Mansbridge took this advice, and threw himself into three inter-related campaigns, for the creation of a system of Church Tutorial Classes, the reform of the Church from within, and 'the application of Christian principles to industry'.[19]

Mansbridge had already proposed the establishment of Church tutorial classes at the annual conference of the diocese of Southwark in December 1915. One of the Church's problems, he argued, was that of recruiting clergy from the working classes. He proposed the formation of tutorial classes which would prepare men 'who had missed educational opportunities in their youth' to go on to a theological college or a university. The idea was warmly welcomed in principle, and a committee was appointed to formulate a practical plan. A subsequent conference accepted the report of the committee, and re-designated the latter the Church Tutorial Classes Committee, charged with the responsibility of launching the scheme.[20]

Progress was delayed, probably by Mansbridge's poor health, until June 1917, when another diocesan conference was called to inaugurate the new movement. To prepare the ground, an article on 'Church Tutorial Classes' was published on 4 May 1917 in the Church journal the *Challenge*, edited by William Temple. It was probably written by Mansbridge. It is in his style, and contains similar ideas and expressions to those found in an article by him on the same subject in the *Church Quarterly Review* of July 1917. The writer in the *Challenge* lamented the alienation from the Church of the more intelligent and thoughtful workers, which was a result not of indifference but of their perception of Christianity, which often appeared as a jumble of out-of-date and untenable ideas about the Creation, miracles and the Atonement. In other words—although the writer made no such specific reference—it was time that the ideas of *Lux Mundi* were put before the workers.

Mansbridge envisaged a system modelled on the tutorial classes movement. Classes would be under the academic oversight of a theological college or the theological faculty of a university; they would be administered by joint committees representing both students and teachers; and the courses would be systematic and prolonged. There would, it was argued, be plenty of men, clerical and lay, who would come forward as voluntary teachers. The classes would differ from those of the WEA in being 'in the best sense propagandist ... the subjects, whatever they be, shall be studied from a distinctly Christian point of view', although the students and tutors together would have 'complete freedom' to choose their course topics and the methods of study.

Some important questions were left unanswered in Mansbridge's speeches and writings about the foundation of the Church tutorial classes. Were they designed to reclaim lost adherents as well as strengthen the faith of existing Church members? Were they intended for all adults, or for all who had been denied full educational opportunity, or for manual workers? All doubts and ambiguities, however, shrivelled up in the heat of Mansbridge's enthusiasm.

> If working men and women will study for long periods without hope of reward (and they have discarded all offers of diplomas and certificates) for the glory of citizenship, it is certain that, even though reluctant Churchmen and women be included, there are numbers who, the plain duty set before them, will study for the glory of God and the extension of His Kingdom on earth.[21]

Both Temple and Mansbridge spoke at the Southwark diocesan conference of 9 June 1917, which effectively launched the new movement. The bishop of the diocese, Dr Burge, and Bishop Gore both lent support. The first classes were formed at Lee and Lewisham later in the same year. A conference held in London in June 1918, under the chairmanship of Gore, appointed a central committee, and gradually the machinery of the Church Tutorial Classes Movement, renamed Association in 1922, was worked out. Mansbridge became a vice-president.[22]

Progress was slow at first and the nationwide links with theological colleges and university departments of theology did not develop as Mansbridge had envisaged. The association made little headway in the north of England until a full-time organizer, Major J. W. Povah, was appointed for the Northern Province in 1928. A rapid growth followed, and by 1930 there were in Great Britain 234 classes (only a minority of them three years in length) with 3,482 students. As the classes were not eligible for government or local authority grant, the teachers were unpaid, and the central organization was maintained only through the generosity of one donor who contributed several thousand pounds. For all its limitations, the Church Tutorial Classes Association made an important contribution to one of Mansbridge's objectives, the development of an educated and thoughtful laity.[23]

The Selborne committee on church–state relations had reported in 1916, with cautious recommendations for greater freedom for the Church of England to manage its own affairs. Arising out of the debate on the report a campaign developed which had amongst its aims not only structural reforms but also a more radical posture on social questions. The 'Life and Liberty' movement, launched publicly in July 1917, had a leadership which could equally well have filled the platform at a WEA rally—Temple (the leading light), Mansbridge, Gore, Tawney, A. L. Smith and Maude Royden. Another prominent member was Bishop Talbot of Winchester. A committee set up in 1916 by the archbishops of York and Canterbury to consider 'The Church and Industrial Life' included Smith, Mansbridge, Tawney, Gore and Talbot. Its report was published in December 1918.[24]

Mansbridge made a vigorous contribution to this campaign. He told a ruri-decanal conference at Woolwich in April 1917 that the Church was essentially a middle-class organization neglecting Labour and consequently being misunderstood by it.

> There should be no distinctions of class whatever in the Church. At present unorganised Labour drifted by the Church—whilst organised Labour steered by it, because they found more comradeship outside.

He urged the Church to take a more active role in such matters as education, children's employment and social welfare.[25]

He repeated these criticisms in June 1917 at a meeting of the Church Reform League which was also addressed by A. L. Smith. Working people suspected that the Church's interest in them was a result of concern about the growing political power of Labour. The thousands of communicants amongst working men and women had no voice in the affairs of the Church. The workers wanted to see in the Church

> some approximation to our Lord's teaching with regard, for instance, to property. The spectacle of the poor clergyman struggling on £100 a year to bring up his family, as contrasted with a priest not far off who held a well-endowed living, excited the disgust of the workers every bit as much as the conditions of the underpaid labourer.

In reviewing proposed structural reforms, Mansbridge urged in particular the need for smaller dioceses, so that bishops could be in touch with the common people. He was caustic about some features of the existing Church machinery, for example, ruri-decanal conferences—'he had never in a long experience of all kinds of movements come across such areas of indiarubber hopelessness'.[26]

Other leaders of the campaign fired off the usual Christian Socialist rockets. Talbot declared that the Church had been unduly subservient to the possessing, employing and governing classes. 'The fundamental evil of modern industrialism', wrote A. L. Smith, 'is that it encourages competition for private gain instead of co-operation for public service.' The example of the WEA encouraged the reformers to think that once again adult education might offer a partial answer to the need for practical action to follow up exhortation. A scheme for 'The Application of Christian Principles to Industry' was worked out, and Mansbridge was asked to develop it on WEA lines. Financial support amounting to £2,000 a year for five years was promised, but nothing came of it. Reflecting on his neglect, Mansbridge confessed in his autobiography that he felt 'indeed cast-down'. He blamed his own 'lack of concentration and … tendency to run after any hare'.[27]

This judgment was perhaps a little harsh, as Mansbridge was doing more than chasing hares during the time which he might have used for the 'Christian Principles' project. At the beginning of 1918, now once more in reasonably good health, he accepted a temporary appointment at the Board of Education. His duties included assisting those responsible for the passage of H. A. L. Fisher's education bill through parliament.[28]

As the war drew to a close, Mansbridge was seconded to help in the running of residential courses for the Australian Army at Cheshunt College, Cambridge. He lectured, took tutorials and marked essays, and greatly enjoyed both his brief experience as a tutor and the pleasures of introducing his students to Cambridge, which he knew so well. He was also in touch with Colonel Lord Gorell, head of the army education section of the War Office, who invited him, as soon as the Australian army school ended, to join the staff of a similar project for British officers at Oxford. In January 1919 Mansbridge took up residence in Trinity College, Oxford, and lectured on civics and related topics for the next two or three months. On one occasion he was reported to the War Office by a major on the course for teaching 'socialism, free love and polygamy', but his reputation survived unscathed. He told Lord Gorell, 'Lecturing on Civics is like a joy ride.'[29]

Mansbridge was greatly impressed by the educational services of the British, Dominion and American armies, which he described as 'The greatest adult education institutions which have yet been created'. He became concerned 'that this impulse is not allowed to run to waste'. Discussions with servicemen from Australia, New Zealand, South Africa and Canada, reinforced no doubt by recollections of his overseas tour in 1913/14, led him to think about 'the possibility of promoting united action between adult educational effort in the British Dominions and indeed ultimately in all countries'.

To meet this need Mansbridge founded the World Association for Adult Education. Its purpose was

> to bring into co-operation and mutual relationships the adult educational movements and institutions of the world, in order that peoples may proceed in greater power through wisdom—the mother of all things—to knowledge, and help to bring about on earth the finer working of such a social and political order as may minister to more complete individual lives, and which the several nations in their degree and place may deem it wise to adopt.[30]

In Mansbridge's view the British Empire could not be held together, nor the League of Nations made effective, without

> the development of common understandings set in common friendship … The League of Nations is, as it were, a rope made up of many strands. Adult education is one of the strands, and by no means the least important.

He described adult education as 'a kind of secular gospel' which offered 'one of the most powerful means of reconciliation between people of different experience and indeed between nations'.[31]

As was his normal practice, Mansbridge set about the establishment of the new association in January 1919 out of the human materials ready to hand, and with constitutional niceties left for later consideration. He recruited several allies from the field of army education—Lord Gorell; Dr H. N. Tory, director of the Khaki University of Canada; the bishop of Bathurst, director of education for the Australian Forces; J. B. Condliffe of the New Zealand Expeditionary Force; and Dr E. W. Pahlow, representative in Britain of the US Army Educational Commission. From the WEA— which was simultaneously planning an International League of WEAs, which could co-operate with the WAAE—came Temple, Zimmern, E. S. Cartwright, Margaret McMillan and Julia Madams. Lord Haldane, whose current concern with adult education is discussed below, promised his support.[32]

The inaugural meeting of the World Association was held in London on 29 March 1919. Haldane gave the keynote speech, repeating the demand of the 'efficiency group' for a 'national minimum' of education, as well as of income and housing. He offered a revealing re-statement of the 'Educate your People' argument upon which Mansbridge had drawn in the articles which led to the foundation of the WEA:

> the education question lies at the root of the social question ... The educated man will not choose bad quality. As a rule the educated man does not drink, and does not take bad wages, and does not live in a slum.

The other speakers included Gorell, the bishop of Bathurst, Pahlow, Temple and two statesmen whom Mansbridge pressed into service because they were available in England—Crawford Vaughan, lately Labour premier of South Australia, and Dr Subotic, foreign minister of Serbia.

Nineteen of the leading supporters, all British, Dominion or American and not including Temple or Haldane, were formed into a provisional committee with power to add to their number. The appointment of provisional officers was confirmed: chairman, Mansbridge; secretaries, Horace Fleming, warden of the Beechcroft Settlement, Birkenhead, and Dorothy Jones. Mansbridge announced, in Gorell's words, 'a deficit of which he was extremely proud', amounting to £48 1s 1d on the first quarter's working.[33]

On June 1919 the provisional commitee turned itself into the governing council of the association, and adopted a provisional constitution and statement of aims. The WAAE was to encourage development and co-operation in adult education throughout the world, by means of an information bureau (in London), a bulletin, conferences, the establishment of branches or commissions, the creation of hostels and the appointment of a representative at the capital of the League of Nations (Geneva). The president was to be appointed annually, from different countries in turn. In the event, Mansbridge was so delighted at securing the services, as the first president, of Thomas Masaryk, president of Czechoslovakia, that he was kept in office from 1920 to 1929. Masaryk never addressed a meeting of the association, although he received a labour delegation, including Mansbridge and J. H. Thomas, which visited Prague in January 1921.[34]

The WAAE conceived the ambitious scheme of turning Crosby Hall, Chelsea, with suitable extensions, into a hall of residence for international adult education. The hall had been removed stone by stone in 1910 from Bishopgate, in the City of London, to a position close to the site of Sir Thomas More's house in Chelsea. An appeal was made for £250,000, but there was little or no response, apart from a conditional offer of £2,000 from the Rhodes Trust. The main work of the association began on a more modest scale. The Cassel Trust gave £500 a year for five years to provide information services. The first *Bulletin*, dealing with the foundation of the WAAE, and the second, an account of the tutorial class movement, apparently written by Zimmern, had both appeared by the end of 1919, and subsequent bulletins came out four times a year. The association was fortunate to have rent-free accommodation at 13 John Street.[35]

The first offshoot of the World Association was the commission on the education of adult seamen, soon named the Seafarers' Education Service. Its origin can be traced back to a conversation which Mansbridge had in the summer or autumn of 1919 at Cuddesdon theological college (where he was a visiting lecturer in civics) with S. N. Minifie Hawkins, who had worked at the Mission for Seamen in Buenos Aires. The latter described how desperate seamen were for any kind of reading matter, and asked Mansbridge whether he could do anything to meet the need. According to Hawkins, Mansbridge said, after a moment's reflection, 'I'll have to do it. Who will give me a start?' Mansbridge sought the support of Lawrence Holt, a member of the family which owned the Blue Funnel Line, who had been a fellow member of the prime minister's committee on the teaching of modern languages. Holt promised to help.[36]

In December 1919 a weekend conference of members of the WAAE and representatives of shipping interests and seamen's unions met under the chairmanship of Crawford Vaughan. It resolved to form what became known as the Seafarers' Education Service. Mansbridge became chairman. In May 1920 the Blue Funnel ship *Aeneas* left London for Brisbane with a library of 150 books on board for the use of the crew. After cautious experiments by several shipping lines, the library service became established as a great boon to seamen and of no small benefit to labour relations on board. The Carnegie United Kingdom Trust and the Chamber of Shipping made grants, which helped to make possible the appointment of George Knowles as organizing secretary in 1921. From 1922 a personal loan scheme, and the issue of reading guides, were introduced, and study advice was offered by correspondence. By 1929, four hundred ships were equipped with libraries, ranging from fifty to three hundred books.[37]

The *Final Report* of the Adult Education Committee of the Ministry of Reconstruction was published in November 1919. Mansbridge was actively involved in the preparation of one of the interim reports on *Libraries and Museums*, published in May 1919, but his contribution to the production of the main report is uncertain. He was absent through ill-health from some of the early meetings. He mentioned the committee only briefly in his autobiography, describing it as 'an interesting committee, composed of diverse elements', which achieved a spirit of unity through the influence of A. L. Smith, the chairman, and Canon R. St J. Parry, of Trinity College, Cambridge. They disarmed the suspicions of two trade union leaders who came from unions which supported the Central Labour College, the National Union of Railwaymen and the South Wales Miners' Federation. The representative of the latter, Frank Hodges, had been a 'Ruskin rebel' in 1909.[38]

The drafting of the *Final Report* was undertaken by four men—Smith, Tawney and the two secretaries of the committee, E. S. Cartwright (organizing secretary of the Oxford tutorial classes committee) and Arthur Greenwood (chairman of the Yorkshire WEA district and currently working at the Board of Education).[39] It turned out to be a hymn of praise to the achievements and ideals of the WEA and the tutorial class movement. Liberal adult education was declared to be a 'universal need', in contrast to technical education, which was important only as a preparation for certain occupations; 'adult education is a permanent national necessity, an inseparable aspect of citizenship, and therefore should be both universal and lifelong'. Economic recovery and social responsibility both depended upon the creation of 'a far wider body of intelligent public opinion' by means of 'a long, thorough, universal process of education continued into and throughout the life of the adult'. The 'freedom of teaching and freedom of expression … the frank interchange of thought and experience' would enable the students 'to rise above their original prejudices and limitations'.

The report regarded adult education as a movement rather than a service, and emphasized its essentially democratic and voluntary character. LEAs were urged to develop non-vocational 'evening centres for humane study', offering courses in music, drama, dance and the domestic and creative arts, but these should be run as far as possible through students' societies.

> The fact that adult education is concerned with men and women of more or less mature experience, who are conscious either of their own needs or of social needs, gives to it a special character. Adult education will clearly thrive only under conditions which allow of the fullest self-determination on the part of the students as regards the studies to be pursued, the choice of the teacher and the organisation of the class ... the advance of adult education can proceed only as quickly as voluntary agencies can stimulate, focus and organise the demand for it.[40]

Mansbridge must have signed the '1919 Report', as it came to be called, with great pleasure. Almost immediately he found himself involved in another important investigation, as a member of the royal commission appointed to examine the financial needs and resources of Oxford and Cambridge. The commission was chaired by H. H. Asquith, the former prime minister, who had lost his seat in the 'khaki election' of December 1918. It was organized so that it could, when required, divide into three separate committees dealing respectively with Oxford, Cambridge and estate management. The members of the Oxford committee included Asquith, Dr T. B. Strong, Sir Henry Miers (now vice-chancellor of Manchester University) and Mansbridge.[41]

In April 1920 Mansbridge completed a history of the WEA down to the time of his resignation in 1915, under the title *An Adventure in Working-class Education*. It was published a few months later, and turned out to be his last major service to the association at national level. In July 1920 he announced that he would not seek re-election as vice-president, because of pressure of other duties. This office was not then, as it is now, essentially honorary in character, and Mansbridge had found himself unable to attend meetings of the central council and executive committee. There is little doubt, however, that he was influenced by other considerations.[42]

Mactavish had been chosen to succeed Mansbridge as general secretary partly because he was considered by the WEA leaders, and particularly by

Tawney, to be the right man to strengthen the weakest link in the association's chain of alliances, that with the trade union movement. It might have seemed that Mansbridge was himself moving in the same direction in 1914/15 through his efforts to secure greater trade union support for tutorial class provision, but it is improbable that he would have countenanced the constitutional arrangements made by his successor. In 1919 the WEA and the Iron and Steel Trades Confederation formed the Workers' Educational Trade Union Committee, which later attracted other unions into membership. Although the WEA provided the secretariat at both national and district level, trade union representatives were in a majority on the committees set up under the scheme. The unions could make use of existing WEA/tutorial class provision, or ask for new programmes, but, in the words of the original constitution, they were to 'retain control over the administration of ... finance, policy and the kind of education provided'.[43]

Mansbridge's concern about this development was probably increased by the transformation in the political role of the trade union movement. Its membership had doubled during the war, and it was now the main support of a Labour party which won twenty-two per cent of the vote in 1918, and had adopted a socialist programme. Mansbridge referred obliquely to the dangers of alliances with sectional interests in the last few pages of *An Adventure in Working-class Education*.

> There may be at any time an influx of those who wish to see the WEA used for immediate economic, social or even political purposes, or who believe in it as a 'Class' instead of a democratic institution. ... The Association must be powerful and confident in its insistence on its own inclusive gospel of education ... There is no other way to maintain its integrity ... On no account ... should it bow the knee in the house of those who promise support and power, undreamed of, if it will chant their songs and utter their dogmas.[44]

He was more specific about his objections to WETUC in an article published two years later in the *Revue internationale du travail*, the organ of the International Labour Office.

> It is too soon to predict the results of this initiative, but it is certain that every action tending to exclude from the work of popular education people of proven good will, such as those who have rallied to the Workers' Educational

Association, will cause irreparable harm to the movement ... if ... it is directed or controlled by one party or one section of the nation it will have to give up the building of the new Jerusalem in 'England's green and pleasant land'.[45]

In 1921 Mansbridge and Haldane founded the British Institute of Adult Education. Although in a formal sense it was a branch of the World Association, the institute was the product of a separate initiative undertaken mainly by Haldane. When he left the government in 1915, Haldane took up the cause of adult education as the 'one great portion of the field of higher education which waited to be developed'. He visited the universities of England and Scotland one after the other and conferred with academic sympathizers. At his London home Haldane had long discussions with his associates in the campaign, principally Mansbridge, Tawney and Harold Laski. In 1918–20 he addressed a large number of meetings in industrial towns to test, and to stimulate popular—mainly working-class—interest in adult education.

'Our common principle', wrote Haldane, 'was one of faith in the effect of higher education on democracy.' Education was a lifelong process. The government should make adult education, with tutors provided by the universities, available to every interested adult. Both the historical evidence of the 1919 Report and the reception accorded to Haldane's speeches in the industrial towns had revealed a strong demand amongst the people for non-vocational education. 'If you want to know more of the reality of this demand, go to Mr. Albert Mansbridge with whom I am working in this matter.' His proposals might easily cost a million pounds a year, but that was a small sum compared to the losses caused by strikes, such as the coal miners' strike of October 1920. Adult education would pay for itself by creating 'a tranquillity which would make an end of strikes and make instead a living reality of government of the people for the people by the people'.[46]

In view of the difficulty of persuading governments of the prophylactic value of adult education, it was fortunate that Haldane was able to tap a rich source of private benefaction. Sir Ernest Cassel, a rich industrialist, told Haldane

> that he wanted to spend a million pounds on bettering the condition of the poor. I replied that his million, if applied thus at large, would do little more

good than if he were to throw a drop of water into a bucket. But if he would spend it on a definite object, such as the higher education of the working-classes, he might do much with it.

Cassel agreed to devote half of his proposed million pounds donation to adult education, and asked Haldane to become chairman of a trust set up for the purpose. Haldane agreed. The Cassel Trust made liberal grants to several adult education bodies, including the WEA, the British Institute and the World Association.[47]

Haldane and Mansbridge conceived of the British Institute of Adult Education as a learned society of activists and supporters which would act as 'a ploughshare breaking up new ground which Adult Education movements would occupy' (Mansbridge) and 'work out standards and forms of organisation or something like a General Staff principle' (Haldane). The institute was formally inaugurated on 28 May 1921, by which time about 180 members had, according to Mansbridge, already been recruited. The provisional constitution explained that the objects were to spread the gospel of adult education, to suggest new developments and to keep up standards, by means of research, publication and conferences. Membership was to be individual, not institutional. Haldane was elected president, with J. R. Clynes, a leading Labour MP, and A. L. Smith as vice-presidents. Mansbridge became chairman, and the duties of honorary secretary and treasurer were undertaken by Oliver Stanley. Subsequently Thomas Harvey Searls was appointed as full-time organizing secretary. The executive committee included Cranage; the Revd F. E. Hutchinson, Marriott's successor at Oxford; Lord Eustace Percy, a prominent Conservative MP; Jack Lawson, a Labour MP who had gone from the Durham coal mines to Ruskin College and back again; William Graham, another Labour MP, who was serving with Mansbridge on the royal commission on Oxford and Cambridge; Harold Laski; and a rich collection of old Mansbridge hands, including Julia Madams, T. W. Price, William Rothenstein (the principal of the Royal College of Art, with whom Mansbridge had worked on the army education schemes in 1918/19), Dr Jane Walker, W. R. Rae of the Co-operative Union Education Committee, Zimmern and Dorothy Jones.[48]

It was fortunate that Mansbridge had such a wide circle of acquaintances, because his idea of a 'representative committee' was often synonymous with a collection of people 'of proven good will' who had helped him in his earlier ventures. The incestuous tendencies of the adult education world were increased at the same time with the appointment by the president of the Board of Education of a committee on adult education 'to promote the development of liberal education for adults' and to stimulate and co-ordinate the efforts of voluntary bodies and LEAs. Temple, now bishop of Manchester, became chairman, and the committee included Mansbridge and several prominent members of the World Association.[49]

The report of the royal commission on Oxford and Cambridge was published in March 1922. Mansbridge commented in his autobiography that he was given every encouragement 'to fight, if need be, for my opinions'. If, in fact, he had to fight to secure recognition and resources for adult education he emerged victorious. The report described extramural work as 'one of the most important modern developments, implying a whole new principle of academic responsibility towards the community at large'. The proposals in the 1919 Report for the establishment at each university of an extramural department with an academic head were endorsed—Cambridge had already taken steps in this direction. It was proposed that centres should be established at Oxford and Cambridge to accommodate administrative services, libraries and study rooms for adult students; that the provision of tutorial classes, extension lectures and summer schools should be expanded; and that additional full-time academic posts should be created. It was envisaged that a full-time tutor would normally live in the region in which his classes were situated, but would spend a short period each year working in the university.[50]

The royal commission recommended the admission of selected adult students, mainly from tutorial classes, to read either for an honours degree or for a diploma course aiming at honours standard within a narrower field. Unlike the 1908 Oxford Report, with which in spirit it was in full accord, the 1922 report accepted the fact that by far the larger contribution to the education of adults would be made through extramural classes and summer schools.

The report laid considerable stress on the need for adult education to be accepted 'as an established and essential part of the normal work of a University'. For this reason it proposed that the additional funds needed for extramural work (over and above normal Board of Education grants), and for mature students, should be provided by the two universities 'out of the funds at their own disposal'. The report called upon the government to replace the temporary grant of £30,000 a year paid to each university since 1920 with permanent annual grants amounting in each case to £100,000 plus £6,000 for adult education and £4,000 for the support of women's colleges. The royal commission did not explain how it reconciled the principle that university adult education should be financed out of money at the disposal of the university with the advocacy of earmarked grants.[51]

In February 1922 Mansbridge sailed from Liverpool to undertake a strenuous lecture tour of North America. He had been invited to give the Lowell Lectures in Boston a year or two earlier, but postponed the visit because of his work on the royal commission. He chose as his topic for the eight lectures given in March, 'The Older Universities of England'. He included an enthusiastic account of the WEA/tutorial class movement, and found that this was the topic asked for in almost all the numerous speaking invitations pressed upon him. He lectured at many universities and colleges, in the north-east and middle-west, and talked to trade union, religious and educational organizations. Conferences and dinners at which he spoke included those of the American University Extension Federation and the recently established Workers' Educational Bureau. Mansbridge visited Canada on his way to and from the United States. He lectured at universities, visited WEA groups and took part in the foundation of a new branch in London, Ontario.[52]

According to press reports, North American audiences were greatly impressed with both Mansbridge and his message. Canadian journals commented that although the WEA had made some progress there—for example, there were seven 'tutorial classes', one year in length, in Toronto—the universities were timid and the trade unions suspicious.

> The visit of so vivid a personality as Mr. Mansbridge, with his whole-hearted belief both in Education and in Labour, should do something to bring them together. His speech was admirable; so were his replies to his hecklers. The ease and racy humour of his style masked, but did not conceal, his moral earnestness.[53]

A Boston newspaper headlined a feature article about Mansbridge, 'Will England Solve the Labour Problem by Giving Adults Education?' and there was considerable discussion about the value of a similar prescription for the United States. The *New York Times*, reviewing the Lowell Lectures and the 1919 Report, argued that the USA needed a co-operative effort by universities, public authorities and labour organizations to promote workers' education on English lines. Because of indifference and mistrust, 'the recent workers' education movement in this country has been, unhappily, largely class conscious'.[54]

Soon after his return to England, Mansbridge was given the honorary degree of Doctor of Laws by the University of Manchester. In 1923 he received a similar honour from Cambridge, as part of the celebrations to mark the fiftieth anniversary of university extension. The committees of the four organizations of which he was chairman—WAAE, BIAE, Seafarers' and the Central Library for Students—raised a subscription to buy his doctoral robes and provide a small present for Mrs Mansbridge. He was also invited to become a member of James Stuart's college, Trinity, and a little later to join the council of Selwyn College, Cambridge.[55]

Mansbridge deeply appreciated the recognition of his work by the university world, and carried his doctoral title with quiet pride. He had, however, little leisure in which to contemplate his own distinction. The four organizations mentioned above all claimed his attention. His pen was busy, particularly with a history of Oxford and Cambridge, *The Older Universities of England*, which was based upon the Lowell Lectures. The book, illustrated with drawings by his son John, who was making a successful career as an artist, appeared in the summer of 1923. It included chapters entitled 'Adaptation to a Democratic Age' and 'The Royal Commission and the Twentieth Century', which described the campaign in which Mansbridge had been engaged, and re-asserted the claims on the ancient universities of both the studious worker and the poor student. Mansbridge's appeal to the conscience of the privileged moved one clergymen who had received an exhibition of £50 a year for three years when an undergraduate at Cambridge fifty years earlier, to refund the money for the use of poor scholars. He told Mansbridge that he had done this because his family was 'in easy circumstances' at the time. 'It is in a sense "Conscience Money".'[56]

Mansbridge was also involved in the follow-up to the report of the royal commission on Oxford and Cambridge, both in public and behind the scenes. He was appointed a member of the statutory commission set up under the Oxford and Cambridge Act of 1923 to draft revised statutes for both the university and colleges at Oxford. In his autobiography Mansbridge commented that he 'enjoyed greatly the task … Once again I made friends, increased my knowledge of Oxford.' He does not, however, mention his efforts to preserve at least part of the grant for extramural work recommended by the royal commission. The publication of the report of the latter coincided with the savage cuts in government expenditure known as the 'Geddes Axe', and it soon became clear that Oxford and Cambridge would not receive in full the proposed grants totalling £220,000. Mansbridge privately urged the Board of Education in February 1923 to accept the principle that 'whatever sum is given to Oxford and Cambridge should be regarded as including a grant in respect of extramural work'. Temple led a WEA deputation to meet the president of the Board in the same month, and warned that if the adult education movement did not receive sufficient funds to maintain the association with the universities it 'would drift into independence and most probably become political in character'. The president (Edward Wood) said that he could not hold out any hope that Oxford and Cambridge would receive the full grant recommended—he did not mention a figure but he was thinking of £60,000 for each university— but that he would consider extramural needs.[57]

In August and September 1923 Mansbridge badgered the Board of Education, through several letters and at least one visit, over the same question. He reminded the Board of the promise recently made on behalf of the government by the Marquess of Bath in the House of Lords,

> if it is found necessary to reduce the grants from the sums mentioned by the Royal Commission, the cut will be made proportionately, so that the women's colleges and the extra-mural boards will get their share of the money.

Unless £3,000 out of the probable £60,000 grant to each university were allocated to adult education, there 'would be a justifiable row' in the House of Commons. When Mansbridge learned of a proposal to earmark sums for women's colleges but not for extramural work, he threatened to make a row himself. He told an official of the Board

> that he might be forced to take the attitude that he was only serving [on the

151

Oxford Commission] on the strength of [the] pledge and that he might have to take an active part in making trouble. At the same time he would be very glad to know immediately what was the real position and what was [the Board's] attitude, as there was just a chance that he would be in a position to allay trouble instead of making it.[58]

In the end adult education at Oxford and Cambridge received about half of the annual grants originally proposed by the royal commission, plus some additional help towards the cost of the new centres. Cambridge set up a Board for Extramural Studies, of which Mansbridge became a member, in 1924, and opened its new building, Stuart House, in February 1927. Oxford established a Delegacy for Extramural Studies, but left its extension lectures and tutorial classes committees as separate providing bodies, each receiving grant from the Board of Education. The new headquarters at Oxford, Rewley House, was also opened in 1927. Mansbridge spoke at both opening ceremonies.[59]

In 1924 the WEA celebrated its coming of age. A special number of the *Highway* carried messages of congratulation, including, of course, one from its founder. Mansbridge also wrote an article for *The Times* about the WEA and the emergence of adult education as a national force. At the time of the actual celebrations, however, he was back in the United States, mainly for the purpose of giving a series of lectures in connection with the golden jubilee of the Chautaqua Summer School. He lectured also at several universities in the middle-west and New York.[60]

By this time Mansbridge's life had settled into a new pattern, albeit a very varied one. The BIAE (1921) turned out to be the last major organization which he founded (in this case in partnership with Haldane), although some of his creations put out new offshoots. He had, however, a good deal of work ahead of him in guiding the development of the several organizations which he chaired. He was also in great demand as a lecturer, both in Britain and in North America. He wrote many articles and, in the 1930s, several more books.

One of Mansbridge's principal concerns was to secure the development of the Central Library for Students into a fully-fledged national central library. This had been recommended in 1919 by the third interim report of the Adult Education Committee of the Ministry of Reconstruction. Some of the administrative proposals of the report, including the transfer of responsibility for library matters from the Local Government Board to the Board of Education, and the extension of library powers to counties (under the control of education committees), were put into effect in 1919/20. As chairman of the executive committee of the CLS, Mansbridge led a deputation to the Board of Education in May 1920, to ask for an annual grant. Because of financial stringency the president, H. A. L. Fisher, turned down the application. He agreed to ask LEAs to consider supporting the library financially in return for the loan of reference books for use by their local students, but by the end of 1923 only nine LEAs were contributing regularly. The CLS was heavily dependent upon the Carnegie United Kingdom Trust, although other bodies such as the Cassel Trust also gave financial support.[61]

Mansbridge found that the subordination of county libraries to education officers and education committees had caused a good deal of resentment amongst professional librarians. He made an effort to undo the damage by supporting in the Adult Education Committee of the Board of Education (not to be confused with the '1919 Committee') the idea of a comprehensive inquiry into public libraries. The permanent secretary to the Board, Sir L. A. Selby-Bigge, told the president in June 1924, 'I gather from Mr. Mansbridge ... that he wants to obliterate the Ministry of Reconstruction's Report and dispel the antagonism which it aroused.' The same minute passed on four suggestions from Mansbridge for the chairmanship of the proposed departmental committee, including Sir Frederic Kenyon of the British Museum, who was chosen.[62]

The Public Libraries Committee, of which Mansbridge himself was a member, reported in 1927. It recommended that the CLS should become a national central library while continuing to support adult classes. The new library should be a separately-administered department of the British Museum, with an interim government grant of £5,000 a year. After further consideration by the British Museum Trustees and the Royal Commission on National Museums and Galleries, the idea of association with the British Museum was dropped. The CLS was reconstituted as the National Central Library, under its own trustees, with an annual government grant of £3,000. The new arrangements came into effect in 1930. Sir Frederic Kenyon became chairman of the executive committee, and Mansbridge chairman of the trustees. With the aid of a further substantial grant from the Carnegie Trust, the central library moved in 1933 from the disused school in Galen Place, Bloomsbury, where it had been housed for some years, into a fine new building in Malet Place. Mansbridge had the pleasure of presenting an address to George V when the king opened the new premises on 7 November 1933.[63]

The British Institute of Adult Education was designed as a learned society promoting research into adult education and providing a forum for the exchange of views. It took part in the campaigns against cuts in Board of Education grants, and for improved financial provision, in the years 1922–26, but it was fighting on behalf of the adult education movement as a whole, and not for the institute itself. The annual conference, which normally alternated between Cambridge (Trinity or Selwyn College) and Oxford (Balliol or New College), became the only common meeting ground for the movement. For contributions to the conferences, the institute had to rely at first mainly upon WEA leaders and university men, including heads of new adult education departments such as Robert Peers of Nottingham and J. H. Nicholson of Bristol as well as old stagers such as Cranage. Every effort was made, however, to interest the LEAs in adult education. Their role was made the principal topic of the second annual conference held in September 1923. The more committed directors of education, including E. Salter Davies of Kent and Henry Morris of Cambridgeshire, and LEA chairmen such as Sir Percy Jackson of the West Riding, soon became familiar figures at Institute functions.

Mansbridge played a leading role in the annual conferences, supported by Mrs Mansbridge as official hostess. In 1926, for example, when Haldane gave his last presidential address before retiring through ill-health, Mansbridge and Gore spoke on 'The Challenge to the Movement' at the final session of the conference. Mansbridge also preached a sermon, 'Except ye become as little children', at the Sunday morning service held in Trinity College chapel.[64]

Mansbridge contributed an essay, 'Ideals as Facts', to a volume on the meaning and purpose of adult education written by members of the institute in 1923. He did not, however, take part in the research programme of the institute, a task for which the talents of other leading members were better suited. Harold Laski, who was vice-chairman until he resigned through pressure of work in 1930, took a leading role in several inquiries, including the first one undertaken 'The Educational Functions of Settlements', and one of the most important, *The Tutor in Adult Education*, which dealt with the supply and training of tutors.

R. S. Lambert, who became editor of the *Listener* in 1929, was involved in inquiries into the role of broadcasting in adult education, and film in national life. Other research topics included science in adult education, audio-visual aids, and education for two disadvantaged groups, the unemployed and prisoners. The institute, or its activists, helped to create machinery to carry out the recommendations of some of the reports, for example the Central Council for Broadcast Adult Education, and the British Film Institute.[65]

In 1925 the British Institute became formally independent of the World Association for Adult Education and moved out of Mansbridge's rent-free but cramped quarters in John Street to rooms in Bedford Square. At about the same time a research library was started, and in 1926 the *Journal of Adult Education* (subsequently *Adult Education*) was launched. Its first editors were Professor J. Dover Wilson and Professor A. E. Heath. The same year saw the first issue of the *Handbook and Directory of Adult Education*.[66]

The work of the British Institute was wide ranging, consistently good in quality and of considerable practical value. The annual conferences might descend occasionally into an exchange of platitudes, but according to a senior official of the Board of Education, writing an internal memorandum in 1927 or 1928,

> The rapid growth of the interest of Local Education Authorities in adult education is attributable in no small measure to the opportunities given by these Conferences for meetings between Chairmen and Directors of Education on the one side and leaders in the Workers' Educational Association and other voluntary bodies who might not otherwise have had occasion to meet on equal terms.

One of the benefits to flow from these contacts was improved financial support for WEA and tutorial classes.[67]

The institute suffered, however, from two serious limitations. Its income was small and precarious, being derived from individual subscriptions, modest grants from the Cassel, Carnegie and Thomas Wall trusts, and the legacy of £2,000 received on the death of Haldane in 1928. No support was received from either public funds or institutional subscriptions. As a result its staff and premises were both inadequate for any activities needing much administrative support. Secondly, its position was ill-defined. It was, *de facto*, the principal national organization for research and consultation in adult education, but it was not formally recognized as such, either by other voluntary bodies such as the WEA, or by the Board of Education (which had its own consultative committee and adult education committee); or even by the World Association, which, after the BIAE had moved out from under its wing in 1925, periodically considered the establishment of a British section.

It may be unfair to attribute these organizational deficiencies to Mansbridge's preference for the 'old boy network', as, for example, Ernest Green did. It is clear, however, that the leadership of the institute was reluctant to consider the introduction of institutional membership, preferring to make periodic appeals for individual support. When R. S. Lambert, at the request of the officers, prepared 'a plan of action' for the institute in 1935, he did not advocate LEA affiliations which, as the LEAs supplied 'the bulk of the attendance at the Annual Conference ... might mean upsetting the present method of electing Council and Committees'. He put forward instead the suggestion of a committee of LEA members, with perhaps at a later date a parallel committee for voluntary bodies. This constitutional problem was still unsolved when Mansbridge retired from the chairmanship in 1940. A solution was forced through soon after the second world war when a group of adult educators impatient with the limitations of the BIAE founded the rival National Foundation for Adult Education, which had institutional membership only. The functions of the two bodies had too much in common for peaceful co-existence, and a merger was quickly arranged. This produced the National Institute of Adult Education, with both institutional and individual membership, and a nationally recognized role.[68]

The Seafarers' Education Service always had a strong claim on Mansbridge's affections. He was chairman from its foundation until 1945, and his faithful aide Dorothy Jones carried out varied secretarial duties from 1920 until 1949. Mansbridge used one of the friendships he had made on the royal commission on Oxford and Cambridge, with Hugh Anderson, master of

Caius College, Cambridge (who came from a shipping family), to arrange at intervals weekend conferences of the SES at Caius College. The service extended to four hundred ships by 1929. The depression of the early 1930s checked development but by 1939 SES libraries, each changed two or three times a year, had been provided for six hundred ships.[69]

In November 1937 Mansbridge seized upon a remark made by the Duke of Kent who, at a reception for the SES, described it, not very accurately, as 'a University of the Sea'. He arranged a meeting of the Commission (the governing body) of the SES at Stoke Rochford, which established the College of the Sea as a section of the SES. Advice on study had been offered to seamen through the SES from time to time, but the college promised tuition in any subject suitable for study by correspondence. The service was free except for a nominal registration charge. Mansbridge became honorary director. He quickly recruited a band of voluntary tutors, many of them eminent scholars and most of them his personal friends. It was almost as though he was trying to prove that he could still move mountains.[70]

The College of the Sea was still in its infancy when the second world war broke out. Within a few weeks Mansbridge had launched the Sea War Library Service, which produced an additional two million books for the men who spent the war at sea. In December 1939 the College of the Sea extended its services to the Royal Navy. Mansbridge abandoned a projected visit to the United States to concentrate on this work, and during most of the war he travelled from his home at Hughenden, near Welwyn Garden City, on three days a week to work in the London headquarters of the SES.[71]

Of all Mansbridge's major creations, the one with the greatest gulf between aspiration and achievement was the World Association for Adult Education. For some years its council was a makeshift collection of British members—drawn from several different organizations or movements but with a few exceptions not formally representing them—together with a few European delegates who had occasion to visit London and such Commonwealth sympathizers who happened to be in Britain. An adult educator from Australia, such as Professor Herbert Heaton, who was visiting or spending a period of study leave in Britain, would be co-opted to represent Australia. It was hoped that national councils would ultimately be established in many countries, to form the basis of a representative world body. Such councils were set up in the Netherlands and Czechoslovakia in 1921, but they were short-lived. In 1926 the American Association for Adult Education was founded, partly as a result of the influence of the World Association and of Mansbridge's speaking tours in the United States. It was recognized in the following year as a national council of the WAAE. At about the same time less formal groups or committees emerged in Germany, Holland, Denmark and Sweden.

The American support was doubly valuable. Because leading American adult educators could afford to travel regularly to Britain, their involvement gave World Association gatherings a more international character. Secondly, the difficult financial situation of the association was eased by American subventions. It was otherwise dependent upon small annual subscriptions—two guineas for institutions, six shillings for individuals—and modest grants from the Cassel and other trusts. At first only one of the two secretaries of the WAAE—Dorothy Jones—was paid. The other, Horace Fleming, was honorary, and tried to do his share from Birkenhead, where he was warden of the Beechcroft Settlement. Gifts from the Thomas Wall Trust and an unnamed American supporter made it possible for Fleming to work full-time in London from May 1924, although a serious illness two years later led to his resignation. With assistance from the same two sources, the WAAE, together with the SES, moved in 1926 from John Street into larger premises in Russell Square, held on a short lease.[72]

Mansbridge pinned his hopes for guiding the World Association from its original, British-dominated phase to a genuinely international organization upon a series of representative conferences. The first world conference was planned for Geneva in 1923, but shortage of money led to its postponement, and it eventually met at Cambridge in August 1929. Two meetings had meanwhile been held on the European mainland, a conference planning committee in Denmark (1926) and a council meeting in Germany (1928).[73]

Shortly before the world conference President Masaryk of Czechoslovakia resigned the presidency of the WAAE and was succeeded by Mansbridge. Four hundred delegates from forty countries assembled for what Mansbridge later described as 'a veritable fountain of inspiration'. Over half of the delegates (including spouses) came from England and Wales (122) and USA (86), Germany coming next with 39. In preparation for the conference the World Association had published a 476-page *International Handbook of*

*Adult Education*, surveying the adult education systems of most of the participating countries.[74]

The conference exposed the conceptual, as well as organizational, difficulties in the way of creating a genuine world association. The institutions, the aims, the methods and the degree of development of adult education varied enormously from country to country. There was no agreed theoretical basis for comparative analysis. Some speakers gave merely descriptive accounts, others spoke vaguely about their aspirations. There were too many formal addresses and too many speakers who overran their time limit. As a result there were few opportunities for genuine discussion, except informally during the gaps in the crowded, week-long programme.

It was nevertheless the general view of those present that the convening of the conference had been a notable achievement, and that the sense of fellowship and unity of spirit were to be treasured. Many tributes were paid to Mansbridge's leadership, and in particular to his enthusiasm and powers of persuasion. He made two major speeches, the presidential adddress and a contribution to a session on 'The Function of the World Association'. The first of these was in the main a declaration of Mansbridge's faith in the spiritual power of adult education.

> Man ... is driven though laborious and baffling days to strive without ceasing to acquire knowledge, express wisdom, in the power of his spirit struggling to free itself and harmonise with the eternal spirit ... The mission and purpose of Adult Education is in the power of the spirit of wisdom, which works persistently to bring all the powers hidden in humanity to fullness of expression ...

This kind of sermonizing can generate a warm glow on one Sunday, with a complete absence of recall a week later. In both speeches, however, Mansbridge showed a firm grasp of practical realities. He repeated the advice he had given to local groups in the early days of the WEA—discover your own needs, no two communities are alike. 'Resist the temptation to imitate', he warned. Successful movements, such as the tutorial classes or the Danish Folk High Schools,

> can only succeed elsewhere, and as a matter of experience do only succeed, when people of the same tradition, in similar environment, facing identical

needs, adopt them … Each community must … develop its own peculiar methods and construct its own institutions … The powers, however, which it invokes to do so are common to all humanity.[75]

On Mansbridge's advice, the conference adopted a revised constitution, which was more representative geographically. The new council met in Sweden in 1930, and in the following year held its annual meeting in Vienna, in association with two small international conferences dealing respectively with 'Radio in Adult Education' and 'Adult Education and Employment'.[76]

As part of the same drive to improve the effectiveness of the WAAE, the quarterly *Bulletin*, which had reached its fiftieth number by November 1931, was replaced by the *International Quarterly of Adult Education*. The articles in the *Bulletin* had varied a great deal in depth and quality, many being merely descriptive. The need was felt for a more substantial journal which would both search for common principles and identify the knowledge, for example about teaching methods, which would be of general application. The publication of the new quarterly, which was edited by J. Dover Wilson, was made financially possible by a grant from the Carnegie Corporation of New York. To emphasize the international character of the journal, articles from non-English speaking contributors were printed in the language of origin with a summary in English, in place of the *Bulletin* practice of having all the full versions in English with summaries in one or two other languages.

It would be difficult to imagine a less auspicious time at which to undertake a new initiative in the field of international co-operation in adult education. The economic crisis caused some voluntary bodies to close down or at least suspend operations, and there were cuts of varying degrees of severity in the grants made by governments in support of adult education. In 1933 the Nazis came to power in Germany, and quickly suppressed the organizations which had sustained adult education in that country and had been collectively one of the main supports of the World Association. After the appearance of the fifth number of the *International Quarterly* in May 1933, the journal ran into financial difficulties. Numbers two and three of Volume II came out as one publication in March 1935, and after the completion of the volume in the following May the journal closed down.[77]

A new series of the quarterly *Bulletin*, more modest in scope than the *International Quarterly*, began in June 1935. The World Association did not attempt another major conference, but continued with other activities, including an information bureau which answered queries from all over the world, and bursaries for visits by tutors. Some of the reports of the latter were published, including John Mack's *Contemporary Adult Education Movements in Switzerland* and W. H. Marwick's *The Present Position of Adult Education in Sweden*.[78]

The outbreak of the second world war severely restricted the role of the WAAE, as well as increasing its financial problems. The wartime annual reports included a forlorn list of European organizations in membership 'as at 1st September 1939'. It was no mean achievement to keep the organization alive during the war. Writing in the February 1944 issue of the *Bulletin*, Mansbridge looked forward to postwar developments which should include an international residential college, special efforts in the reconstruction of Europe and new initiatives amongst colonial peoples. However, the establishment of Unesco provided a new framework for international co-operation in adult education, and whatever the desirability of creating a parallel non-governmental organization, Mansbridge was too old for such a venture. The last number of the *Bulletin* came out in February 1946, and the WAAE closed down shortly afterwards.[79]

Mansbridge's relations with the organizations of which he was chairman or president during the 1920s and 1930s were very different from his earlier role in the WEA. He was not employed by any of the organizations, nor was he burdened with their day-to-day administration. He was thus able to undertake many speaking engagements, both at home and in North America. Although he had little contact with the WEA at national level, he spoke to a number of district and branch gatherings. He enjoyed visiting public schools to lecture about education. As his lectures were very much like sermons, they were readily adapted to the many pulpits which he occupied as a distinguished Anglican layman.[80]

Mansbridge's visits to North America in 1922 and 1924 have already been described. He sailed in December 1925, accompanied by Mrs Mansbridge, for a lecture tour which occupied several months. They spent seven weeks in Berkeley, California, where Mansbridge delivered the Earle Lectures; went on to Canada for five weeks; and returned to the United

States to visit Denver, Pittsburgh, Chicago, New York and several other cities. Mansbridge gave ninety lectures in the United States and fifty-one in Canada. As in Australia, Frances Mansbridge was also persuaded to lecture, mainly to women's organizations. The Mansbridges were well received wherever they went, and were delighted to see evidence of growing support for adult education in North America.[81]

Mansbridge returned to Pittsburgh in June 1927 to give the Commencement Oration at the University, and receive the honorary degree of Doctor of Laws. He realized that his audience, numbering six thousand, regarded the Oration as a penance which they had to undergo before receiving, or seeing their children receive, their degrees. He responded to the challenge with an inspirational address, 'The Waters of Learning', which he described later as possibly the best of his career. Shortly afterwards the city department of education closed all its schools for a day to allow four thousand teachers to hear a similar lecture.[82]

The next American visit by the Mansbridges was to Newfoundland in 1929. It was planned by John Lewis Paton (son of John Brown Paton, the distinguished Congregationalist), a close personal friend, who had resigned as high master of Manchester Grammar School to head the new Memorial College at St John's. Both Albert and Frances had to deliver many speeches, because they found that the bodies concerned with education were organized on separate denominational lines—Anglican, Nonconformist and Roman Catholic. During the visit Mansbridge helped to launch the Newfoundland Association for Adult Education.[83]

In the Birthday Honours List of June 1931, Albert Mansbridge became a Companion of Honour. The following year saw the publication of his book on one of his closest friends and allies, Margaret McMillan, who had died in March 1931. It was arranged that the profits of both author and publisher (Dent) would go to the maintenance of the Camp School founded at Deptford by Margaret McMillan. In November 1933 Mansbridge completed a history of the Co-operative Permanent Building Society, of which he had been a director since 1910. Entitled *Brick upon Brick*, it was published in 1934. The first edition of sixty thousand was exhausted within the year, and it was reprinted.[84]

Mansbridge was invited to Boston in 1934 to give a second series of Lowell Lectures. He took as his theme 'An English Gallery', and described the work of many of his famous collaborators. He also spoke at several universities elsewhere in the United States.[85]

Charles Gore died in January 1932. Mansbridge began work on a biography of his dear friend and mentor, but ran into difficulties. The Revd Dr Leonard Prestige was appointed official biographer, and although Mansbridge was urged by mutual friends to press on with his own book, he was reluctant to do so. He handed his own material over to Prestige, and contented himself with publishing as a short memoir a series of lectures which he gave in 1934 at Cuddesdon theological college about Gore and Bishop Talbot, who had died in January of that year. Mansbridge gave his royalties from this book to the Church Tutorial Classes Association.[86]

Mansbridge described the pattern of his life at about this time in a letter to Elizabeth Haldane, sister of Lord Haldane who had died in 1928. He was president of the World Association; chairman of BIAE, SES, the Thomas Wall Trust and the trustees of the National Central Library; vice-chairman of the Church Tutorial Classes Association, the Cambridge joint committee and the CJAC; a lecturer at Cuddesdon; 'etc. etc.'—the latter including membership of the consultative committee of the Board of Education, to which he had been re-appointed in 1929. 'Unless some good fairy smiles on us I expect to be mainly responsible for the Finance of the National Library … I am hopelessly overwhelmed, and I am getting warning signs … after it all I have to earn my living except for £200.' Half of the latter sum came from the civil list pension, which had been increased from the original £70 in 1924. The other £100 may have been an honorarium attached to the chairmanship of the Thomas Wall Trust. Mansbridge's main source of income was his directorship of the Co-operative Permanent Building Society, which was worth £700–£800 a year in the 1930s.[87]

In the correspondence of both Albert and Frances Mansbridge in the 1930s, there are frequent references to overwork. He wrote to a friend in April 1937 that he was 'just back from a heavy day at Cuddesdon College … If I do not do all I should wish, please remember that I am over-whelmed—and don't know which way to turn.' In the same year he took on the additional responsibility of vice-chairmanship of the governors of Rachel McMillan Training College for nursery school teachers at Deptford, named after Margaret McMillan's sister.[88]

Mansbridge continued as a member of the consultative committee of the

Board of Education until 1939. He was, he wrote, 'by many years, father of the Committee'. The last committee project with which he was involved was the Spens Report on secondary education, although he told a friend, 'I did little to influence it'. In *The Trodden Road* Mansbridge observed, 'It is probable that I have signed more Government reports on education than any other person.'[89]

The Mansbridges paid two further visits to North America. In January 1937 Mansbridge shared with J. B. Conant, president of Harvard University, the distinction of addressing the annual gathering of the Association of American Colleges, in Washington. He took as his subject 'The Effect of the Colleges of Oxford and Cambridge on the development of Liberal Education'. It had long ceased to be remarkable that Jude the Obscure had become the voice of Christminster. He also visited Pittsburgh where the university had almost completed the building of a huge gothic tower known as 'The Cathedral of Learning'. Mansbridge proposed that subscriptions should be collected from England to provide an 'English Room' in the building. The suggestion was warmly welcomed, although the room, a lecture room in Tudor style, was not ready until shortly after Mansbridge's death in 1952. In the summer of 1938 he lectured in Newfoundland, Nova Scotia and New Brunswick at the invitation of the Canadian Education Association, and received yet another LLD, from the University of Mount Allison, New Brunswick.[90]

In later years Mansbridge used to recall how, on his American lecture tours, he would offer a choice of a dozen lecture titles with the advice, 'Choose which you like—you will get the same lecture!'[91] Despite this sensible economy of effort, he built up over the years a stock of scripts for lectures and sermons, and it occurred to him that a selection from these and his published articles 'might ... make a little book'. In 1937 he invited his brother-in-law, J. C. Pringle, to make a suitable selection and asked Leonard Clark to edit the book. 'The Power of the Spirit' and 'Sources of Power' were two suggested titles. The work proceeded slowly, partly because Clark was waiting for Mansbridge to write a new paper to fill a gap in the collection.

Early in 1939 Mansbridge put aside work on the collected pieces, and began to write *The Trodden Road*, which was, in his own words, 'a testament of experience, inspiration and belief'. This was ready before the end of the year, and came out in the spring of 1940. Its appearance spoiled the market for the other work, which was eventually published, entitled *The Kingdom of the Mind*, in 1944.[92]

In 1945 Albert and Frances Mansbridge moved in semi-retirement to Paignton in Devon. He resigned the chairmanship of the Seafarers' Education Service, the last remaining voluntary post to claim a substantial part of his time. He continued to serve as a director of the Co-operative Permanent Building Society (of which he had been president from 1942 to 1946), until the end of 1951. He gave occasional lectures, and worked on another book, *Fellow Men*, sub-titled 'A Gallery of England 1876–1946'. Published in 1948, it described the people 'who have compelled my admiration or from whom I have learned' during the seventy years of his life. One of them was Professor H. H. Turner of Oxford, who had forecast in 1908 that Mansbridge would do 'many more fine things'.[93]

Leonard Clark, who reviewed *Fellow Men* in the *Yorkshire Post*, pointed out to Mansbridge one significant omission from the 'gallery'—Frances Mansbridge. He also suggested that it was time that both Albert and Frances received some further public honour. Mansbridge was well aware that without the devotion and hard work of 'Tot'—his pet name for Frances— he could never have achieved his successes. She had been much more than the loving wife behind the great man. She had worked alongside him in the WEA, particularly in the women's movement and at summer schools; lectured in Australia and North America; acted as hostess to the British Institute conferences for nearly twenty years; and helped in many other ways. He responded warmly to Clark's suggestion, saying 'of course, if anything is done it should be for Frances … I'd like Tot to have a D.B.E. of course, or even a C.B.E.', and in another letter, 'Tot is old now … I would love to see her few last years inspired by recognition … My only regret about the C.H. … was that it was only for me.' Mansbridge revealed to Clark that Ramsay MacDonald had been approached after the award of the CH (in 1931) with the suggestion of a knighthood for Mansbridge, but had said that the standing of the CH precluded such an award. Mansbridge wrote to George Isaacs, a Labour minister, and Clark raised the matter with some other Labour MPs, but nothing came of it.[94]

It would not have been surprising if Mansbridge had been offered some kind of title. A substantial number of Labour ministers and MPs in the 1945 parliament had been WEA tutors or students. The prime minister, Clement

Attlee, knew Mansbridge and his work well enough. He agreed to take part in the presentation to Mansbridge of the latter's portrait, painted by his son John, at a ceremony held in the House of Commons in May 1947, but was prevented from doing so at the last moment. In the following year Attlee offered a life peerage to the general secretary of the WEA, Ernest Green, who refused it.[95]

Tot was not the only one who was getting old. Mansbridge admitted to Clark in June 1948, 'I find getting about not easy.' He still made occasional public appearances. In May 1949 he spoke at a rally at University College, Exeter, on one of his favourite themes, 'Workmen Scholars'. He told a friend that giving the lecture made him feel forty years younger. In the following month he opened the Hudson Shaw Memorial Garden, at St Botolph's Church, Bishopsgate, in the City of London, of which Shaw had been the vicar.[96]

In 1950, when the Mansbridges celebrated their golden wedding, Albert's health began to fail. He wrote in October of that year, 'I find work increasingly difficult … I had a fall which may have affected me.' He was ill again in the following summer, with chest trouble and rheumatism. Frances wrote to the Clarks, 'He looks very frail'. Mansbridge was feeling 'much better' in October 1951 and was 'trying to get to writing again'. In June 1952 he wrote, 'I have been tired but soon, if not now, I am certain to be better.' It was not to be. His body was worn out, a prey now to the multiple afflictions of old age. Friends who called to see him in his last weeks found him very weak, but cheerful and happy to talk about mutual friends and cherished ideals. He died in a Torquay nursing home on 22 August 1952, in his seventy-seventh year.[97]

# 8

## The Man and the Movements

The active life of Albert Mansbridge falls naturally into four divisions. In the first he was searching for an outlet for his idealism and energy. The second saw the creation of the WEA and the tutorial class movement, and the transplantation of both to Australia. In the third phase Mansbridge founded several new organizations designed to reinforce and extend the work of adult education at home and overseas. In the last and longest phase, which began in 1922–23 with his first American lecture tour and his two honorary doctorates, Mansbridge was established as the leading figure in British adult education and its principal spokesman overseas, but with his energies increasingly devoted to preaching rather than pioneering.

There can be little doubt that the outstanding achievements of Mansbridge's life belong to the second phase: uniting a wide range of working-class organizations in an educational crusade; forming an alliance on equal terms between the WEA and the universities; gaining the support of influential people in the Church and the 'Establishment'; securing Board of Education grants for tutorial class work without restricting academic freedom; and breathing into the whole movement a joyful spirit of evangelical fervour—these victories had all been won by 1914.

The second and third phases of his working life were separated by a severe illness and a slow return to health. Both W. H. Hosford, who worked with Mansbridge in the WEA central office from 1909 to 1914, and R. H. Tawney thought that the attack of cerebro-spinal meningitis had permanent effects. According to Tawney, Mansbridge 'never fully recovered the power and sense of strategy which had made him so brilliant a pioneer of adult education'. Hosford considered that after his illness 'he was not quite the same man—slower in thought and speech and movement'. Both men saw the rest of Mansbridge's life as an unavailing struggle to match the remarkable successes of his earlier years. Dorothy Jones who, outside his immediate family, had the longest close association with Mansbridge, disagreed with Tawney and Hosford. In her view he recovered all his power and energy, 'indeed he was so energetic at times that we tried to hold him back'.[1]

Mansbridge was thought by people who met him for the first time after 1918 to be remarkably vigorous. As late as 1945 George Keeton wrote that his 'abundant vitality seems inexhaustible. It is as though he draws upon some inner well of energy from which he is perpetually refreshed.' He certainly retained the power to attract allies and disciples. The tributes paid to his powers of persuasion by speakers at the World Conference of Adult Education in 1929 were typical of many such statements. The deputy vice-chancellor of Cambridge University described Mansbridge as 'that very accomplished and persuasive magician'. A senior official of the Board of Education, W. R. Davies, spoke about 'the powers of persuasion' which Mansbridge exercised 'successfully and repeatedly upon Education Ministers in England … it does not matter what their political party … he gets his own way with them'. Some allowance has to be made for the hyberbole of the conference platform, but the internal memoranda of the Board of Education in the 1920s show that Mansbridge was held in high regard and his views respected. He was also prepared, at least in the early 1920s, to be a hard man in private, as he showed by threatening the Board of Education with trouble over the grants for extramural work at Oxford and Cambridge. Mansbridge was certainly a calmer man in the 1920s than in his WEA days. His zeal lacked the frenetic touch which had worried his friends, but that could have been the result of middle age rather than meningitis.[2]

The contrast between Mansbridge's achievements before and after the first world war may be attributed more confidently to changes in circumstances than to a decline in his powers, even if the latter cannot be altogether ruled out. In Edwardian England many people and groups in the working-class movement, the Church, the universities and the 'Establishment', were in varying degrees attuned to the wavelengths on which he learned, after his early mistakes, to transmit his message. The workers' aspirations, the anxiety of the Church to do something about social evils without becoming too overtly political, the rise of new universities and the pressure to reform the ancient ones, concern about the increasing industrial and political power of labour—these currents could all be harnessed through Mansbridge's organizing skill, missionary zeal and 'gift of tongues'. The currents flowing in his favour during the 1920s were fewer and weaker. He worked hard for the development of a National Central Library, but was held up both by governmental parsimony and by the slow pace of ministerial decision-making—six years from the appointment of the Kenyon committee to the establishment of the library. The Seafarers' Education Service developed as quickly as shipping companies could be persuaded that it was worth financing.

Mansbridge had more room to manœuvre with the other two organizations founded shortly after the war, the World Association and the British Institute. The deficiencies of the former were, however, beyond his power to remedy. He could not call into being suitable adult education movements in many different countries, although he was able on his lecturing tours to encourage developments in North America. His hopes that the WAAE would eventually live up to its name were disappointed. Effective co-operation and exchanges of ideas on a worldwide scale had to await the development of speedy and relatively cheap air travel. The World Association may be regarded as a brave attempt at an impossible target, and its limited success in spreading knowledge about adult education is not to be despised.

The achievements of the BIAE are discussed in Chapter 7. It can be argued that it should have been developed at some stage from its original voluntary and unofficial role into an institutionally-based, officially recognized national body. To do this, however, it would have been necessary for LEAs in general to be willing to play an active part in the development of adult education. LEAs such as the London County Council or the West Riding of Yorkshire, which were strong supporters of non-vocational education for adults, were far from typical. There were rather more authorities like the East Riding of Yorkshire which was prepared to contribute 'not more than £100 a year' to a scheme for the county organized by the WEA and otherwise financed by WEA supporters, the Cassel Trust and Board of Education grants. The East Riding Education Committee resolved in 1924, 'That whatever the advantages of Adult Education under proper control may be, it is not desirable under the present stringent financial conditions to commit the ratepayers to any great expenditure of public money in this direction.'[3] It was no small achievement for the British Institute, mainly through its annual conference, to persuade most LEAs to take enough interest in adult education to grant-aid tutorial and other WEA classes.

The history of LEA involvement in adult education between the wars has yet to be written, but it would appear that Mansbridge's informal, old-boy-network approach was working as well as could be expected for most of this period. It is quite possible that a chance was lost about 1936, when the period of financial restraint begun by the economic crisis of 1931 had ended, some universities were talking about new initiatives to reach potential students not catered for by the WEA and the tutorial class movement, and the important experiment of the Cambridgeshire village colleges was in progress. In 1936, however, Mansbridge was sixty years of age, and perhaps for this reason was not disposed to lead the BIAE on new paths.

Mansbridge's influence on the development and policy of the WEA after he resigned the office of vice-president in 1920 was slight. Mactavish had been brought in as general secretary in 1916, largely at the behest of Tawney, with the deliberate intention of drawing the WEA into closer partnership with the organized labour movement, and particularly the trade unions. Mansbridge's reservations about the formation of the WETUC have already been mentioned, but he had other reasons for disapproving of his successor. The shrewdness and subtlety which had so often guided Mansbridge to success seem to have been wholly lacking in Mactavish. The WEA campaign about H. A. L. Fisher's education bill in 1917/18 was intended to be a careful blend of support for the bill against its conservative critics and pressure on Fisher to strengthen some of its provisions. Mactavish concentrated on the second of these objectives at the expense of the first. Temple, Gilbert Murray and A. L. Smith had their work cut out to prevent an open breach between the WEA and Fisher, who accused Mactavish of 'bitterly attacking the Bill as an altogether cowardly, if not aristocratic measure'.[4]

Mactavish, who was a committed socialist, did not draw the clear distinction between political and educational roles on which Mansbridge had always insisted. In 1921 he had to be persuaded by Temple and Tawney not to stand as a Labour candidate for the London County Council. During the following year the WEA central executive committee spent a good deal of time arguing about whether Mactavish's socialist opinions expressed in speeches and articles were having an adverse effect upon the work and the financial position of the WEA. The matter was settled by a re-affirmation of the non-party character of the association, and a reminder to Mactavish that his right of free public speech as an individual was contingent upon his ensuring that the WEA was seen not to be committed by his views.[5]

Mactavish received some support in the executive committee from G. D. H. Cole, who was becoming a power in the association. Cole looked forward to the time when the WEA would be financed wholly by the labour movement and could do without the Board of Education grants and the conditions attached to them.[6] His was a minority view, but there was broader support for the idea that the WEA was the 'educational wing of the labour movement', the other wings being the TUC and the Labour party. Mansbridge had always paraded the all-party character of the national support for the WEA. In the 1920s nearly all of the national officers of the WEA were members of the Labour party. This was not easy to avoid as so many leading supporters of the movement who had previously been uncommitted or members of the Liberal party—including Haldane, Zimmern and Temple—had joined the Labour party, but Mansbridge would have done everything possible to recruit at least one or two token Conservatives.

Mansbridge may at the same period have caused some irritation in the WEA leadership through the actions of some of his other organizations. When the Central Library for Students was given a new constitution in 1921, a place was reserved for the CJAC but not, until two years later, for the WEA. There was some concern about the role of the BIAE, particularly as it seemed to be treating the WEA and tutorial classes as separate movements, until a visiting deputation from the British Institute removed those fears. An article in the *Scotsman* in 1921 forecast that the influence of the World Association would save the WEA from extremists in the labour movement. Mactavish wrote an angry rejoinder in the *Highway*, inviting the WAAE to disclaim any desire to 'play chaplain to the WEA', but no reply is recorded either in the journal or in the WEA minutes.[7]

In public Mansbridge defended the WEA against accusations of political bias. In private he complained that it was turning away from its former ideals, 'I sometimes think remembered only by me', as he wrote to Sir

171

Michael Sadler.[8] Reuben George joined in the argument by pleading, as a socialist, for a halt in the drift towards 'class education' and for the preservation of 'the WEA spirit', which in Mansbridge's time had united people of all political and religious views and had buried questions of class 'fathoms deep'.[9]

The coolness between Mansbridge and the WEA at national level (he remained on very friendly terms with some branches and districts) was no doubt regretted by others as well as the faithful Reuben George. Mansbridge was, however, partly to blame because the range and balance of his opinions had shifted. In the formative years of the WEA he had made demands for educational reforms which were both radical and specific—secondary education for all, a school-leaving age of sixteen, maintenance allowances for poorer pupils, entry to the university for all who could benefit. While insisting that the WEA must avoid any sectarian or party commitment, he had from time to time supported criticisms from within the movement of industrial and social conditions inimical to educational progress. These arguments were contained within a broad spectrum of views about the nature and purpose of adult education for workers—that knowledge was power, that knowledge brought responsibility and wisdom, and that knowledge was to be valued for its own sake.

After leaving the WEA Mansbridge's commitment to the first of these ideas, never as strong as his faith in the other two, weakened, and he tended more and more to advocate education for its own sake. He came near to denying that adult education had any social purpose at all. He romanticized about miners and factory workers who did not mind 'working long hours at low pay' as long as they could 'discuss Greek history with men like Alfred Zimmern, Greek poetry with men like Gilbert Murray and Greek philosophy with men like W. H. Hadow'.[10] In his twenty-first birthday message to the WEA he wrote,

> The old original faith of the W.E.A., that man is destined, if he would live aright, to develop his mind and body in the power of the spirit, not because it will serve some specific purpose, but because it is the law of his being, still stands to me as the reason for education in our time.[11]

Abandoning the idea of 'education for emancipation' in favour of the belief that 'education *is* emancipation' relieved Mansbridge of the difficulty of reconciling demands for radical educational reform with his insistence upon political neutrality. The shift exposed, however, a more fundamental problem, to which Mansbridge does not seem to have given much thought. He argued that the WEA had been built upon 'man's natural hunger and thirst for truth, beauty and goodness', that students joined the classes, 'making tremendous sacrifices, because they desire more light in their souls and a greater warmth in their hearts'. They were 'yearning after spiritual perfection ... Our members are the apostles of a new state—a Christian state in which the grabber and the profiteer and the sweater will find it impossible to breathe.'[12]

Mansbridge never believed that more than a relatively small proportion of the working class, as indeed of other classes in society, had a taste for serious intellectual pursuits. If therefore the workers with the ability to understand the nature and causes of poverty, ill-health and bad housing were to turn away from industrial and political action to savour more fully purely intellectual delights, were they not betraying their fellow workers and their families? Was this not going back to 'singing a lot of hymns to help the unemployed'?

T. W. Price, writing in 1924, put the view which was generally supported in the WEA, then and in Mansbridge's time.

> Education for its own sake may be excellent, but education as a means to service is a tenfold better ideal, and is the bedrock upon which the faith of the WEA is founded.[13]

It was not surprising, therefore, that as a new generation of WEA leaders emerged who had not been close to Mansbridge during the pioneering years, they were inclined to regard him as an Edwardian relic. His name appeared on WEA writing paper as the founder, but his opinions do not seem to have been sought. Mansbridge once said to Hosford, 'They treat me as if I were already dead.'[14]

Mansbridge complained to Leonard Clark in 1943 that the WEA had ignored all his books. This had certainly not been true of his books about the pioneering days, *University Tutorial Classes* (1913) and *An Adventure in Working-class Education* (1920), although they had long been out of print. The books written in 1932–35 about Margaret McMillan, the Co-operative Building Society and Talbot and Gore did not directly concern the WEA.

He must have felt that inadequate attention had been paid to *The Trodden Road*, but this had appeared in the spring of 1940, when the WEA was wrestling with the problems created by the outbreak of war. When *The Kingdom of the Mind* was about to be published in 1944, Mansbridge suggested to its editor, Leonard Clark, that he should bring it to the notice of the WEA; 'if they knew it, it is fundamental for them'. Ernest Green, the WEA general secretary, replied to Clark that he would be 'delighted to see that Mansbridge's book is reviewed in the *Highway*', and offered to circulate a publicity leaflet to WEA branches. Mansbridge's recognition of these offers, in letters to Clark, was rather grudging, and he commented later, 'As far as the WEA is concerned, suggest what you will to them. I keep off the grass.' Green wrote a glowing review of the book, published in the *Highway* of February 1945, praising Mansbridge's 'creative genius' and describing him as 'an idealist with a practical mind … who hates oppression and injustice'.[15]

The development of Mansbridge's views was to some extent influenced by the company he kept. After his resignation from the general secretaryship of the WEA he was no longer in close and regular contact with the working-class movement, although he kept in touch with individual working-class friends and with some WEA branches. The organizations which he started and the committees with which he was involved, in the period 1916–22, brought him a new circle of friends, mainly academics, churchmen and businessmen. He did not lean towards any political party, but he valued the support and friendship of prominent Conservatives, including two presidents of the Board of Education, Edward Wood and Lord Eustace Percy. He commented in *The Trodden Road* that Margaret McMillan had, 'strangely enough' gained more support from Liberals and Conservatives than from the Labour party. 'My experience was not unlike hers. Although never hindered by Labour politicians, and, indeed, supported by the most outstanding of them, yet their attitude was never so generous as that of the Conservatives.'[16]

His honorary degrees, his membership of senior common rooms in Oxford, Cambridge and London and later of the Athenaeum Club, and his international reputation as a distinguished educationist tended to identify Mansbridge with the 'Establishment'. He was even on terms of respectful friendship with Queen Mary. He was received by the queen in July 1919, when he told her about the work of the WEA, the World Association and the Central Library for Students.[17] Queen Mary sent donations from time to time for Mansbridge's good causes. The Mansbridge MSS contain letters from the queen's private secretaries written in the years 1922–24, and a large number of letters covering the period 1940–52. Queen Mary encouraged Mansbridge to offer detailed comments on current events. Only one of his letters has been preserved in the royal archives, but it is possible to infer the substance of his observations from the replies. In 1924 he assured the Queen that the leaders of the new Labour government were reasonable and responsible men. He repeated the message in 1945. Lady Cynthia Colville, a lady-in-waiting, wrote to Mansbridge on 25 August 1945,

> Queen Mary commands me to thank you very much indeed for your delightful letter of the 21st August and to tell you with what deep interest Her Majesty heard your views upon the new Government and upon recent events. The Queen shares your view that they have made an excellent start … My youngest son [who] has been working for years in the secretariat at Downing Street … had told me that 5 or 6 members of the new Govt. were remarkably fine, upright and patriotic men, notably Mr. Lawson. Your estimate of them and of the role the WEA has played in preparing such men for their new responsibilities has greatly interested the Queen.

Queen Mary found Mansbridge's reviews of current affairs always 'most interesting and encouraging … You always contrive to make one see these in a truer—and therefore more cheerful—perspective than the Press or the B.B.C., and for this Her Majesty is really grateful.' In 1942 the queen anxiously sought Mansbridge's opinion 'on the subject of the increase of Communism'.[18]

The replies from the ladies-in-waiting to Mansbridge's letters were always warm and friendly, frequently quite long and detailed, and usually included good wishes for Mrs Mansbridge. It helped, of course, that Mansbridge was devoted to the monarchy. 'It is good that people feel that the Royal Family is, as it were, the highest expression of our common life. One never hears in ordinary intercourse anything contrary to this, as one has heard at times in the past.'[19] The queen was 'delighted' at the description of King George V which appeared in *Fellow Men*. Lady Cynthia Colville recalled with how much sympathy King George had quoted John Wheatley, the only left-wing socialist in the Labour cabinet of 1924, as saying to him, 'Brought up, eleven of us in one room, are you surprised that I am a socialist, and that I want to see living conditions entirely changed?' She felt that Mansbridge's impression of the late king 'brings out so well the essential simplicity, kindness and intense sincerity of his character'.[20]

Mansbridge's correspondence with Queen Mary must be seen in its proper context. In the first place, he was an assiduous letter-writer, and kept in regular contact with a wide circle of friends. Secondly, he showed as deep an interest in the affairs of his poorest friends as of his richest, and was always ready to offer practical help when it was needed. One of his friends was H. Wooldridge, a stalwart of the Reading WEA and active in trade union, Co-operative and Labour party affairs despite the misfortune of losing a leg in an industrial accident at the age of eighteen. In 1912 his fourteen-year-old daughter Emma had just started as a pupil teacher when he broke his other leg. Mansbridge came to his aid in characteristic fashion, sending him a weekly allowance of a few shillings out of his own pocket and giving him a copy of Norman Angell's *The Great Illusion* to read. Four years later Mansbridge found Emma a place at Goldsmiths' College, and seems to have helped with her expenses. In 1926, having failed to secure a public scholarship for the Wooldridges' other child, Harry, to go to King's College, London, Mansbridge raised a private subscription by circularizing his friends. He kept up a regular correspondence with Wooldridge over a period of at least seventeen years. Most of the surviving letters are, of course, from Wooldridge, and they are divided between descriptions of WEA and labour activities in Reading, and comments upon the books he had read.[21]

Some of Mansbridge's friendships began with a helping hand. When he could not draw on trust funds to which he had access, he would dip into his own pocket. In 1928 he arranged for the Thomas Wall Trust to provide a bursary for Leonard Clark, who wanted to train as a teacher. He kept up a regular correspondence with Clark, and encouraged his writing of poetry. The relationship ripened into a close friendship between the Mansbridges and the Clarks.[22] He never seems to have helped anyone in an impersonal way. When he met a railway porter whose wife was seriously ill, he took a personal interest in the man as well as arranging financial help. During the second world war he lost touch with George Alcock, the railwayman who had been a member of the provisional committee of the WEA in 1903.

When he wrote to Alcock in 1948, the latter's reply was a catalogue of wartime misfortunes, with his wife killed and house destroyed in an air raid. Mansbridge immediately wrote offering both sympathy and financial help, although the latter was not needed.[23]

Mansbridge seems to have been indifferent to material possessions beyond the need to make reasonable provision for his wife and family. Frances Mansbridge had to be a frugal housekeeper in the early years of their marriage, but later in life they lived in simple comfort without money worries. When Mansbridge died his assets, all bequeathed to Frances, were valued at £10,650. He never regarded his pen as a source of extra income, and gave away most of the royalties from his books.[24]

Mansbridge's published writings fall into several distinct categories. *University Tutorial Classes* and *An Adventure in Working-Class Education* are accounts of his pioneering work in the WEA. They are the best written and perhaps the most valuable of his books. His autobiographical writings are *The Making of an Educationist* (1929), a little book of only thirty-five pages, and the first section of *The Trodden Road* (1940). They give valuable insights into his childhood and youth, add some interesting and more personal details to the accounts of the WEA, and describe his work after 1916 in a compass that is excessively brief for the scale of his activities. In both works, however, Mansbridge was careless about dates. The first tutorial class was said to have begun in 1906 in one book and 1907 in the other. The correct date was 1908. He wrote that he left the employment of the Co-operative Building Society early in 1905. It was actually a year later. A visit to Pittsburgh in December 1936/January 1937 was described as taking place after Christmas 1937. There are several other errors of this kind, most of them of little importance, but his memory sometimes played tricks by placing events in the wrong order. For example, he sat for his Oxford scholarship in October 1894, a few months before Charles Gore was appointed canon of Westminster, and not, as he implies in *The Trodden Road*, some time later.[25]

A third section of his writings consists of histories of institutions or movements with which he was associated—*The Older Universities of England* (1923), *Brick upon Brick* (1934) and a detailed account of adult education movements in England and Scotland which appeared in 1906.[26] All of these seem to have been carefully researched.

Another important group is made up of his biographical works, all posthumous—a full-length book on Margaret McMillan, and shorter accounts in *Edward Stuart Talbot and Charles Gore*, Part II of *The Trodden Road*, Part II of *Fellow Men* (1948), and several printed memorial lectures, the subjects of which include George Cadbury and Haldane.[27] In addition Part I of *Fellow Men* contains within the compass of thirty-eight pages brief references to over ninety people not dealt with in the second part of the book or in *The Trodden Road*. It would be inappropriate to assess his short pieces critically as biography. They depict his heroes (with two heroines, Margaret McMillan and Dr Jane Walker, who both figure in *The Trodden Road*) and one would not expect more than the occasional wart to be allowed to blemish the portraits. What is significant—apart from the abundant evidence of a keen interest in his fellow men—is the selection.

A few Labour leaders, including MacDonald, Lansbury and Shackleton, are mentioned in Part I of *Fellow Men*, but with the exception of Haldane no political figure appears in the main gallery. Haldane was exceptional among leading politicians in making adult education a principal concern. His influence on Mansbridge seems to have been surpassed only by that of Charles Gore. The largest group consists of university men such as Canon Parry of Cambridge and Professor H. H. Turner of Oxford. Next in order of numbers come the churchmen who had been leading supporters of Mansbridge—Gore, Temple, Barnett and J. B. Paton. Businessmen with the same qualification included Thomas Wall and H. R. Dent, the publisher. Morant appears, of course, together with two other men who for part of their lives were public servants: John Buchan, Lord Tweedsmuir; and Philip Kerr, Marquess of Lothian.

The gallery includes only two working men, Reuben George, who appears in both *The Trodden Road* and *Fellow Men*, and Alfred Williams. George was, like Mansbridge, a native of Gloucester, who moved as a young man to Swindon. After his right hand had been mutilated in an accident in the wagon works where he was employed, he became an insurance agent. He was an ardent socialist, a member of the SDF—in Mansbridge's words, 'the leading soap-box orator of the town—his slogan being: "Down with everything that is up".' After attending a course of extension lectures given by Hudson Shaw, he won a scholarship to the Oxford summer meeting, and fell in with the WEA group there. As a result 'he got converted and at once started to be an apostle of sweetness and light'. He became a pillar of the WEA, in Swindon, in the Western district and nationally. He was elected to borough and county councils, interesting himself mainly in education; served as mayor of Swindon; and unsuccessfully contested Chippenham as a Labour parliamentary candidate. He lived a simple life, a life of unselfish service to his fellow men, and when he died the whole town turned out to mourn. The bishop of Bristol officiated at his funeral, and Mansbridge preached the sermon.[28]

Alfred Williams (1877–1929) was frequently cited by Mansbridge to illustrate one of his favourite themes, 'workmen-scholars'. For twenty years he worked, mainly as a hammerman, in the railway works in Swindon. He studied in the early morning before going to work, at meal-times and in the evening. He taught himself French, Latin and Greek, and, during army service in India in the first world war, Sanskrit. He wrote four books on industrial and rural life as well as some volumes of poetry, and published translations of classics from Latin, Greek and Sanskrit—a total of thirteen works. Williams spoke at many WEA meetings, and was the subject of a book by Leonard Clark.[29]

The ideas expressed in the fifth main category of Mansbridge's writings— about his beliefs and sources of inspiration—help to explain his choice of two working-men who lived very simply but climbed to great heights through devotion to scholarship or disinterested public service. These writings—Part III of *The Trodden Road*, and most of the essays and lectures published in *The Kingdom of the Mind*—show a profound respect for the dignity of manual labour. In a sermon preached in 1918 in Salisbury Cathedral, he said,

> Labour has for its purpose the strength and glory of human life. It ... has always been in its essence the sweetest, the most uniform of all human occupations. Yet, in our stupidity, we have thought it to be inferior and even degrading. Even when we have not been oppressors, we have stood by, sheltering behind some artificial economic doctrine whilst the workers have been sacrificed on the altar of the false god of profit.[30]

Mansbridge considered that 'the greatest happiness of the ordinary man lies in making things'. The growth of mass production had 'steadily diminished ... the area of employment for fine craftsmanship'. He looked

179

to the expansion of craft education in LEA evening institutes to provide an alternative means of satisfying the creative urge. He never imagined that more than a relatively small minority would be able to, or would wish to, meet the intellectual demands of the university tutorial class:

> only a small proportion of working men and women, as, indeed, of other men and women, possess the student mind and have, together with interest in a subject, the ability to persist in it. Adult Education should cover the whole of life; everything that is legitimate should be included in its scope, whether it be manual or mental.

For the same reason, he was critical of what he saw as the excessively literary bias of some schools, and argued for the complementary encouragement of craft skills. Mansbridge was fond of quoting or paraphrasing St Paul's reference to 'a diversity of gifts ... but the same spirit'. For example, 'A man who seeks training out of harmony with his gifts ... is hindering his education.'[31]

Almost every page of Mansbridge's 'inspirational' writings shows that the mainspring of his life and thought was a Christian faith that was intense and simple.

> In common with men of all time I have sought for the vision of God ... I have learned that the greatest discernible work in the world, whether in scholarship or in practical affairs, has been accomplished by those who did it confessedly in the power of their spirits.

He was very critical of outward observances which did not touch the soul.

> I have known men, not only in the world of business but in working-class organisations, become rapacious and selfish, wax fat and overbearing, as their unsatisfied appetites fed on success. Often they were pillars of churches, utilizing Sunday as a day of glossy glory.

He was also scathing about clergymen whose concern for status or possessions made it 'hard for a meanly clad man or woman to enter many churches and chapels'.[32]

'The overwhelming need of the present', Mansbridge argued, was that 'Man must be brought to realize that the only things that matter are the

180

forces of reality, which proceed from the Throne of God.' He was fond of talking about 'the forces of reality' and about 'positive and true qualities', by which he meant forces in harmony with the divine will. In his later years he became convinced that these forces were of positive value to physical as well as spiritual health. He wrote in *The Trodden Road*, 'I realized that my rightness or health of body as of mind depended in the main on my conscious and regular opening of myself to the rhythm of the good.' This practice 'increases the health of the body and renders it increasingly immune to disease.' He carried the idea further in unpublished notes and conversations with friends; 'the true functioning of limbs, organs and thoughts depends upon God-created forces ... If all men relied solely upon these forces, disease would vanish from their lives.'[33]

He devised his own spiritual exercises, which he described as a daily 'bath in reality'. Dr Ronald Hope of the Seafarers' Education Service understood him to be talking about a 'bath in grace', but in Mansbridge's conception reality and grace were more or less synonymous:

> begin by welcoming the God-created real forces into any part or organ of his being that he can conceive, perhaps giving increased welcome into any part which aches or is not working normally ... it lifts one's outlook and thoughts to higher levels ... In a sense it is prayer ... prayer should be gratitude rather than asking.

He did not rule out the use of doctors and medicines where necessary, but claimed that he had managed without them for many years by using his method: 'rejoice in the working of the Natural forces ... welcome them through the pores of the whole body'.[34]

There is no doubt that, in matters of the spirit as well as in attitudes to education, Mansbridge was profoundly influenced by Charles Gore. In one of his essays on the latter, he quoted from Gore's Bampton Lectures of 1890 on the theme of the Incarnation.

> To you ... brethren ... the document of God's offer in Jesus Christ is once again presented. It is black with the signatures, it is red with the seals of those who ... have given in their assent 'that God is true' ... You cannot evade your responsibilities; you must at the last issue confess or deny; you must sign or repudiate.

Mansbridge commented, 'It was the appeal of his life ... Ever after it would seem the vision he then saw so clearly sufficed him. He had seen the Lord and was satisfied.' Mansbridge himself drew strength from the simplicity of his own faith. He had little interest in doctrinal controversies. 'I am inspired and sustained by Faith, which is the greatest power I possess ... As ... my positive and true qualities develop, my comprehension of God will develop also.'[35]

The mantle of simplicity which fitted Mansbridge's religious beliefs so well was, however, a rather threadbare garment for an educationist. As his role gradually changed from innovator to sage, his educational ideas did not develop in depth or complexity. His favourite definition of the method and purpose of education, which he used repeatedly, was, 'In the power of the Spirit, through knowledge and training, to order the material of the world for the welfare of man and the glory of God.' This basic idea was sometimes expressed in more colourful language.

> The end of education is a joyous life for all men, shot through indeed with that inevitable sorrow of earth destined one day to be caught up again in the certain joy of heaven. Wisdom, knowledge, training, are all part of the matter, the spirit fuses them, and man goes forth on his quest and adventure ...[36]

The terms used over and over again in Mansbridge's writings on education, such as 'sufficient', 'real', 'right direction', were never adequately defined. He was happy to use them if they carried the spirit of his message. This was particularly true of those published works, including nine of the seventeen papers in *The Kingdom of the Mind*, which are transcripts of lectures or sermons. One of Mansbridge's own favourites amongst his public addresses was 'The Waters of Learning', the commencement oration given at the University of Pittsburgh in 1927. Amongst its key passages are the following:

> The universities of the New World, when true to their mission, are gathering places of the waters of learning, sending out streams of fertilising power, which have left a multifarious people, untrammelled, adventurous and alert, until the day of their great opportunity, which although not yet, is surely near at hand.
> The big thing in the life of a nation is the spirit of her people. If that is working freely and magnificently as a dynamic force, then mighty buildings,

mills of steel and repositories of treasure make up a glorious vesture indeed to be worn with grace; but, if that spirit works enslaved and feebly, then buildings, steel and gold become a burden and a reproach, the instruments of vice and destruction.

Strip away the 'rhetorical ornament', to quote Marriott's criticism of Mansbridge's Oxford paper in 1899, and what is left?[37] Mansbridge's work translated more effectively from the spoken to the written form when he was not trying so hard to be profound. His lecture on 'The Dynamic of Life', given at a conference of industrial managers and foremen in 1932, was a homely and humorous address, in which he drew upon his own experiences, and the example of some of his distinguished friends, to provide a mixture of moral uplift and practical advice on human relations. He urged the managers to believe in their staff, to devolve responsibility, to make room for different kinds of ability and to look for more talent in 'awkward' youngsters than in those who were neat and docile. When he came to the 'power of the spirit' theme, which appears in most of his inspirational speeches and writings, he tried to develop it in simple language. St Paul, he explained, had said most of what he wanted to say in the discourse on charity in his first letter to the Corinthians.

> For charity, or love, means leaving behind all selfish isolation, and entering into a vaster life ... It means the sense of unity, and of willing sacrifice for the whole of which we are a part, that is the mother of all virtues. We gain strength from it ... because it lifts us out of the weakness, the captivity of selfishness ... those who live in the spirit become, as it were, power-houses, both receiving and giving out all that is best and truest.[38]

The impact of Mansbridge's addresses cannot be judged by reading them as literature. The atmosphere, the voice and above all the personality of the man are wanting. Many of his friends would have agreed with Percy Redfern that he was 'an orator rather than a writer. His words most come to life when transformed by the passion of his personality.'[39] There is abundant evidence of his ability to move and inspire audiences of widely differing characters. When Christopher Turnor wrote to Mansbridge in 1940 after reading *The Trodden Road*, he still remembered vividly the impact of Mansbridge's speech to the dinner at the Working Men's College in 1913, just before the visit to Australia, and particularly the reaction of the editor of *The Times* which is described in Chapter 5.[40]

Harold Begbie was fascinated by Mansbridge's voice, 'its tremendous, hissing, almost fanatical intensity ... This voice is the man himself.'[41] William Temple was struck by

> his astonishing power of presenting his case in precisely the form that would most appeal to his audience on any occasion ... He did not present different aspects of the Association [the WEA] to different people; he always gave them the whole truth; but by a gift of almost universal sympathy he was able to take the standpoint of those whom he was addressing ... employing by a sure instinct the phraseology that was natural to them.[42]

Some of the friends who knew Mansbridge only in his later years saw him essentially as a man with a spiritual message. George Keeton, who worked closely with him in the World Association and the London Institute for World Affairs, summed him up more accurately as 'a curious mixture of prophetic fire and business shrewdness'.[43] Werner Picht had made a similar point in 1912 when he wrote of the WEA, 'here at last the organising and the prophetic spirit meet'.[44] Without his remarkable talents as an organizer and manipulator, Mansbridge's evangelical zeal and 'gift of tongues' might have achieved very little.

In one of his gloomier moments, harassed by the problems encountered in setting up the Central Joint Advisory Committee for Tutorial Classes, Mansbridge lamented to Zimmern,

> Why on earth did I become an educationist—not that but a mover of pieces about. All my instincts are domestic—to work from 9 am to 6 pm writing invoices and then home to tea, that's my line, to meddle about in a garden and all one's happiness to depend on whether a rose blooms or no.[45]

But it was not Mansbridge's destiny to cultivate his garden and live as a private man. He and Frances had been guided by the right instincts when, on their courtship walks, they had resolved 'to do good work'.[46] He was fortunate in finding a cause to which his talents were so well suited, and rich in the friendships which helped him to find his way.

Four days before he died, Mansbridge woke from a sleep and said, 'I have had a lovely talk with Charles Gore.'[47] It was fitting that his thoughts were with Gore at the end, for it was in the latter's house that he had first glimpsed the promised land of knowledge and wisdom which was his inspiration for the rest of his life. It was there, wrote Mansbridge, that he had made his 'entry into a bigger world of affairs', and had received encouragement for 'every thought and aspiration'.[48]

Two memorial services were held after Mansbridge's death, one in Gloucester cathedral, where his ashes were laid to rest, and the other in the church of St Martin in the Fields, in the centre of London. After the latter service Maude Royden wrote to Frances Mansbridge, 'That was a beautiful service and what a tremendous crowd! ... I kept thinking how many of those serried ranks of men must have owed their entrance into a new world of light and beauty to your husband.'[49] Tawney read the lesson, and the preacher was Bishop Bell of Chichester, who as a young curate had met Mansbridge at the Oxford summer school in 1909 and fallen under his spell. He, too, paid tribute to Mansbridge's 'extraordinary gift for convincing men and women of all classes and creeds, and enlisting them in his crusade'. Bishop Bell attributed his achievements to the inter-weaving of three factors, his zest for knowledge, his deep love of humanity and his profound religious faith.

> It was these three united that made him the great prophet-founder of the W.E.A. ... Albert Mansbridge was a great man ... his life was a dedicated life, dominated by a single purpose ... May God in His mercy raise up many more brave and generous spirits in this country who, after his example, will dedicate their lives to the service of mankind.[50]

# References and Notes

## Location of Manuscript Sources

Birmingham University
  Joint Board with WEA                  Birmingham Central Library

British Institute of Adult Education    NIACE
                                          21 de Montfort Street
                                          Leicester

Central Joint Advisory Committee        Rewley House MSS and
  for Tutorial Classes                     WEA Central Archives

Leonard Clark MSS                       Mills Memorial Library
                                          McMaster University, Hamilton
                                          Ontario (where they are known as
                                          the Mansbridge MSS)

Ed (PRO Reference)                      Public Record Office, Kew

Manchester University Joint Committee   John Rylands Library
  and Extension records                   University of Manchester

Mansbridge MSS                          British Library
                                          ADD MS 65231

Reading WEA branch records              Thames and Solent WEA District
                                          6 Brewer Street, Oxford

Rewley House MSS                        Bodleian Library, Oxford

Rochdale WEA branch records             Rochdale Public Library

Royal Army Educational Corps MSS        National Army Museum
                                          Hospital Road, Chelsea

Ruskin College MSS                      Ruskin College, Oxford

South Wales WEA Records                 South Wales WEA District
                                          11 Station Terrace
                                          Crowbridge Road West, Cardiff

Stuart House MSS                        Cambridge University Library

WEA Central Archives                    University of North London

World Association for Adult Education   NIACE, Leicester

Zimmern MSS                             Bodleian Library, Oxford

186

## Published Works: place of publication London unless otherwise stated

### 1: The young and enthusiastic Co-operator

1  A. Mansbridge, *The Trodden Road* (1940), 9–13, and *The Making of an Educationist* (1929), 12.

2  *The Trodden Road*, 15–17.

3  *The Trodden Road*, 10–13; *The Making of an Educationist*, 10–11.

4  *The Trodden Road*, 18–20, 43; information from the Mansbridge family.

5  *The Making of an Educationist*, 13.

6  H. Begbie, *Living Water: being chapters from the romance of the poor student* (nd [1918]), 176–177.

7  *The Trodden Road*, 231; *The Making of an Educationist*, 14.

8  *The Trodden Road*, 23, 236; *The Making of an Educationist*, 17.

9  *The Trodden Road*, 24–36; Begbie, 177–178.

10  *The Trodden Road*, 36.

11  Mansbridge, 'Some Aspects of Oxford: from a worker's point of view', *Millgate Monthly* 1:12 (September 1906), 716.

12  A. Mansbridge to Thomas Mansbridge [nd], Mansbridge MSS; *Co-operative News*, 6 August 1898.

13  *The Making of an Educationist*, 18; *The Trodden Road*, 24.

14  *The Trodden Road*, 24–29; *The Making of an Educationist*, 15; C. Gore, *The Sermon on the Mount* (1896).

15  *The Trodden Road*, 30–38; correspondence in Mansbridge MSS 1895–96.

16  *The Trodden Road*, 3, 29, 38–44.

17  Margot C. Finn, *After Chartism* (Cambridge, 1993), 106–110, 132–134, 140–141, 151–152; J. Birchall, *Co-op: the people's business* (Manchester, 1994), chapters 3 and 4; Co-operative Congresses 1896 and 1897, *Reports*; *Co-operative News*, May–August 1899.

18  B. Jennings, *The University Extension Movement in Victorian and Edwardian England* (Hull, 1992), 2–3; E. Welch, *The Peripatetic University : Cambridge Local Lectures 1873–1973* (Cambridge, 1973), chapter 2; N. A. Jepson, *The Beginnings of English University Adult Education* (1973), 24, 66, 81, 83; J. F. C. Harrison, *Learning and Living, 1790–1960* (1961), 221–225.

19  Jepson, 82–87, 101; Stuart Marriott, *Extramural Empires: service and self-interest in English university adult education 1873–1983* (Nottingham, 1984), 21–34.

20  W. H. Draper, *University Extension 1873–1923* (Cambridge, 1923), 42.

21  Jennings, 3–4.

22  Jennings, 4–5; Jepson, chapter 9; H. J. Mackinder and M. E. Sadler, *University Extension, Past, Present and Future* (1891), 49.

23  Draper, 60–63, 148–149; J. A. R. Marriott, *Memories of Four Score Years* (1946), 105–116; *Co-operative News*, 2 September 1899.

24  Jepson, 99, 128.

25  Harrison, 239–240; R .D. Roberts, *Eighteen Years of University Extension* (1891), 59–60.

26  B. Jennings (ed), *Pennine Valley: a history of upper Calderdale* (Otley, 1992), 183–186; R. Halstead, 'Working men and university extension', *Oxford University Extension Gazette*, May 1893.

27  Oxford Extension Delegacy, *Annual Reports 1887–1900*; *Co-operative News*, 7 December 1895, 5 August and 23 September 1899, 5 January 1901.

28  J. Burrows, *University Adult Education in London: a century of achievement* (1976). 8, 18–19; J. A. R. Pimlott, *Toynbee Hall* (1935), 59–71; R. A. Evans, 'The University and the City: the educational work of Toynbee Hall 1884–1914', *History of Education* 11:2 (1982), 113–115.

29  Co-operative Congresses 1896 and 1897, *Reports*; *Co-operative News*, May–August 1899.

30  *Co-operative News*, 25 May 1895, 26 November 1898; Co-operative Congress 1898, *Report*; *University Extension Journal*, May and October 1897.

31  *Co-operative News*, 24 July 1897.

32  *Wheatsheaf*, November 1897.

33  *Co-operative News*, 3 July 1897, 6 August 1898.

34  *Co-operative News*, 1898, various references; Co-operative Congress 1898, *Report*, 72, 157–159; *The Trodden Road*, 58.

35  Jennings, *Pennine Valley*, 183.

36  *Co-operative News*, 22 October 1898, 15 July 1899.

37  *Co-operative News*, 19 August 1899; *Oxford Journal*, 19 August 1899; *Oxford Chronicle*, 19 August 1899.

38  Gore to Mansbridge 24 and 26 August 1899, Mansbridge MSS; *Co-operative News*, 26 August 1899.

39  Lectures and Addresses no 50, Mansbridge MSS.

40  *The Making of an Educationist*, 18–19; *The Trodden Road*, 58–59.

41  *The Trodden Road*, 29, 44–45; C. A. Wase to Mansbridge 2 May 1899, W. Strann to clerk of Islington Vestry 25 January 1900, Mansbridge MSS.

42  M. E. Sadler to Mansbridge 2 May and 13 July 1899; J. M. Knight to London School Board 4 July 1899; G. H. Poulton to Islington Vestry 29 January 1900, Mansbridge MSS; *The Trodden Road*, 42–43.

43  *The Trodden Road*, 45; *Co-operative News*, 29 March 1902.

44  *The Trodden Road*, 45.
45  Correspondence with John Carter, J. L. Paton and others, 1901–02, Mansbridge MSS.
46  Correspondence: Mansbridge to Mrs Mansbridge April 1902, Mansbridge MSS; *Co-operative News*, 12 April 1902.
47  G. J. Holyoake, *A History of Co-operation* (1908), 622–626, 634–635, 648, 662–675.

## 2: The Founding of the WEA

 1  *Co-operative News*, 27 May 1899, 15 July 1899, 2 June 1900, 1902–03 various references; Co-operative Congress 1903, *Report*, 79 and 1925 *Report*, 10.
 2  H. J. Twigg, *An Outline of Co-operative Education* (Manchester, 1924), 31; *University Extension Journal*, October 1899; *Co-operative News*, 24 February 1900, 31 August 1901.
 3  *Young Oxford*, vols 1–4; the general circular of Ruskin Hall, bound at the end of volume 2.
 4  *Young Oxford*, 1:1 and 2.
 5  A. Mansbridge, *An Adventure in Working–class Education* (1920), 11.
 6  Royal Commission on Trade Disputes and Trade Combinations 1903–06, *Report*, Cd 2825 of 1906; P. Bagwell, *The Railwaymen* (1963), 206–226.
 7  William Beveridge, *Power and Influence* (1953), 25.
 8  *The Trodden Road*, 60–61.
 9  T. W. Price, *The Story of the Workers' Educational Association 1903–24* (1924), 15–16; Lectures and Addresses no 50, Mansbridge MSS; WEA Central EC Minutes, Report on provisional work, 1 October 1903.
10  *Co-operative News*, 22 October 1898, 17 May 1902; Price, 16; *The Trodden Road*, 61; *An Adventure in Working–class Education*, 12; WEA Central EC, Minutes of Provisional Committee July–August 1903.
11  WEA, *The Working Classes and Higher Education* (conference papers, 1903); WEA, *The Higher Education of Working Men* (conference report 1903); *Co-operative News*, 29 August, 12 September 1903; Price, 17; *An Adventure in Working–class Education*, 14; WEA Central EC Minutes 28 July–1 October 1903.
12  *Co-operative News*, 28 December 1901, 19 December 1903; *The Trodden Road*, 67; B. Jennings, 'Robert Halstead', in J. M. Bellamy and J. Saville (eds), *Dictionary of Labour Biography*, VI (1982), 1–7.
13  WEA Central EC Minutes 1903–06; *Co-operative News*, 26 December 1903.
14  *Co-operative News*, 13 August 1904.

15  *Co-operative News*, 15 October 1904.

16  *Co-operative News*, 8 October 1904; Price, 19–20; *The Trodden Road*, 62–63; W. J. Souch, *The History of the Reading Branch of the Workers' Educational Association 1904–54* (Reading, 1954), 6–9; Reading Branch Minutes 1904.

17  Price, 24; *University Extension Journal*, February and April 1903; *Co-operative News*, 19 November 1904.

18  Souch, 7–8; Price, 19–21; *The Trodden Road*, 62–63; WEA Central EC Minutes 1 December 1904; Mansbridge, article in *University Extension* 1904–05, no 1; Reading Branch Minutes 23 November 1904.

19  WEA Central EC Minutes December 1904–March 1905; Rochdale Education Guild Minutes April–November 1905; Price, 21–5; *Rochdale Observer*, 12 April 1905; *University Extension* 1904–05, no 3.

20  *Co-operative News*, 13 August, 19 November 1904; Rochdale Education Guild, *Handbook and Calendar 1908–09*, 21; PRO Ed 24/461.

21  *Co-operative News*, 19 August 1905; WEA, *Attendance at Evening Schools* (Memorandum to Board of Education, 1905), published 1906.

22  *An Adventure in Working–class Education*, 17; Ed 24/461.

23  W. E. Bullock, *Should Co-operators Support the Workers' Educational Association?* (paper read at Derby 28 July 1906 and published as a pamphlet); WEA Central EC Minutes 13 January 1906; Consultative Committee of the Board of Education, *Report on the Attendance, compulsory or otherwise, at Continuation Schools*, Cd 4757–8 of 1909.

24  WEA Central EC Minutes 24 February 1905 and AGM Minutes 14 October 1905; *Co-operative News*, 21 October 1905.

25  WEA AGM Minutes 14 October 1905.

26  WEA Central EC Minutes 2 December 1905.

27  WEA Central Finance Committee Minutes 6 October 1908; *An Adventure in Working–class Education*, 24, 69–72.

28  Draft statement of aims, *Official Report of the Inaugural Conference of An Association to Promote the Higher Education of Working Men* (1903).

29  WEA, *Annual Reports 1905–07*.

30  WEA, *Annual Reports 1905–07*; *Co-operative News*, 16 December 1905; *University Extension* 1906–07, no 2, 17.

31  *University Extension* 1904–05, no 3, 19, 1905–06 no 3, 15; Price, 30; Rochdale Education Guild Minutes 1905–06.

32  Price, 30; WEA, *Annual Report 1906–07*.

33  Price, 30; A. Mansbridge, 'Workpeople and the university', *University Review* 1:4 (August 1905); WEA, *Annual Report 1906–07*.

34  A. Mansbridge, *University Tutorial Classes* (1913), 16–17.

## 3: Oxford and Working-Class Education

1   J. A. R. Marriott, 'The higher education of working men', *Fortnightly Review* New Series 80 (July–December 1906), 247; Henrietta Barnett, *Canon Barnett: his life and work* (two vols, 1918) II, 195; G. D. H. Cole, *The World of Labour* (1915), 15, 288–290.

2   Marriott, 247, 251–255.

3   A. E. Zimmern, 'Oxford in the new century', *Independent Review* 11:37 (October 1906), 95–104; *Hansard*, 24 July 1907, CLXXVIII, 1526–33.

4   R. Terrill, *R. H. Tawney and His Times* (1973), 23–29; F. A. Iremonger, *William Temple: his life and letters* (Oxford, 1948), chapters 3 and 4; Jose Harris, *William Beveridge: a biography* (Oxford, 1977), 48–51, 61–63, 76–81; correspondence between Temple, Tawney and Zimmern, October–November 1905, Zimmern MSS.

5   S. A. Barnett, 'University settlements', *University Review* 1:2(June 1905), 129–135.

6   *The Trodden Road*, 64; *An Adventure in Working–class Education*, 16–17; Harris, 52; A. Wright, *R. H. Tawney* (Manchester, 1987), 4–5; WEA AGM Minutes 14 October 1905; *Ilford Recorder*, 30 June 1906.

7   Henrietta Barnett, II, 110–111.

8   *Westminster Gazette*, 15 February–10 March 1906.

9   E. Jenks to S. A. Barnett, 19 May 1906, R. H. Tawney to A. E. Zimmern, 21 May 1906, Zimmern MSS.

10   Mansbridge to Zimmern, 26 June 1906, Zimmern MSS; *The Trodden Road*, 20; H. P. Smith, *Labour and Learning* (Oxford, 1956), 23; WEA, *Annual Report 1905–06*.

11   Zimmern, 'Oxford in the New Century'.

12   *Hansard*, 24 July 1907.

13   Zimmern, 'A College head on university reform', *Fortnightly Review* New Series 82 (July–December 1907), 744.

14   Mansbridge, *University Tutorial Classes*, 18; Price, *The Story of the Workers' Educational Association 1903–24*, 31; Rochdale Education Guild, Minutes of Conference, 18 July 1907.

15   *University Tutorial Classes*, 19–20.

16   Correspondence relating to the establishment of tutorial classes 1907–08, Rewley House MSS; *Oxford Chronicle*, 16 August 1907.

17   Details of the speeches at the conference come from a manuscript in the WEA Central Office archives which is apparently a verbatim record of the major contributions, and from the *Oxford Chronicle*, 16 August 1907. The speech of

J. M. Mactavish is reproduced, in a slightly shortened form, in *University Tutorial Classes*, 194–197.

18  WEA, *Papers submitted to the National Conference, 10 August 1907* (1907); Terrill, 37–38.

19  *An Adventure in Working-class Education*, 38; *Justice*, 24 August 1907; *Clarion*, 16 August 1907.

20  Price, 37.

21  Price, 37; *University Tutorial Classes*, 26; *Oxford Chronicle*, 16 August 1907.

22  Correspondence relating to the establishment of tutorial classes 1907–08; R. Morant to Mansbridge 4 December 1911, Mansbridge MSS.

23  *University Tutorial Classes*, 21, 27; Price, 37.

24  W. W. Jackson, 'Some problems of university reform', *Fortnightly Review* New Series 82 (July–December 1907), 562–574; J. A. R. Marriott, 'Oxford and the nation', *Nineteenth Century* 62 (July–December 1907), 674–688.

25  Mansbridge to Zimmern 20 August 1907, Zimmern MSS; WEA Central EC Minutes 19 October 1907.

26  WEA Central EC Minutes 19 October 1907; correspondence relating to the establishment of tutorial classes 1907–08.

27  Correspondence relating to the establishment of tutorial classes 1907–08; Price, 32; *University Tutorial Classes*, 19.

28  Price, 33–34; Early Documents on Tutorial Classes, Rewley House MSS; R. A. Lowe, 'Some forerunners of R. H. Tawney's Longton tutorial class', *History of Education* 1:1 (January 1972), 43–56; Wright, *R. H. Tawney*, 5–6.

29  Correspondence relating to the establishment of tutorial classes 1907–08; Tutorial Classes Committee Early Papers; 'Workers' Joint Committee' file, in 'Miscellaneous Early Extension Files'; all Rewley House MSS.

30  J. A. R. Marriott, *Memories of Four Score Years* (1946), 139.

31  Correspondence relating to the establishment of tutorial classes 1907–08.

32  WEA, *Annual Report 1908–09*.

33  Correspondence relating to the establishment of tutorial classes 1907–08; J. M. Mactavish to Zimmern 14 September 1908, Zimmern MSS.

34  Sylvia Harrop (ed), *Oxford and Working-class Education* (new edn, Nottingham, 1987), 141–142.

35  Harrop (ed), 150–154, 158–160.

36  Correspondence relating to the establishment of tutorial classes 1907–08.

37  Correspondence relating to the establishment of tutorial classes 1907–08; correspondence in Zimmern MSS; WEA Central EC Minutes 2 December 1908.

38  Marriott to Dr T. B. Strong 26 June 1908, 'Workers' Joint Committee' file;

memoranda in same file; *Oxford and Working–class Education*, 131–134.

39 *Oxford and Working–class Education*, 184; 'Workers' Joint Committee' file.

40 *Toynbee Record* 21:3 (December 1908), 40–42.

41 Mansbridge, 'What workpeople want from Oxford', *Socialist Review* 3 (March–April 1909), 173–177.

42 *Nation*, 6 February 1909.

43 *The Times*, 25 January 1909.

44 *Morning Leader*, 2 December 1908.

45 F. C. S. Schiller, 'Oxford and the working man', *Fortnightly Review* 93 (1913), 766–778.

46 *Nineteenth Century* 65 (March 1909), 521–534.

47 *Oxford Magazine* 27, 205–206; *Oxford Chronicle*, 12 February 1909; information from Elliott Dodds and Nathaniel Micklem.

48 H. H. Turner to Zimmern 15 February 1909 and correspondence April 1912, Zimmern MSS.

49 *Labour Leader*, 27 November 1908; J. R. MacDonald to Mansbridge 4 December 1908, Tutorial Classes Committee Early Papers III, Rewley House MSS.

50 E. N. Bennett, 'What can Oxford offer to the working man?', *Socialist Review* 2 (January 1909), 852–856; W. A. Spooner, 'Oxford University reform : is a commission necessary?', *Church Quarterly Review* 65 (January 1908), 415–442; *Morning Post*, 19 February 1908.

51 F. W. Kolthammer, 'Oxford and working–class education', *Sociological Review* 2 (1909), 74–80.

52 W. Runciman to Mansbridge 17 February 1909, Cuttings File C, Mansbridge MSS.

53 H. Barnett, *Canon Barnett: his life and work*, II, 110–111; L. Goldman, *Dons and Workers: Oxford and adult education since 1850* (Oxford, 1995), 156–158; Mansbridge to Zimmern 17 November 1909, Zimmern MSS; A. Mansbridge, *How the Workpeople of England can utilize the Universities* (Manchester, 1910), 5.

54 Lord Curzon, *Principles and Methods of Universities Reform* (Oxford, 1909), 50–51, 61–65.

55 *Nation*, 10 July 1909.

56 *Nation*, 3 September 1910; H. P. Smith, *Labour and Learning*, 56.

57 *Cambridge Review*, 17 October 1907.

58 S. Ball, 'What Oxford can do for workpeople', WEA, *Papers submitted to the National Conference, 10 August 1907*.

59 D. H. S. Cranage, 'The University and the democracy', *Cambridge Review*,

17 October 1907; R. D. Roberts, 'The inwardness of the university extension movement', *University Review* 2:6 (October 1905).

60 *Hansard*, 24 July 1907.

61 *Nation*, 5 August 1911; WEA, *Annual Report 1907–08*; Burrows, *University Adult Education in London*, 36–37; W. A. Devereux, *Adult Education in Inner London* (1982), 122–123; S. Marriott, 'Oxford and working–class adult education: a foundation myth re-examined', *History of Education* 12:4 (1983), 287–288; Mansbridge, *University Tutorial Classes*,17; WEA Central EC Minutes 8 May, 11 December 1909.

62 *University Tutorial Classes*,17; WEA, *Annual Reports 1908–10*.

63 *Nation*, 5 August 1911.

64 *University Tutorial Classes*, 16; Mansbridge to Zimmern 2 March 1909 and [nd, May 1910], Zimmern MSS.

65 B. Bowen Thomas, 'R. D. Roberts and adult education', in B. B. Thomas (ed), *Harlech Studies* (Cardiff, 1938), 23–30.

66 H. H. Turner to Mansbridge 9 December 1908, Tutorial Classes Committee Early Papers I, Rewley House MSS.

## 4: Mansbridge the Evangelist

1 Mansbridge, *An Adventure in Working–class Education*, xviii, 23; R. H. Tawney, 'An Experiment in democratic education', *Political Quarterly*, May 1914, 73; articles by Mansbridge in *Highway*, October 1908–1913.

2 A. E. Zimmern, 'Education and the working–class', *Round Table*, no 14, (March 1914), 265–266.

3 WEA, *Annual Report 1906–07*; Bristol WEA, *Annual Report 1907–08* (copy in WEA Central Archives).

4 Rochdale Education Guild Minutes 1905–06; *Rochdale Observer*, 12 April 1905.

5 Rochdale Education Guild Minutes 1905–10 and *Handbook 1908–09*; Tutorial Classes Committee Early Papers II, Rewley House MSS; *Rochdale Observer*, 18 April 1908.

6 S. Yeo, *Religion and Voluntary Organisations in Crisis* (1976), 253; Ruth Hinder to F. Padley 5 February 1950; and J. Harris to F. Padley 5 March 1950, Reading WEA branch records.

7 T. W. E. Spir to F. Padley 6 January 1950; and Ruth Hinder to F. Padley 5 February 1950, Reading WEA branch records.

8 *Yorkshire Herald*, 5 April 1906; *Darwen News*, 7 April 1906; *Preston Guardian*, 7 April 1906; *Arrow*, May 1906; *South Wales Argus*, 25 April 1906.

9 *Northern Echo*, 17 September 1906; *Railway Review*, September–October

1906; *Kettering Leader*, 28 September 1906; *Sheffield Independent*, 1 October 1906.

10  Printed notice of Cricklewood meeting in Mansbridge MSS; *Co-operative News*, 6 October 1906.

11  *South Wales Daily News*, 8 October 1906; *Durham County Advertiser*, 12 October 1906; *Durham County Gazette*, 12 October 1906; WEA Central EC Minutes 8 December 1906.

12  WEA, *Annual Reports 1906–08*.

13  WEA, *Annual Reports 1905–07*; WEA AGM Minutes 14 October 1905; WEA Central EC Minutes December 1905–May 1906, 9 October 1909, 19 November 1910; Early WEA Districts file, Rewley House MSS; *Highway* December 1908; Mansbridge to Zimmern [nd, ?December 1909], Zimmern MSS; *The Workers' Educational Association 1909*.

14  Tutorial Class Papers 1909–11, Rewley House MSS; A. Mansbridge, *Arnold Toynbee* (1906); *C.W.S. Annual 1906*, 259–98; *Co-operative News*, September 1906–December 1911.

15  *An Adventure in Working–class Education*, 29–30.

16  WEA Central EC Minutes 9 February, 13 July 1907, Finance Committee Minutes 5 March, 7 July 1907.

17  Tutorial Class Papers 1909–11, Rewley House MSS.

18  WEA, *Annual Report 1908–09*; Central EC Minutes 25 February, 8 May 1909, 19 November 1910; *An Adventure in Working–class Education*, 29.

19  Central Joint Advisory Committee Minutes 2 October 1909, 26 February 1910, Rewley House MSS.

20  Iremonger, *William Temple: his life and letters*, 76–77.

21  Cambridge Syndicate Letter Book February 1909–October 1911, Stuart House MSS.

22  Mansbridge to Zimmern 17 November 1909 and 2 March 1910, Zimmern MSS.

23  Mansbridge, *University Tutorial Classes*, 142–163.

24  *University Tutorial Classes*, 136–141; Central Joint Advisory Committee Minutes 1 July 1910, 7 July 1911, 18 January 1913.

25  Tutorial Classes Committee Papers 1909–11, Rewley House MSS; Manchester University Joint Committee Minutes 24 April 1909, 1 May 1912, and Minutes of Senate Representatives on the Joint Committee 19 December 1911.

26  Tutorial Classes Committee Early Papers III, Early Documents Tutorial Classes Committee, 10 December 1909, 28 August 1911, Rewley House MSS.

27 Tutorial Classes Committee Papers 1909–11, Tutorial Classes Committee 1911, Rewley House MSS; S. C. Moore, 'The industrial evolution of a manufacturing village', *Economic Journal* 21 (1911), 613–624; Moore, 'An Industrial Survey', typescript, copy in possession of the author.

28 Tutorial Classes Committee Early Papers I, and E. S. Cartwright to Mansbridge in Early Documents Tutorial Classes Committee, Rewley House MSS.

29 *Highway*, August 1912.

30 Mansbridge to F. W. Kolthammer 3 January 1912, 'Tutorial Class Student Essays 1911', Mansbridge to Tawney 7 November 1911, Tutorial Classes Committee Papers 1909–11 and other references in the same file, Rewley House MSS; *University Tutorial Classes*, 140–141.

31 Mansbridge to Zimmern, [nd, May 1910], Zimmern MSS.

32 *University Tutorial Classes*, chapters V–VII; Tutorial Classes Committee 1911, Rewley House MSS; W. J. Ashley, review of *The Agrarian Problem in the Sixteenth Century*, *Economic Journal* 23 (1913), 85–89.

33 *University Tutorial Classes*, 116; Manchester Joint Committee Minutes 1909–13; Birmingham University Joint Board Minutes 1910–13.

34 *University Tutorial Classes*, 118–120.

35 *University Tutorial Classes*; CJAC Minutes 1910–12; WEA Central EC Minutes 17 February, 20 March 1912.

36 1913–14 Class Papers, Rewley House MSS.

37 *University Tutorial Classes*, 99–110, 188–193; WEA, *Annual Reports 1909–13*; Tutorial Classes Committee Papers 1909–11, Tutorial Classes Committee Early Papers III, Early Documents Tutorial Classes Committee, Rewley House MSS.

38 *University Tutorial Classes*, 107; Tutorial Classes Committee Papers 1909–11, Rewley House MSS; CJAC Minutes 7 July 1911; WEA Central EC Minutes 22 September 1913; Cambridge Joint Committee Minutes September–December 1913, Stuart House MSS.

39 WEA, *Annual Report 1912–13*; WEA Central EC Minutes 22 September 1913 and AGM Minutes 16 May 1914.

40 WEA, *Annual Reports 1908–13*; WEA Central EC Minutes April 1907–May 1908, Central Council Minutes 9 July 1910, 18 March 1911, and Minutes of National Demonstration, 16 October 1908; *Highway* 1908–11.

41 *Highway*, May, October, November 1909, June 1910, May 1911; WEA Central EC Minutes 19 September 1910, Central Council Minutes 7 May 1910, AGM Minutes 15 Oct 1910; H. G. Wood and A. E. Ball, *Tom Bryan, first Warden of Fircroft* (1922), 44–56.

42 *The Trodden Road*, 70.

43   WEA, *Annual Report 1907–08*.
44   WEA, *Annual Reports 1909–14*; WEA AGM Minutes 1909–13.
45   *Highway*, February 1910; Mansbridge to Zimmern [nd, February 1910], Zimmern MSS; Mansbridge to W. Aston, Wrexham 2 and 8 February 1910, Early Documents Tutorial Classes Committee, Rewley House MSS.
46   *Justice*, 12 October 1907, 19 December 1908; *Clarion*, 1 November 1907; *New Age*, 10 June 1909; Tawney to E. S. Cartwright 7 April 1911, Tutorial Classes Committee Early Papers III, Rewley House MSS; Mansbridge to Zimmern 17 November 1909, Zimmern MSS.
47   WEA AGM Minutes October 1908.
48   *The Trodden Road*, 68; Mansbridge to Zimmern [nd, May 1910], Zimmern MSS.
49   WEA, Speeches delivered at the Seventh Annual Meeting; WEA AGM Minutes 1909 and 1911; *An Adventure in Working–class Education*, 35; Goldman, *Dons and Workers*, 326.
50   *Highway*, February 1912.
51   WEA, *Annual Report 1908–09*; WEA AGM Minutes Oct 1911; *Cambridge Independent Press*, 14 August 1908; *Highway*, December 1909–February 1912.
52   Mansbridge, *The Education of the People*, reprinted from the official report of the Church Congress [nd].
53   L. V. Gill to Mansbridge 13 October 1907, in WEA Central EC Minute Book.
54   Information from W. H. Hosford; Mansbridge to W. T. Cope, Longton 22 October 1908, Tutorial Classes Committee Early Papers III, Rewley House MSS; Mansbridge to Zimmern [nd, May 1910], Zimmern MSS.
55   *Highway*, September 1910; WEA Central EC Minutes 10 July 1909; *The Trodden Road*, 105–106.
56   J. B. Paton to Frances Mansbridge 29 December 1910, Mansbridge MSS.
57   *The Trodden Road*, 162–163.
58   WEA Central EC Minutes 11 December 1909, 19 November 1910, March 1911–December 1912; WEA, *Annual Report 1912–13*; Tutorial Classes Committee Minutes 1 November 1911, Rewley House MSS; Mansbridge, *Brick upon Brick* (1934), 66.
59   WEA Central EC Minutes 1911–13.
60   Central EC Minutes 1911–13 and Central Council Minutes 18 March 1911, 13 July 1912; WEA, *Annual Report 1912–13*; C. R. Williams, 'Fifty years of adult education in South Wales', in *South Wales WEA District, Jubilee Year* (Cardiff, 1957), 5–10; South Wales/Wales District Minutes 1909–11; CJAC Reports 1910–14.

61 WEA Central EC Minutes 14 December 1912, 15 February 1913; Tutorial Classes Committee Minutes 21 July 1913, Rewley House MSS; Joint Committee Minutes 16 January 1914, Stuart House MSS; *The Trodden Road*, 72.
62 H. Clay to Mansbridge 3 June 1913, Mansbridge MSS.
63 *Highway*, June 1913; *The Trodden Road*, 72–73.

## 5: Friends and Enemies

1 H. P. Smith, *Labour and Learning*, 8.
2 *The Trodden Road*, 72–73; C. Turnor to Mansbridge 30 April 1940, Mansbridge MSS.
3 G. R. Searle, *The Quest for National Efficiency: a study in British politics and political thought 1899–1914* (Oxford, 1971), 1–13, 62–65, 75–78; H. G. C. Matthew, *The Liberal Imperialists : the ideas and politics of a post–Gladstonian elite* (Oxford, 1973), 224–230, 238–241; E. Ashby and Mary Anderson, *Portrait of Haldane at Work on Education* (1974), 103–111; D. Sommer, *Haldane of Cloan: his life and times* (1960), 124; *The Trodden Road*, 147; R. B. Haldane, *Education and Empire* (1902), 32–36; Mansbridge, 'The Functions of a modern university', *University Review* 6:33, 165.
4 Mansbridge, 'Workpeople and the university', *University Review* 1:4, 398; PRO Ed 24/199; C. F. G. Masterman, *The Condition of England* (1st edn 1909, Methuen edn 1960), 112.
5 Haldane, 32–40.
6 *The Trodden Road*, 147; Matthew, 129–130, 227–230.
7 WEA, *Attendance at Evening Schools* (1905); PRO Ed 24/197, 199, 461.
8 R. Morant to Mansbridge 4 December 1911, Mansbridge MSS.
9 Masterman, 53.
10 P. d'A. Jones, *The Christian Socialist Revival 1877–1914* (Princeton, New Jersey, 1968), 85, 164–184, 194–197, 213.
11 W. Temple, 'The Church and the Labour party', *Economic Review*, April 1908, 196–200.
12 J. M. Winter and D. M. Joslin (eds), *R. H. Tawney's Commonplace Book* (Cambridge, 1972), 30–31, 53, 61; R. H. Tawney, *The Acquisitive Society* (1921), 227–228.
13 *R. H. Tawney's Commonplace Book*, 52; R. Terrill, *R. H. Tawney and his Times* (1974), 37; Tawney, 'The theory of pauperism', *Sociological Review* 2 (1909), 361–374; J. M. Winter, 'R. H. Tawney's early political thought', *Past and Present* no 47, May 1970, 72–76; S. Ball, 'The moral aspects of socialism', *International Journal of Ethics* 6 (April 1896), 290–332; A. M. McBriar,

*Fabian Socialism and English Politics 1884–1918* (Cambridge, 1962), 74, 168.

14 S. Collini, *Liberalism and Sociology: L. T. Hobhouse and political argument in England 1880–1914* (Cambridge, 1979), 4, 51–67, 78–83; L. T. Hobhouse, *Democracy and Reaction* (1904), 227–229; Hobhouse, *Liberalism* [nd, 1911], 149–150, 159; Hobhouse, 'The historical evolution of property, in fact and in idea', in C. Gore (ed), *Property, its Rights and Duties* (1913), 21–22; Hobhouse, leading article in *Manchester Guardian*, 7 July 1899, quoted in P. F. Clarke, 'The Progressive movement in England', *Transactions of the Royal Historical Society* 5th series, 24 (1974), 167.

15 Book in the author's possession; *Nation*, 17 August 1907.

16 M. Richter, *The Politics of Conscience : T. H. Green and his age* (1964), 15–19, 30–35, 89–125, 284–296, 324–325; P. W. G. Lawson, 'Influences on the thought of the Lux Mundi school of theology' (unpublished MA thesis, University of Leeds, 1969), 18–20.

17 Lawson, 10–16, 27; Jones, chapter 1, 85, 164–167; Mansbridge, *Edward Stuart Talbot and Charles Gore* (1935), 88.

18 Hobhouse, *Manchester Guardian*, 7 July 1899; Jose Harris, 'Political thought and the Welfare State 1870–1940 : an intellectual framework for British social policy', *Past and Present* 135 (May 1992), 123, 137–138.

19 Maisie Ward, *Gilbert Keith Chesterton* (1944), 143.

20 Temple, 'The Church and the Labour party', 200–202.

21 T. A. Jackson, *Solo Trumpet* (1953), 60–64, 90, 97, 143–144, 153, 156–162; T. Bell, *Pioneering Days* (1941), 35, 40–41.

22 Bell, 56–57; J. Broom, *John Maclean* (Macdonald, Loanhead, 1973), 58–65; Nan Milton, *John Maclean* (Pluto Press, 1973), 40–41, 149.

23 *Young Oxford* I, nos 1, 3, 7, 9.

24 W. W. Craik, *Central Labour College* (1964), 37–39; H. Sanderson Furniss, *Memories of Sixty Years* (1931), 89–90; E. B. Forrest, 'A Labour college', *Independent Review* 9:31 (April 1906), 80–90; H. B. Lees Smith, 'Economic theory and proposals for a legal minimum wage', *Economic Journal* 17 (1907), 508–509.

25 Ruskin College Strike Records Vol I, Ruskin College MSS; Craik, 41–42, 48; 'Ruskin College' in Miscellaneous Early Files, University Extension, and Tutorial Classes Committee Early Papers II, Rewley House MSS; WEA Central EC Minutes 14 October, 2 December 1905.

26 Strike Records Vol I; Furniss, 90; *Oxford Chronicle*, 2 April 1909.

27 Craik, 38–39, 52–54; Furniss, 86–87, 97; L. T. Dodd and J. A. Dale, 'The Ruskin Hall movement', *Fortnightly Review* New Series 67 (1900), 334; W. H. Seed (ed), *The Burning Question of Education* (Oxford, 1909), 1–8; R. Lewis,

'The South Wales miners and the Ruskin College strike of 1909', *Llafur* 2:1, (Spring 1976), 57–72; *Clarion*, 8 May 1909.

28  J. Lawson, *A Man's Life* (1944), 102.

29  Strike Records Vol I; Craik, 28, 51–52; Furniss, 83, 92; Committee of Ruskin Students, *Ruskin College and Working–class Education* (Oxford, [nd]); *The Times*, 16 August 1907.

30  Furniss, 83–85, 92–94, 100–101; Seed, 7, 12.

31  Seed, 8–11; WEA Central Office, MS Report of Oxford Conference 1907.

32  Furniss, 92; Seed, 11; C. S. Buxton in *Cornhill Magazine*, August 1908.

33  Craik, 61–62; Furniss, 95; Strike Records Vol I; *Ruskin College and Working–class Education*; *Clarion*, 4 December 1908.

34  Strike Records Vol I; Furniss, 94–100.

35  Craik, 64 and chapter 5; Furniss, 99; Strike Records Vol I; *Oxford Chronicle*, 11 December 1908; Ruskin College, *Annual Report 1909*.

36  *The Story of Ruskin College* (3rd edn, Oxford, 1968), 17; Craik, 79–84; Furniss, 108–110; *Ruskin College and Working–class Education*; *Justice*, 28 August 1909; *Railway Review*, 3 September 1909.

37  *Railway Review*, 6 August 1909; Craik, chapter 6; Furniss, 103–104.

38  P. S. Bagwell, *The Railwaymen* (1963), 676; *Clarion*, 2 April 1909; Craik, 72–74; Strike Records Vol II.

39  *Clarion*, 8 May 1909; Craik, 67.

40  Craik, 74–75; *Oxford Chronicle*, 2 April 1909.

41  *Railway Review*, 2 July, 17 September 1909; J. C. Finch, Barry ASRS to Mansbridge 16 December 1907, Correspondence about the establishment of Tutorial Classes 1907–08, J. Murgatroyd to Mansbridge 4 December 1908, Tutorial Classes Committee Early Papers I, Rewley House MSS.

42  *Railway Review*, 2–16 July 1909; Craik, 86.

43  Bagwell, 678–679; *Railway Review*, April–October 1909.

44  *The Story of Ruskin College*, 18–19; Ruskin College, *Annual Reports 1909–10*; Strike Records Vol II.

45  Craik, 92–93.

46  Jackson, *Solo Trumpet*, 150–151

47  B. Simon, *Education and the Labour Movement 1870–1920* (1974), 318–325.

48  J. Saville, *The Labour Movement in Britain* (1988), 32.

9  B. Jennings, *Knowledge is Power: a short history of the WEA 1903–78* (Hull, 1979), 37–39.

50  Carolyn Steadman, *Childhood, Culture and Class in Britain: Margaret McMillan 1860–1931* (1990), 180.

51  J. Rée, *Proletarian Philosophers: problems in socialist culture in Britain 1900–40* (Oxford, 1984), 19–21.

52  Anne Phillips and Tim Putnam, 'Education for emancipation: the movement for Independent Working–class Education 1908–28', *Capital and Class* 10 (1980), 22–24; H. Pollins, *The History of Ruskin College* (Oxford, 1984), 36.

53  J. F. and Winifred Horrabin, *Working–class Education* (1924), 56–68.

54  W. H. Marwick, *A Short History of Labour in Scotland* (Edinburgh, 1976), 87–8; Nan Milton, *John Maclean*, 42–3; Nan Milton (ed), *John Maclean, In the Rapids of Revolution: essays, articles and letters 1902–23* (1978), 123.

55  Mary Stocks, *The Workers Educational Association: the first fifty years* (1953), 50.

56  Letter Frank Pickstock to B. Jennings [nd, received 18 December 1979], copy in WEA Central archives.

57  R. Miliband, *Capitalism and Democracy in Britain* (Oxford, 1982) and *Parliamentary Socialism* (2nd edn 1972); R. T. Fieldhouse, 'The 1908 Report: antidote to class struggle?', in Sylvia Harrop (ed), *Oxford and Working–class Education*, 45.

58  J. P. M. Millar, *The Labour College Movement* (1979), 131–132; Chushichi Tsuzuki, 'Anglo–Marxism and working–class education', in Jay Winter (ed), *The Working Class in Modern British History* (Cambridge, 1983), 198–199.

## 6: Expanding the WEA

1  Ann McKee, *Belfast Trades Council: the first hundred years 1881–1981* (Belfast, 1983), 16–17; *Highway*, May 1910; WEA, *Annual Reports 1909–11*.

2  CJAC *Reports 1910–14*; *Highway*, May 1911, November 1912.

3  Mansbridge, 'A Survey of working–class educational movements in England and Scotland', *C.W.S. Annual 1906*, 268.

4  J. S. G. Shearer, 'The Universities and adult education in Scotland', *Studies in Adult Education* 1 (1979), 140–150, and 'Town and Gown together' (reprinted from the *College Courant*, University of Glasgow, June and December 1976), 1–9; I. Bryant, *Radicals and Respectables: the adult education experience in Scotland* (Edinburgh, 1984), 1–10.

5  WEA, *Annual Reports 1905–10*; *Highway*, June 1909.

6  *Highway*, June 1913; WEA, *Annual Reports 1912–18*; Marwick, *A Short History of Labour in Scotland*, 87–8; 'The Universities and Adult Education in Scotland', 146–151.

7  The account of the visit of the Mansbridges to Australia draws heavily upon the unpublished text of the Mansbridge Memorial Lecture, entitled 'Mansbridge

and the WEA in Australia', given in Sydney in 1969 by Vernon Crew, then a resident tutor in the Department of Continuing Education at the Australian National University. A condensed version, 'Mansbridge and his mission to Australia', was published in *Australian Highway*, December 1969. The lecture and the published version are used by kind permission of Mr Crew, and are jointly cited as the Crew MS.

8 E. Jenks, 'Extension work in Victoria', *University Extension Journal*, 15 May 1892; Crew MS.

9 Crew MS; F. A. Iremonger, *William Temple: his life and letters*, 129–31.

10 E. M. Higgins, *David Stewart and the WEA* (Sydney, 1957), 21.

11 Mansbridge, *The Trodden Road*, 72; Crew MS; *Highway*, June 1913.

12 *The Trodden Road*, 74–78; Crew MS; Lectures and Addresses no 18, Mansbridge MSS.

13 *Highway*, June, September, December 1913, December 1914; *The Trodden Road*, 74; Crew MS.

14 Crew MS; *Highway*, December 1913.

15 *Highway*, November 1913; Crew MS.

16 *Highway*, November 1913, March 1914; Lectures and Addresses no 18; G. P. Barber to Mansbridge 4 September 1913, Mansbridge MSS; *The Trodden Road*, 77; V. Crew, 'The Beginnings of the WEA in Queensland', *Australian Journal of Adult Education* 9:2 (July 1969), 72–83; B. H. Molesworth, 'Workers education in Queensland 1913 to 1937', *Australian Journal of Adult Education* 8:2 (July 1968), 59–61; *Worker*, Brisbane, 18 April 1918.

17 *The Trodden Road*, 74–78; Crew MS.

18 L. T. Leathley, 'The beginnings of the WEA in Victoria', *Australian Journal of Adult Education* 3:1 (July 1963), 32–34; *Highway*, October 1913; Minutes of Conferences, WEA of Victoria, 1913–14, Clyde Cameron College, Wodonga, Victoria.

19 *Highway*, December 1913, December 1914; F. A. Bland, 'The WEA in Australasia', *WEA Education Year Book 1918*, 335–338; Crew MS.

20 Crew MS; Higgins, 19–20.

21 Higgins, 13–16.

22 Higgins, 19–22.

23 *The Trodden Road*, 76–79; *Highway*, October 1913; Crew MS.

24 Lectures and Addresses no 18; *Highway*, March, June 1914; Higgins, 23; Crew MS.

25 *The Trodden Road*, 77; Higgins, 19–20.

26 *Highway*, June, November, December 1913, February 1914; Barber to Mansbridge 2 September 1913; *The Trodden Road*, 79–81; 'A long–delayed letter', Mansbridge MSS; Bland, 'The WEA in Australasia', 338; Higgins, 29; A. B. Thompson, *Adult Education in New Zealand* (New Zealand Council for

Educational Research, 1945), 66, 72–84; J. B. Condliffe, *The Beginning of the WEA* (Wellington, NZ, 1968), 11–15.

27  'A long–delayed letter'.

28  Bland, 335–338.

## 7: Many More Fine Things

1  WEA, *Annual Report 1913–14*; Tutorial Classes Committee Minutes 23 May 1914, Rewley House Papers.

2  WEA Central EC Minutes 7 January 1914, 20 September 1915, Central Council Minutes 11 July 1914; *Annual Report 1913–14*.

3  *Annual Report 1913–14*; WEA Finance Committee Minutes November 1913–March 1914.

4  *The Trodden Road*, 83; *The Times*, 30 January 1914.

5  Dorothy Jones to W. J. Conybeare 19 June 1914 and J. A. Dale 17 June 1914, Mansbridge MSS.

6  *The Trodden Road*, 63–64, 83; *Answers*, 27 January 1934; Mansbridge, *Fellow Men* (1948), 26; information from John Mansbridge.

7  WEA Central EC Minutes 2 July 1914, Central Council Minutes 7 November 1914.

8  Cambridge Joint Committee Minutes February 1915, Stuart House MSS; WEA Central EC Minutes 6 March, 15 May 1915.

9  Mansbridge to Central EC 14 September 1915, in CEC Minute Book; WEA, *Report of 12th Annual Meeting 15–16 Oct 1915*.

10  Information from Dorothy Jones.

11  WEA Central EC Minutes 20 September 1915, Central Council 20 November 1915.

12  Central Council 20 November 1915; Lectures and Addresses no 50, Mansbridge MSS.

13  *The Trodden Road*, 84; WEA Central EC Minutes 19 February, 17 November 1916; CJAC Minutes 12 January, 13 July 1917; Cambridge Joint Committee Minutes 27 November 1917, Stuart House MSS; *Highway*, August 1917; Mansbridge to Patrick Gower 22 March 1924, Mansbridge MSS.

14  WEA Central EC Minutes 19 February 1916; *The Trodden Road*, 84–85; T. W. Price to Mansbridge 22 April 1916, Mansbridge MSS.

15  CJAC Minutes 16 July 1915, 14 January 1916; WEA Central EC Minutes 6 March 1915; *The Trodden Road*, 93–95.

16  *The Trodden Road*, 93; *Fellow Men*, 97–101; *DNB 20th Century 1931–40* (Kerr); *Who Was Who 1961–70* (Drummond).

17  *The Trodden Road*, 93.
18  *Yorkshire Evening Post*, 28 August 1916; *Times Educational Supplement*, 10 May 1917; F. J. Taylor, 'The Making of the 1919 Report', *Studies in Adult Education* 8:2 (October 1976), 138, 143.
19  Information from John Mansbridge and Dorothy Jones.
20  *Educational Times*, December 1915.
21  Mansbridge, 'Church Tutorial Classes : a proposal for the further education of adult churchmen and women', *Church Quarterly Review*, July 1917.
22  J. W. Povah (ed), *Students and the Faith* (1927), 36–45.
23  *The Trodden Road*, 102–103; Church Tutorial Classes Association, Memorandum from Central Council of Church for Religious Education, July 1943, Mansbridge MSS.
24  Iremonger, *William Temple*, chapters 13 and 15; *Challenge*, 22 June 1917; *Manchester Guardian*, 19 July 1917; *The Times*, 18 December 1918; *Morning Post*, 19 December 1918; Archbishops' Committee, *Christianity and Industrial Problems* (1918).
25  *Woolwich Pioneer*, 27 April 1917.
26  *Church Times*, 29 June 1917; *Challenge*, 29 June 1917.
27  *The Trodden Road*, 130–131; *The Times*, 19 December 1918; *Morning Post*, 19 December 1918.
28  *The Trodden Road*, 85–86; R. Morant to Mansbridge 21 January 1918, Mansbridge MSS.
29  Lord Gorell, *One Man ... Many Parts* (1956), 207–210; Mansbridge to Gorell September 1918–February 1919, Box RR 9/Ill, RAEC Archives (I am indebted for this reference to Major G. E. F. Beard); *The Trodden Road*, 86–90.
30  *The Trodden Road*, 96; WAAE, *Bulletin I* (1919), *IV* (November 1920).
31  WAAE, *Bulletin I*; *Co-operative News*, 20 September 1919; *Observer*, 12 October 1919.
32  *Highway*, May, July 1919; WEA Central Council Minutes 25 January 1919; R. B. Haldane, *An Autobiography* (1929), 149.
33  WAAE, *Bulletin I*; *Sunday Times*, 30 March 1919.
34  WAAE, *Bulletin I*, *VII* (February 1921).
35  WAAE, *Bulletin III* (February 1920), *VIII* (May 1921); *Co-operative News*, 20 September 1919.
36  R. Hope, *In Cabined Ships at Sea* (1969), 9, 24; *The Trodden Road*, 100–101.

37  *The Trodden Road*; Hope, 13, 21–22, 27–29, 48; WAAE, *Bulletin VIII*.
38  Taylor, 'The Making of the 1919 Report',143; H. Wiltshire (ed), *The 1919*

*Report* (Nottingham, 1980); *The Trodden Road*, 167.

39  Taylor, 144–146.

40  *The 1919 Report*, 4–5, 86–91, 150, 168–171.

41  Royal Commission on Oxford and Cambridge Universities, *Report*, Cmd 1589 of 1922.

42  WEA Central EC Minutes 23 July 1920.

43  T. W. Price, *The Story of the WEA 1903–24*, 56; A. J. Corfield, *Epoch in Workers' Education* (1969), 7–17, 244.

44  *An Adventure in Working–class Education*, 64–65.

45  Mansbridge, 'L'Association pour l'instruction des travailleurs', *Revue International du Travail* 6:3 (September 1922), 361.

46  Haldane, *An Autobiography*, 292–296; *Observer*, 14 November 1920; National Library of Scotland MS 5999 f 182.

47  Haldane, 297–298.

48  *The Trodden Road*, 99–100; D. Sommer, *Haldane of Cloan : his life and times* (1960), 333–334; WAAE, *Bulletin IX* (August 1921); BIAE, *List of Original Members* (1922).

49  Haldane, 296; *The Trodden Road*, 99; WAAE, *Bulletin IX, XIII* (May 1922).

50  *The Trodden Road*, 121; Royal Commission on Oxford and Cambridge Universities, *Report*, 41, 127–131.

51  *Report*, 57, 120–128, 160–163.

52  WAAE, *Bulletin III* (February 1920), *XIII* (August 1922); *Liverpool Daily Post*, 18 February 1922; *New York Times*, 9, 23 April 1922; *Toronto Daily Mail*, 18 March 1922.

53  *Canadian Forum* [nd, cutting in NIACE library]; *Varsity* [Toronto], 28 February 1922.

54  *Boston Evening Transcript*, 5 April 1922; *New York Times*, 23 April 1922.

55  J. L. Paton to Mrs Mansbridge 3 April 1922, Charles Wase to Mansbridge 4 July 1923, L.J. Thomson to Mansbridge 27 April 1923, Mansbridge MSS; *Morning Post*, 7 July 1923; *The Trodden Road*, 6, 126.

56  E. N. Wix to Mansbridge 10 Oct 1923, Mansbridge MSS.

57  *The Trodden Road*,124; PRO Ed 24/1913.

58  *Hansard* Fifth Series, Lords, Vol 53, 740; Ed 24/1914.

59  WEA Central EC and Finance Committee Minutes 1924–26; Oxford Delegacy Minutes 1924–27, Rewley House MSS; Welch, *The Peripatetic University*, 143–147; *The Trodden Road*, 127.

60  *Highway*, Summer 1924; *The Times*, 10 July 1924; WAAE, *Bulletin XXI* (August 1924), *XXIV* (May 1925).

61  T. Kelly, *A History of Public Libraries in Great Britain 1845–1975* (2nd ed,

1977), 215–216, 319; WAAE, *Bulletin XIX* (February 1924).

62 PRO Ed 24/1197 (I am indebted for this reference to Frank Withers).

63 Kelly, 234, 318–320; *The Trodden Road*, 95–96, 295–296; BIAE 9th AGM 24 May 1930.

64 BIAE General Purposes Committee 18 February 1922, 1st AGM 15 July 1922, Annual Conference Papers and Reports; WAAE, *Bulletin XX* (May 1924), *XXIV* (May 1925).

65 Haldane, *An Autobiography*, 299–301; O. Stanley (ed), *The Way Out* (Oxford, 1923); BIAE, *Interim Report on the Educational Functions of Settlements* [nd, about 1922] and *Guildhouse* [nd, about 1925]; BIAE and Tutors' Association, *The Tutor in Adult Education* (Dunfermline, 1928); BIAE, Minutes of AGMs, printed statements of aims and objects [about 1930] and present activities [about 1931], and R. S. Lambert, 'Outline of a plan of action', 1935.

66 BIAE GP Committee Minutes 18 February 1925, 5th AGM Report 1926; WAAE, *Bulletin XXVIII* (May 1926).

67 Ed 24/592; BIAE GP Committee Minutes 26 May 1924, 'Outline of a plan of action'; *The Trodden Road*, 100.

68 BIAE GP Committee Minutes 4 May, 21 September 1928, Reports of 9th AGM 1930 and 19th 1940, publicity leaflets [about 1930–about 1934]; NIAE, papers on BIAE and NFAE, 1945–49.

69 Mansbridge to L. Clark 27 April 1945, Clark MSS; Hope, 4–5, 27–28, 146; *Fellow Men*, 69–72.

70 *The Trodden Road*, 101–2; Hope, 5, 50–57.

71 Mansbridge, letter to *The Times*, 4 September 1939; Archbishop Lang to Mansbridge 28 September 1939, Mansbridge MSS; Memorandum on College of the Sea, Clark MSS; Hope, 5.

72 Various references in WAAE, *Bulletins*.

73 WAAE, *Bulletin XXX* (November 1926), *XXXVIII* (November 1928).

74 *The Trodden Road*, 97; WAAE, *International Handbook of Adult Education* (1929); WAAE, *World Conference on Adult Education, Cambridge 1929* (1930), ix–xxiv.

75 *World Conference on Adult Education*, 23–26, 497–504, 541–543 and various references; WAAE, *Bulletin XLIII* (November 1929).

76 WAAE, *Bulletin XLVI* (November 1930), *XLVII* (February 1931), *XLIX* (August 1931), *L* (November 1931); WAAE MSS, Conference on Educational Broadcasting, Vienna, 1931.

77 *International Quarterly of Adult Education* 1 (1932–33), 2 (1933–35).

78 WAAE, *Bulletin 2nd series XIX* (November 1939).

79 WAAE, *Bulletin 2nd series XXXVI* (February 1944), *XLIV* (February 1946).

80   *The Trodden Road*, 128–129.

81   *The Trodden Road*, 109; *Co-operative News*, 3 July 1926; WAAE, *Bulletin XXVI* (November 1925), *XXVIII* (May 1926), *XXIX* (August 1926).

82   *The Trodden Road*, 109; L. Clark (ed), *The Kingdom of the Mind* (1946 edn), 96–105.

83   *The Trodden Road*, 111–113; *Fellow Men*, 80; *Evening Telegram* [St John's, Newfoundland], 8 June 1936.

84   Mansbridge, *Margaret McMillan, Prophet and Pioneer* (1932) and *Brick upon Brick: the Co-operative Permanent Building Society 1884–1934* (1934).

85   *The Trodden Road*, 7.

86   Bishop of Peterborough to Mansbridge 2 April 1933, Mansbridge to Miss Gore 28 August 1933, Mansbridge MSS; Mansbridge, *Edward Stuart Talbot and Charles Gore* (1935); G. L. Prestige, *The Life of Charles Gore* (1935), vii–viii.

87   Mansbridge to Elizabeth Haldane [nd, ?1934], National Library of Scotland MS 6037 f261; Mansbridge to Patrick Gower 22 March 1934, Mansbridge MSS; information from Co-operative Permanent (now Nationwide) Building Society.

88   Correspondence between Albert and Frances Mansbridge and Leonard Clark 1937–39, Clark MSS.

89   Mansbridge to Clark 6 January 1939, Clark MSS; *The Trodden Road*, 128.

90   *The Trodden Road*, 113–115; *Washington Evening Star*, 14 January 1937; Mansbridge to Clark 4 February 1937, 25 October 1938, Clark MSS; University of Pittsburgh, *English Room in the Cathedral of Learning* (Pittsburgh, 1952).

91   Hope, *In Cabined Ships at Sea*, 4.

92   Correspondence between Mansbridge, Clark and J. C. Pringle 1937–40, Clark and Mansbridge MSS.

93   *Building Societies Gazette*, September 1952; H. H. Turner to Mansbridge 9 December 1908, Tutorial Classes Committee Early Papers I, Rewley House MSS.

94   Mansbridge to Clark 8 February–29 June 1948, Clark MSS.

95   *British Weekly*, 15 May 1947; E. Green, 'The retreat from utopia', MS WEA Central archives.

96   Mansbridge to Clark June 1948– September 1949, Clark MSS; Mansbridge to F. H. Bentley 29 May 1949, Mansbridge MSS.

97   Mansbridge to Clark 31 October 1950, 1 October 1951, 7 June 1952, Frances Mansbridge to Clark 1 August 1951, Clark MSS; Sir R. W. Livingstone to A. E. Zimmern 9 November 1956, Zimmern MSS; information from Mr and

Mrs F. Pickstock; death certificate, General Register Office, London.

## 8: The Man and the Movements

1 *Manchester Guardian*, 25 August 1952; W. H. Hosford MS, 'The triumph and tragedy of Albert Mansbridge' and notes on this by Dorothy Jones, copies in WEA Central archives.

2 G. W. Keeton, 'An Educational pioneer', *World Affairs*, April 1945; WAAE, *World Conference on Adult Education*, 1, 552; PRO Ed 24/592, 1914.

3 East Riding Education Committee Minutes 21 January 1924 and various references 1920–24 (East Riding Public Library, Beverley).

4 Ed 24/1911.

5 WEA Central F and GP Committee 4 July 1921, EC and F and GP Committees April–December 1922.

6 G. D. H. Cole, 'What Labour wants from Education', *Plebs* 8:10, November 1916, 217–220.

7 WEA Central EC and F and GP Committees March 1921– April 1923; *Highway*, April 1921.

8 *Sunday Times*, 2, 9 January 1921; Mansbridge to Sir Michael Sadler 16 April 1920, Leeds University Archives.

9 *Highway*, September 1920.

10 H. Begbie, *Living Water: being chapters from the romance of the poor student* [nd, 1918], 184, 187.

11 *Highway*, Summer 1924.

12 Begbie, 184–185; *Boston Evening Transcript*, 5 April 1922.

13 *Highway*, November 1920

14 Hosford, 'Triumph and tragedy'

15 Mansbridge and E. Green to Clark July 1943–Oct 1944, Clark MSS.

16 *The Trodden Road*, 157.

17 *The Times*, 10 July 1919; *Times Educational Supplement*, 17 July 1919.

18 Sir Harry Verney to Mansbridge 17 January 1924, Lady Cynthia Colville to Mansbridge 25 August 1945, 2 June 1947, Lady Constance Milnes Gaskell to Mansbridge 5 August 1942, Mansbridge MSS.

19 Mansbridge to Lady Cynthia Colville 26 May 1944, Windsor Castle Library RA Geo.V CC47/2157. The extract from this letter is reproduced by gracious permission of Her Majesty the Queen.

20 Lady Cynthia Colville to Mansbridge 7 February 1947, Mansbridge MSS.

21 H. Wooldridge correspondence and memoranda 1912–29, Mansbridge MSS.

22 Clark MSS, various references.

23  G. H. Newbery to Mansbridge 3 October 1946, G. Alcock to Mansbridge 17 Sept, 3 December 1948, Mansbridge MSS.

24  General Register Office, Grant of Probate, 27 November 1952.

25  Mansbridge, *The Making of an Educationist*, 25; *The Trodden Road*, 28–39, 64, 67, 113, 123.

26  Mansbridge, 'A Survey of working–class educational movements in England and Scotland', *C. W.S. Annual 1906*, 259–298.

27  *George Cadbury, Adult Schools and Adult Education*, First George Cadbury Memorial Lecture (Selly Oak, 1927); *The Dedication of Life*, Second Haldane Memorial Lecture 1930 (reprinted in *The Kingdom of the Mind*, 127–144).

28  *The Trodden Road*, 174–179; *Fellow Men*, 43–45; *The Kingdom of the Mind*, 169–170.

29  *The Kingdom of the Mind*, 169–170; *The Trodden Road*, 180–185; L. Clark, *Alfred Williams* (Oxford, 1945).

30  *The Kingdom of the Mind*, 59.

31  *The Trodden Road*, 220, 246–247, 277–278; Address to London Missionary Society 21 February 1939, Mansbridge MSS.

32  *The Trodden Road*, 218–219, 272.

33  *The Trodden Road*, 226–227, 270.

34  Hope, *In Cabined Ships at Sea*, 1; memoranda and letters to F. H. Bentley, Mansbridge MSS.

35  Mansbridge, *Edward Stuart Talbot and Charles Gore*, 44; *The Trodden Road*, 220–221, 271.

36  *The Trodden Road*, 71; *The Kingdom of the Mind*, 113.

37  *The Kingdom of the Mind*, 103.

38  *The Kingdom of the Mind*, 145–156.

39  *Co-operative Review* (1945), 70.

40  C. Turnor to Mansbridge 30 April 1940, Mansbridge MSS.

41  Begbie, *Living Water*, 174.

42  *Highway*, Summer 1924.

43  Keeton, 'An educational pioneer'.

44  *Highway*, July 1912.

45  Mansbridge to Zimmern 2 March 1910, Zimmern MSS.

46  *The Trodden Road*, 44.

47  Information from John Mansbridge.

48  *The Making of an Educationist*, 16.

49  Copy of address by bishop of Tewkesbury in Gloucester cathedral, Maude Royden to Frances Mansbridge 13 November 1952, Mansbridge MSS.

50  Copy of address by bishop of Chichester, Mansbridge MSS.

# Index

# Leeds Studies in Continuing Education

*Edited by Stuart Marriott, formerly Research Professor, University of Leeds*

A BACKSTAIRS TO A DEGREE: DEMANDS FOR AN OPEN UNIVERSITY
IN LATE VICTORIAN ENGLAND Stuart Marriott

SIR MICHAEL SADLER: A BIBLIOGRAPHY OF HIS PUBLISHED WORKS
O S Pickering

THE DEMISE OF THE LIBERAL TRADITION: TWO ESSAYS ON THE FUTURE
OF BRITISH UNIVERSITY ADULT EDUCATION
Alastair D Crombie and Gwyn Harries-Jenkins

ADULT EDUCATION AND THE COLD WAR: LIBERAL VALUES
UNDER SIEGE 1946–51 Roger T Fieldhouse

UNIVERSITY ADULT EDUCATION IN CRISIS
John McIlroy and Bruce Spencer

THE EXAMINER: JAMES BOOTH AND THE ORIGINS OF COMMON
EXAMINATIONS Frank Foden

LEARNING THROUGH LABOUR: TRAINING, UNEMPLOYMENT AND
THE STATE 1890–1939 John Field

THE EDUCATION OF PART-TIME TEACHERS IN FURTHER AND ADULT
EDUCATION: A RETROSPECTIVE STUDY Frank Foden

CONTINUING EDUCATION IN HIGHER EDUCATION: ACADEMIC SELF-CONCEPT
AND PUBLIC POLICY IN THREE EUROPEAN COUNTRIES
Colin Titmus, Joachim H Knoll and Jürgen Wittpoth

ADULT EDUCATION FOR INDEPENDENCE: THE INTRODUCTION OF UNI-
VERSITY EXTRA-MURAL WORK INTO BRITISH TROPICAL AFRICA
Colin Titmus and Tom Steele

ENGLISH–GERMAN RELATIONS IN ADULT EDUCATION 1875–1955:
A COMMENTARY AND SELECT BIBLIOGRAPHY
Stuart Marriott